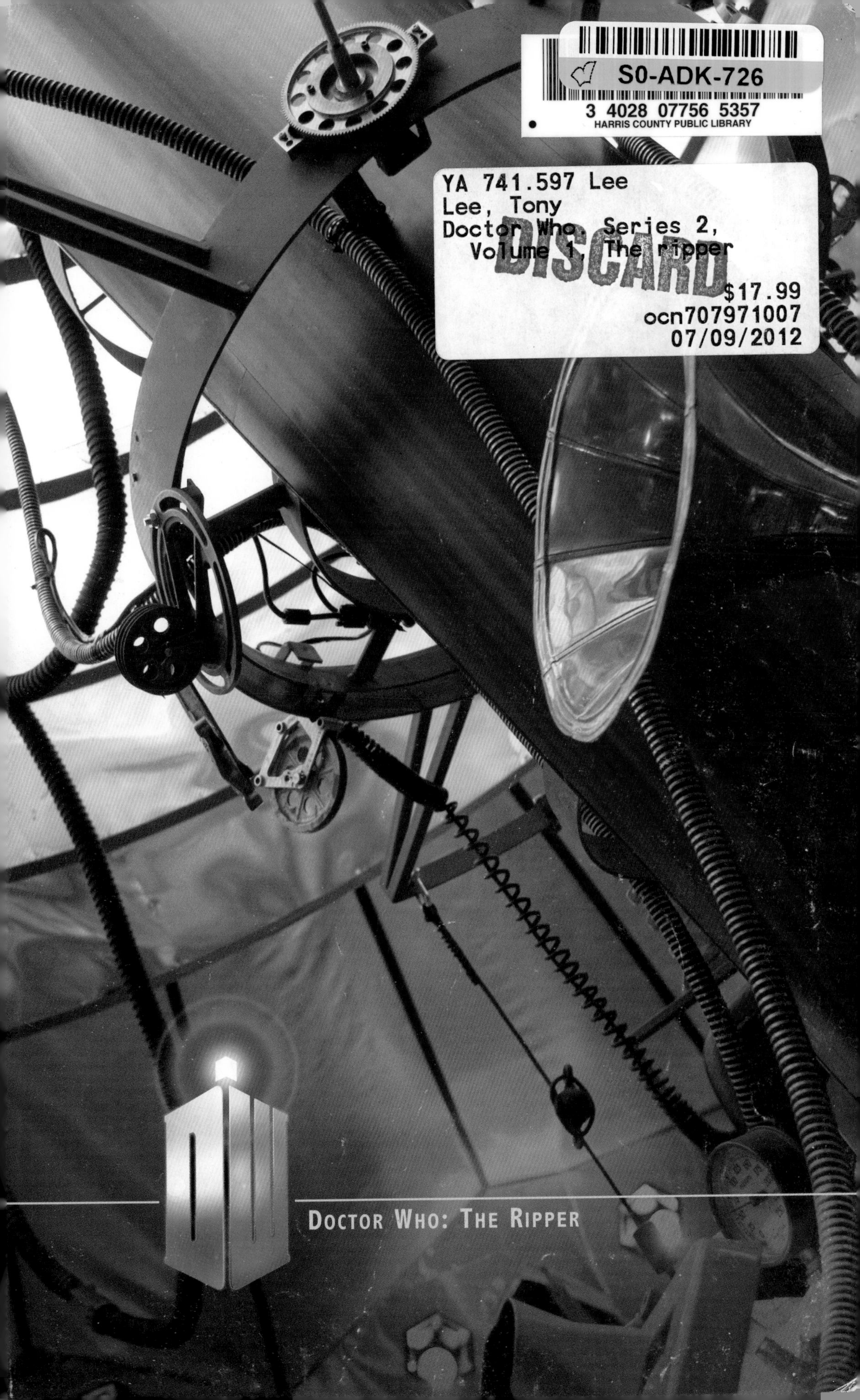

Doctor Who: The Ripper

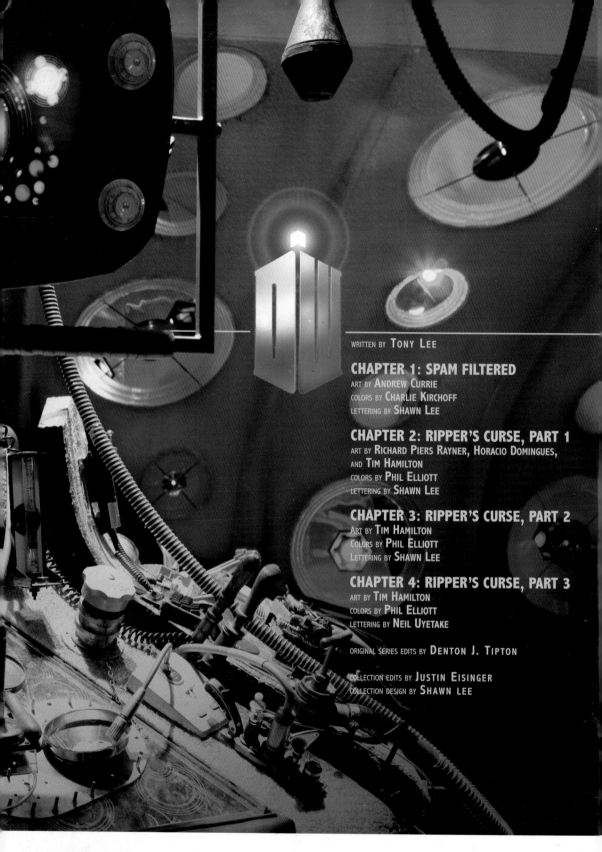

WRITTEN BY TONY LEE

CHAPTER 1: SPAM FILTERED
ART BY ANDREW CURRIE
COLORS BY CHARLIE KIRCHOFF
LETTERING BY SHAWN LEE

CHAPTER 2: RIPPER'S CURSE, PART 1
ART BY RICHARD PIERS RAYNER, HORACIO DOMINGUES,
AND TIM HAMILTON
COLORS BY PHIL ELLIOTT
LETTERING BY SHAWN LEE

CHAPTER 3: RIPPER'S CURSE, PART 2
ART BY TIM HAMILTON
COLORS BY PHIL ELLIOTT
LETTERING BY SHAWN LEE

CHAPTER 4: RIPPER'S CURSE, PART 3
ART BY TIM HAMILTON
COLORS BY PHIL ELLIOTT
LETTERING BY NEIL UYETAKE

ORIGINAL SERIES EDITS BY DENTON J. TIPTON

COLLECTION EDITS BY JUSTIN EISINGER
COLLECTION DESIGN BY SHAWN LEE

Special thanks to Gary Russell, David Turbitt, and Ed Casey for their invaluable assistance.

ISBN: 978-1-60010-974-4   14 13 12 11   1 2 3 4
www.IDWPUBLISHING.com

Ted Adams, CEO & Publisher
Greg Goldstein, Chief Operating Officer
Robbie Robbins, EVP/Sr. Graphic Artist
Chris Ryall, Chief Creative Officer/Editor-in-Chief
Matthew Ruzicka, CPA, Chief Financial Officer
Alan Payne, VP of Sales

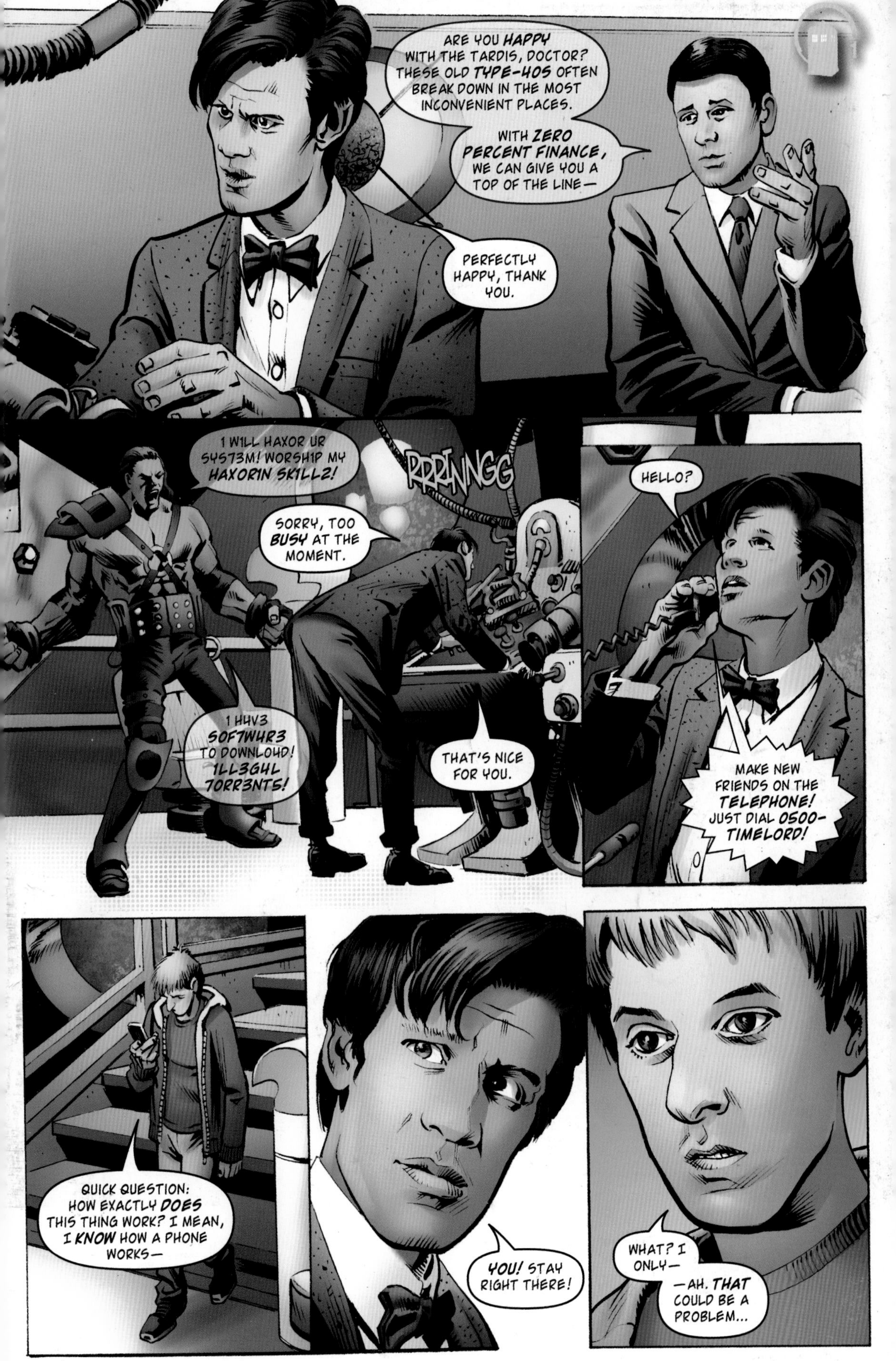

ARE YOU HAPPY WITH THE TARDIS, DOCTOR? THESE OLD TYPE-40S OFTEN BREAK DOWN IN THE MOST INCONVENIENT PLACES.
WITH ZERO PERCENT FINANCE, WE CAN GIVE YOU A TOP OF THE LINE—
PERFECTLY HAPPY, THANK YOU.
1 W1LL HAXOR UR SYS73M! WORSH1P MY HAXOR1N SK1LLZ!
SORRY, TOO BUSY AT THE MOMENT.
1 H4V3 SOF7WHR3 TO DOWNLOHD! 1LL3GHL 7ORR3NTS!
THAT'S NICE FOR YOU.
RRRINNGG
HELLO?
MAKE NEW FRIENDS ON THE TELEPHONE! JUST DIAL 0500-TIMELORD!
QUICK QUESTION: HOW EXACTLY DOES THIS THING WORK? I MEAN, I KNOW HOW A PHONE WORKS—
YOU! STAY RIGHT THERE!
WHAT? I ONLY—
—AH. THAT COULD BE A PROBLEM...

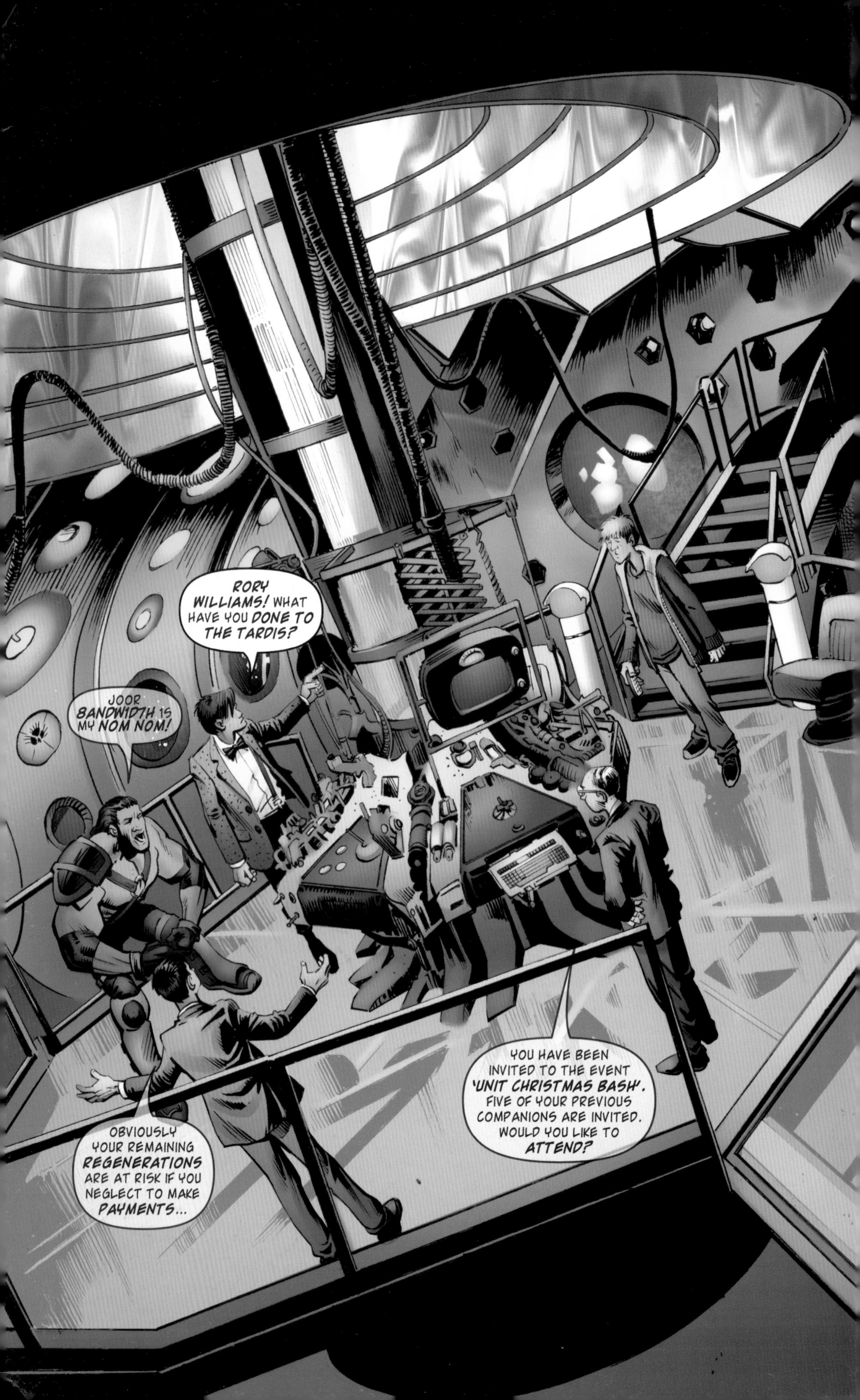
RORY WILLIAMS! WHAT HAVE YOU DONE TO THE TARDIS?
JOOR BANDWIDTH IS MY NOM NOM!
YOU HAVE BEEN INVITED TO THE EVENT 'UNIT CHRISTMAS BASH'. FIVE OF YOUR PREVIOUS COMPANIONS ARE INVITED. WOULD YOU LIKE TO ATTEND?
OBVIOUSLY YOUR REMAINING REGENERATIONS ARE AT RISK IF YOU NEGLECT TO MAKE PAYMENTS...

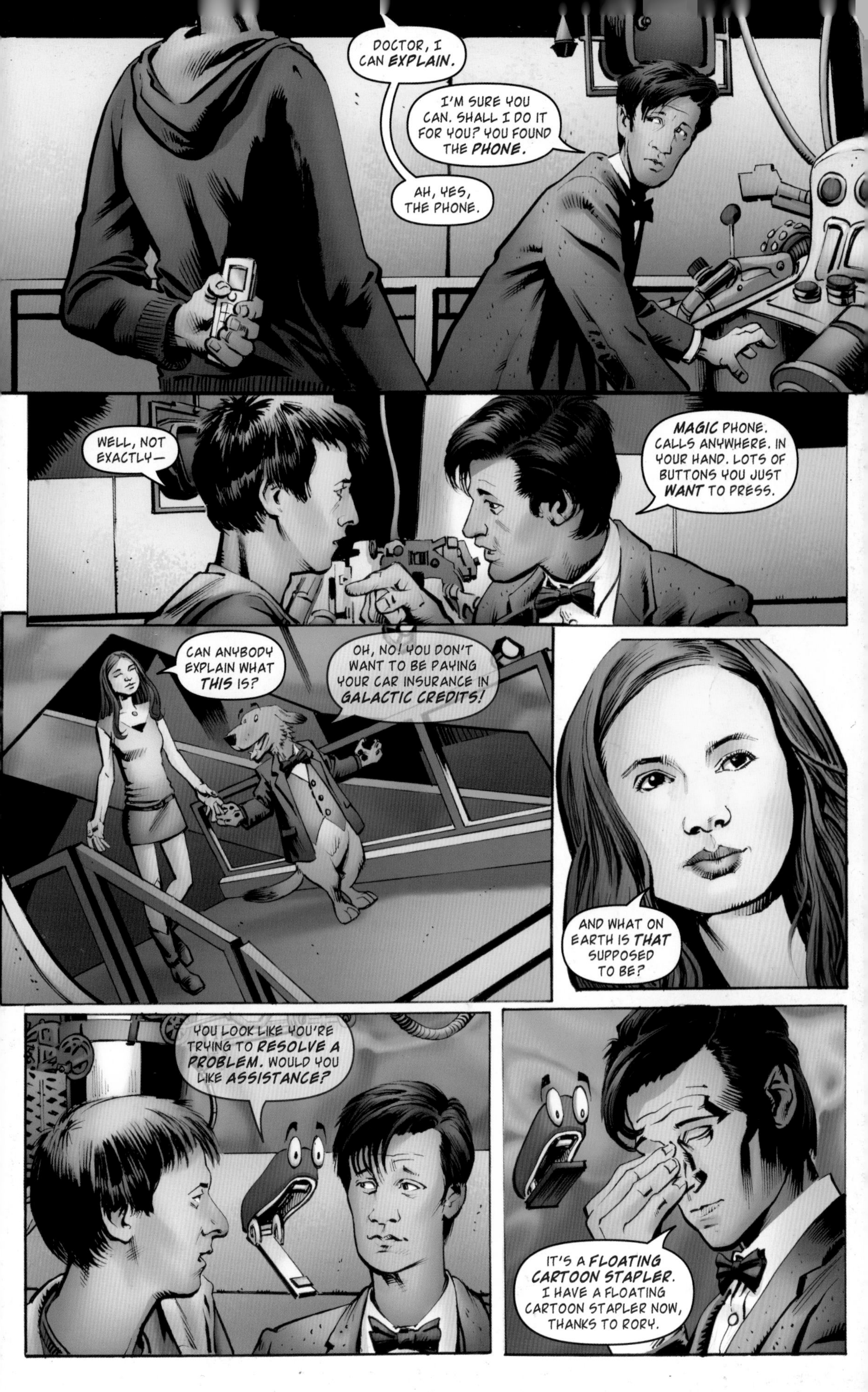
DOCTOR, I CAN EXPLAIN.
I'M SURE YOU CAN. SHALL I DO IT FOR YOU? YOU FOUND THE PHONE.
AH, YES, THE PHONE.
WELL, NOT EXACTLY—
MAGIC PHONE. CALLS ANYWHERE. IN YOUR HAND. LOTS OF BUTTONS YOU JUST WANT TO PRESS.
CAN ANYBODY EXPLAIN WHAT THIS IS?
OH, NO! YOU DON'T WANT TO BE PAYING YOUR CAR INSURANCE IN GALACTIC CREDITS!
AND WHAT ON EARTH IS THAT SUPPOSED TO BE?
YOU LOOK LIKE YOU'RE TRYING TO RESOLVE A PROBLEM. WOULD YOU LIKE ASSISTANCE?
IT'S A FLOATING CARTOON STAPLER. I HAVE A FLOATING CARTOON STAPLER NOW, THANKS TO RORY.

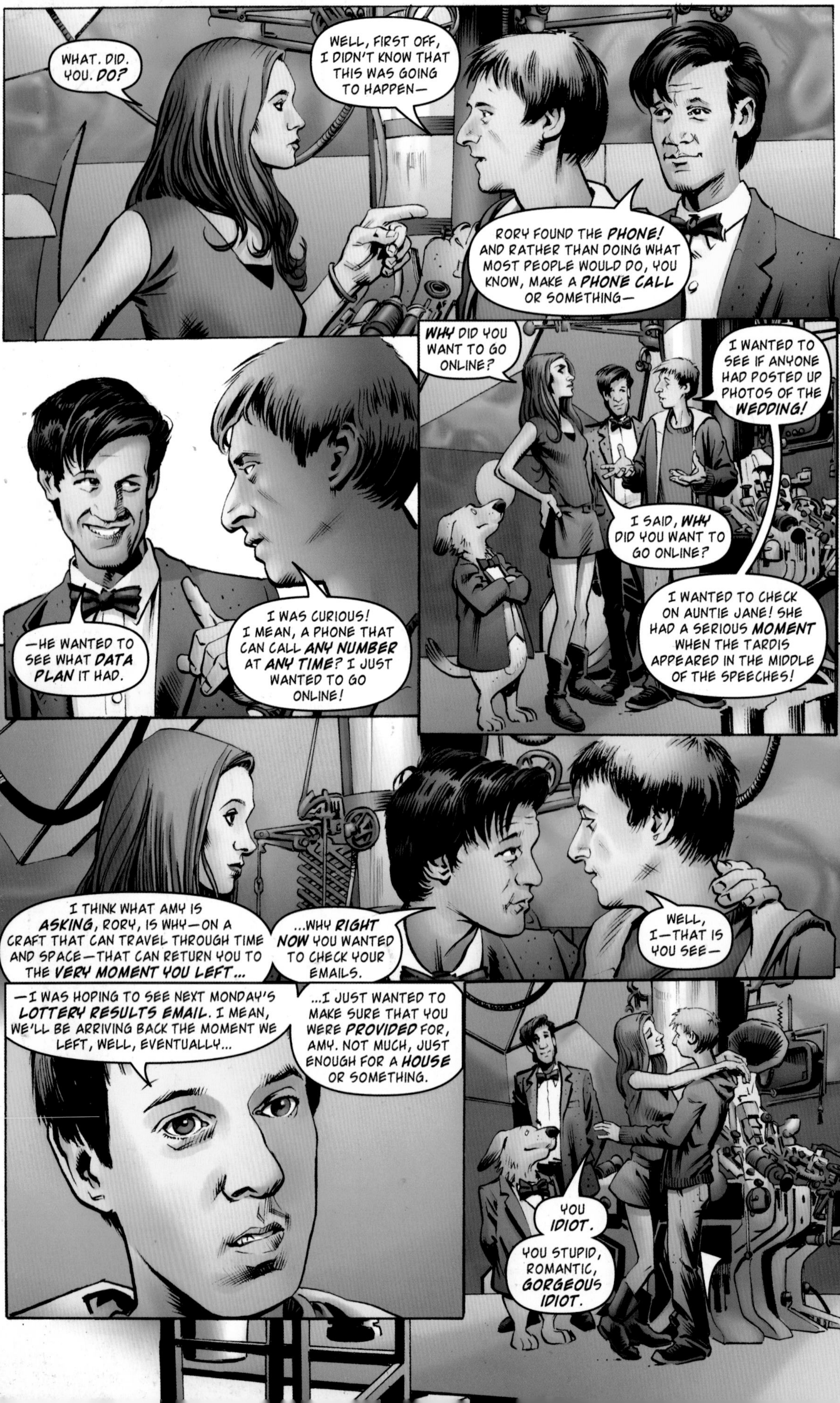
WHAT. DID. YOU. DO?
WELL, FIRST OFF, I DIDN'T KNOW THAT THIS WAS GOING TO HAPPEN—
RORY FOUND THE PHONE! AND RATHER THAN DOING WHAT MOST PEOPLE WOULD DO, YOU KNOW, MAKE A PHONE CALL OR SOMETHING—
—HE WANTED TO SEE WHAT DATA PLAN IT HAD.
I WAS CURIOUS! I MEAN, A PHONE THAT CAN CALL ANY NUMBER AT ANY TIME? I JUST WANTED TO GO ONLINE!
WHY DID YOU WANT TO GO ONLINE?
I WANTED TO SEE IF ANYONE HAD POSTED UP PHOTOS OF THE WEDDING!
I SAID, WHY DID YOU WANT TO GO ONLINE?
I WANTED TO CHECK ON AUNTIE JANE! SHE HAD A SERIOUS MOMENT WHEN THE TARDIS APPEARED IN THE MIDDLE OF THE SPEECHES!
I THINK WHAT AMY IS ASKING, RORY, IS WHY—ON A CRAFT THAT CAN TRAVEL THROUGH TIME AND SPACE—THAT CAN RETURN YOU TO THE VERY MOMENT YOU LEFT...
...WHY RIGHT NOW YOU WANTED TO CHECK YOUR EMAILS.
WELL, I—THAT IS YOU SEE—
—I WAS HOPING TO SEE NEXT MONDAY'S LOTTERY RESULTS EMAIL. I MEAN, WE'LL BE ARRIVING BACK THE MOMENT WE LEFT, WELL, EVENTUALLY...
...I JUST WANTED TO MAKE SURE THAT YOU WERE PROVIDED FOR, AMY. NOT MUCH, JUST ENOUGH FOR A HOUSE OR SOMETHING.
YOU IDIOT.
YOU STUPID, ROMANTIC, GORGEOUS IDIOT.

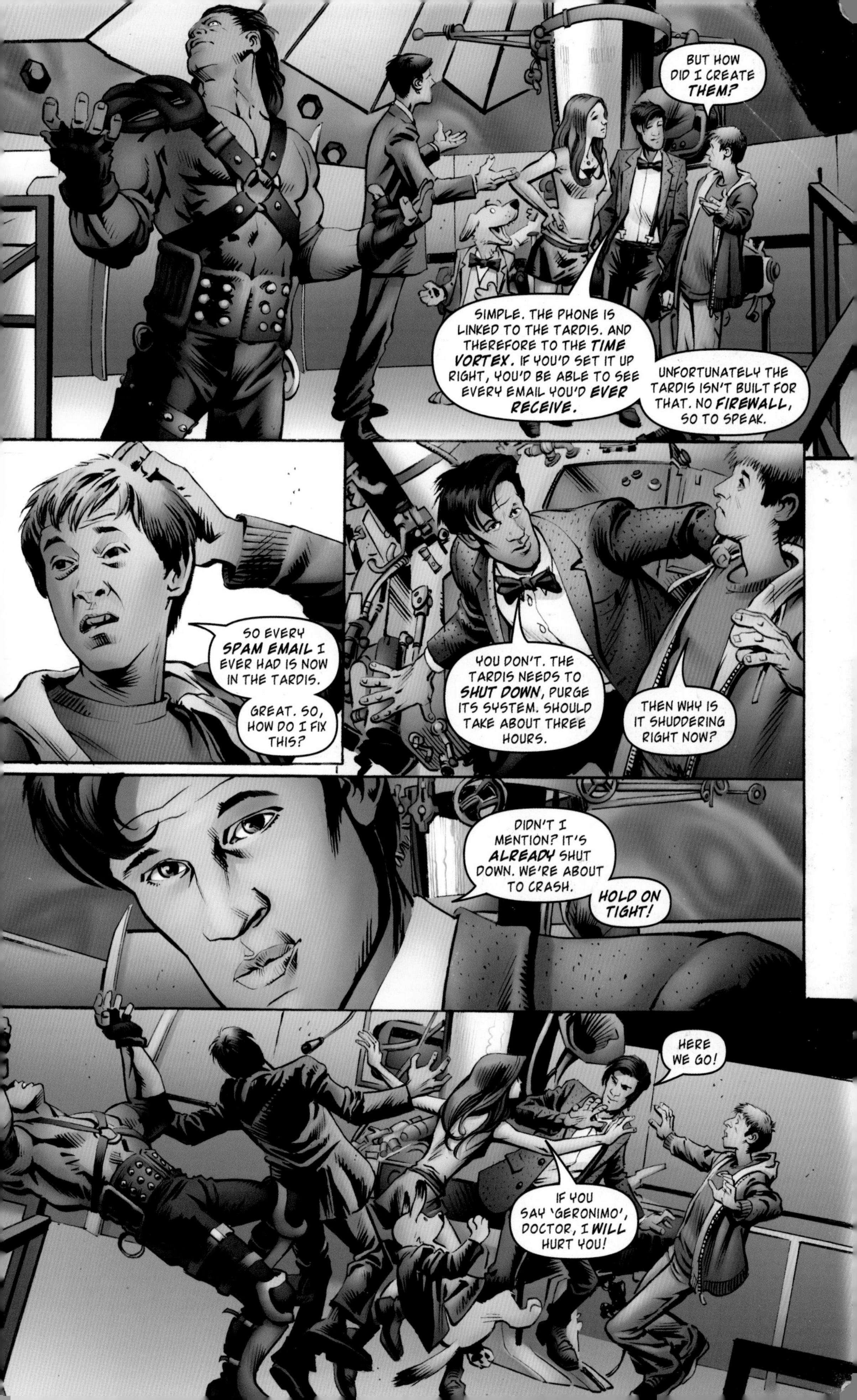
BUT HOW DID I CREATE *THEM?*
SIMPLE. THE PHONE IS LINKED TO THE TARDIS. AND THEREFORE TO THE *TIME VORTEX.* IF YOU'D SET IT UP RIGHT, YOU'D BE ABLE TO SEE EVERY EMAIL YOU'D *EVER RECEIVE.*
UNFORTUNATELY THE TARDIS ISN'T BUILT FOR THAT. NO *FIREWALL,* SO TO SPEAK.
SO EVERY *SPAM EMAIL* I EVER HAD IS NOW IN THE TARDIS.
GREAT. SO, HOW DO I FIX THIS?
YOU DON'T. THE TARDIS NEEDS TO *SHUT DOWN,* PURGE ITS SYSTEM. SHOULD TAKE ABOUT THREE HOURS.
THEN WHY IS IT SHUDDERING RIGHT NOW?
DIDN'T I MENTION? IT'S *ALREADY* SHUT DOWN. WE'RE ABOUT TO CRASH.
HOLD ON TIGHT!
HERE WE GO!
IF YOU SAY 'GERONIMO', DOCTOR, I *WILL* HURT YOU!

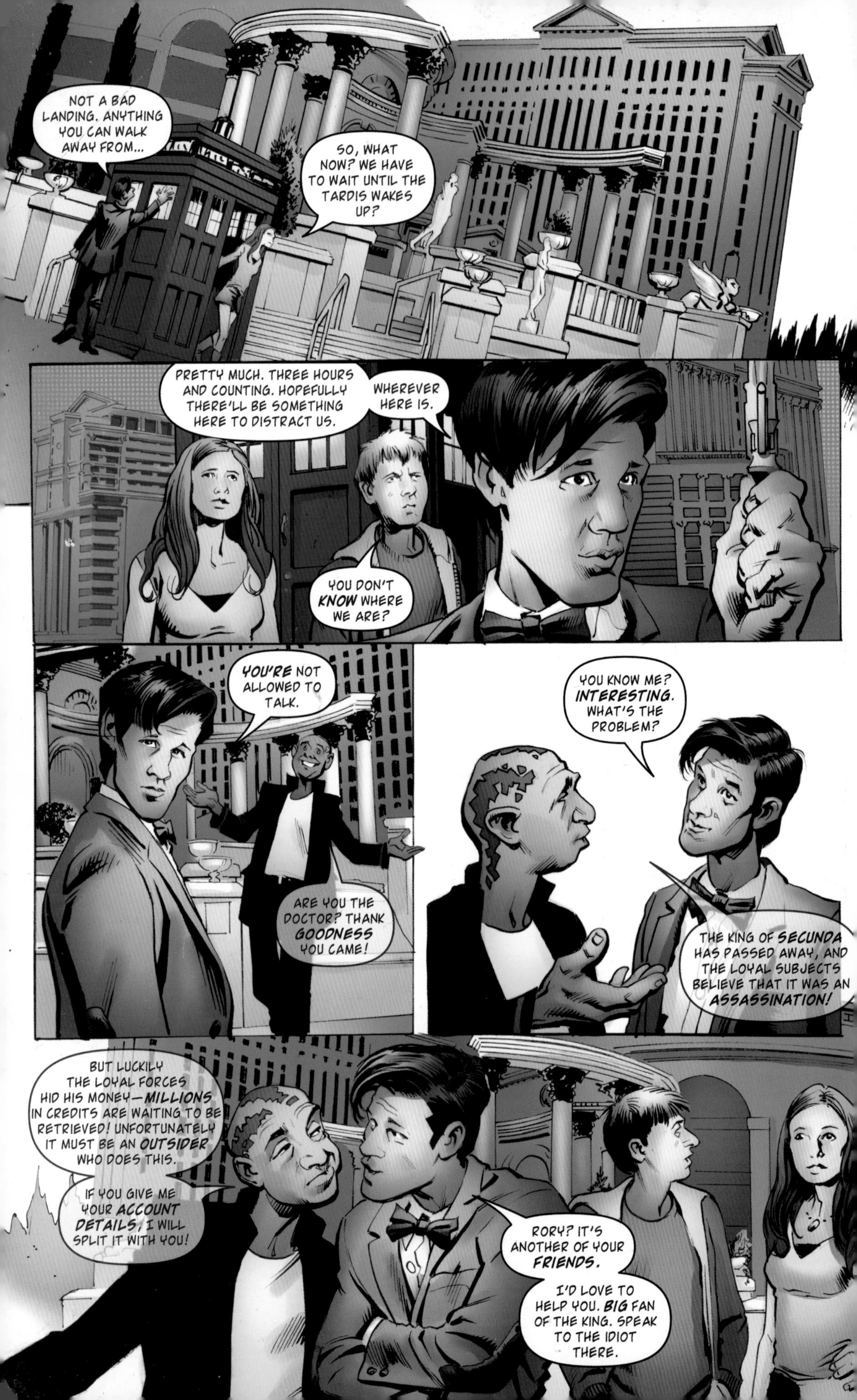
NOT A BAD LANDING. ANYTHING YOU CAN WALK AWAY FROM...
SO, WHAT NOW? WE HAVE TO WAIT UNTIL THE TARDIS WAKES UP?
PRETTY MUCH. THREE HOURS AND COUNTING. HOPEFULLY THERE'LL BE SOMETHING HERE TO DISTRACT US.
WHEREVER HERE IS.
YOU DON'T KNOW WHERE WE ARE?
YOU'RE NOT ALLOWED TO TALK.
ARE YOU THE DOCTOR? THANK GOODNESS YOU CAME!
YOU KNOW ME? INTERESTING. WHAT'S THE PROBLEM?
THE KING OF SECUNDA HAS PASSED AWAY, AND THE LOYAL SUBJECTS BELIEVE THAT IT WAS AN ASSASSINATION!
BUT LUCKILY THE LOYAL FORCES HID HIS MONEY—MILLIONS IN CREDITS ARE WAITING TO BE RETRIEVED! UNFORTUNATELY IT MUST BE AN OUTSIDER WHO DOES THIS.
IF YOU GIVE ME YOUR ACCOUNT DETAILS, I WILL SPLIT IT WITH YOU!
RORY? IT'S ANOTHER OF YOUR FRIENDS.
I'D LOVE TO HELP YOU. BIG FAN OF THE KING. SPEAK TO THE IDIOT THERE.

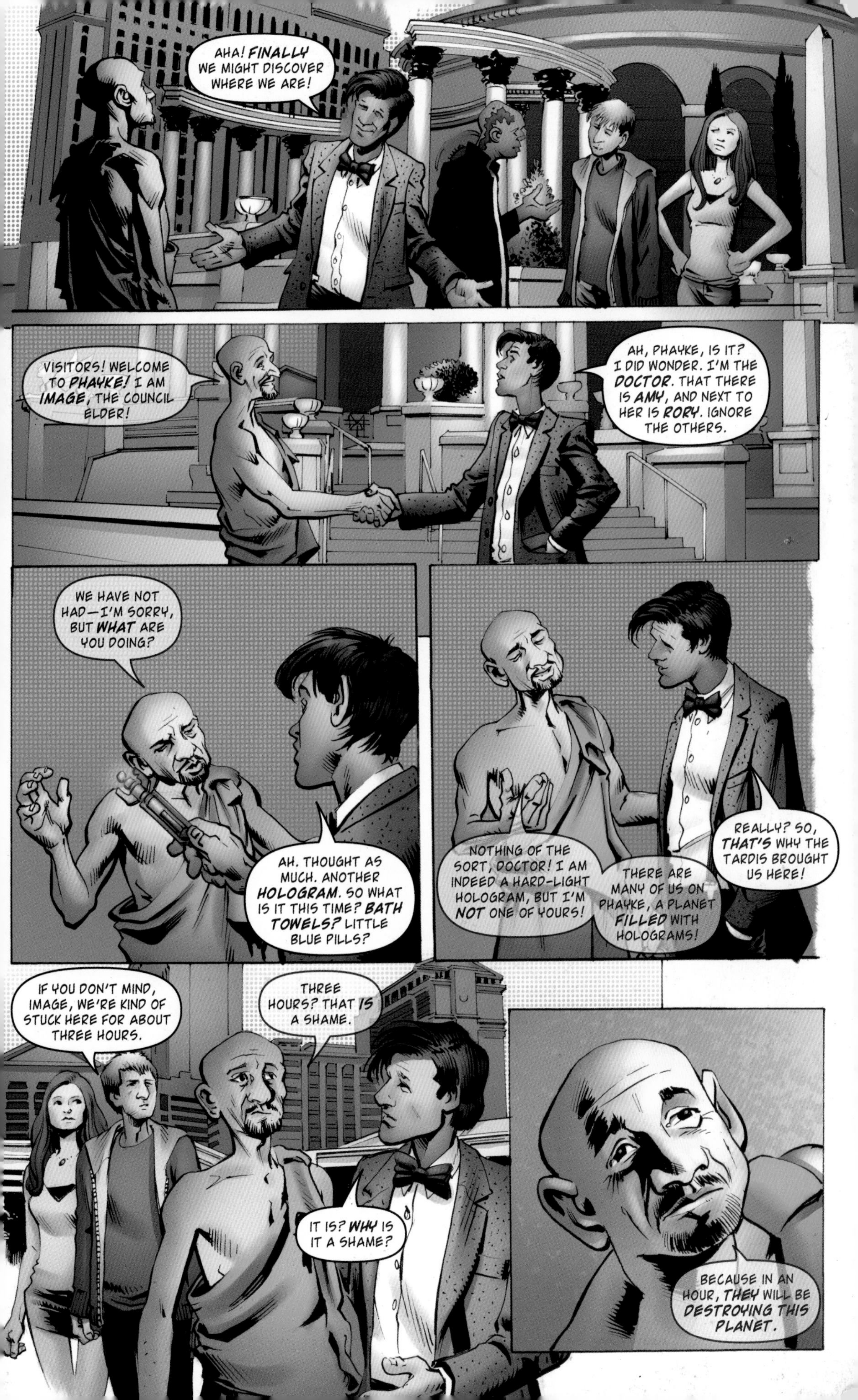
AHA! FINALLY WE MIGHT DISCOVER WHERE WE ARE!
VISITORS! WELCOME TO PHAYKE! I AM IMAGE, THE COUNCIL ELDER!
AH, PHAYKE, IS IT? I DID WONDER. I'M THE DOCTOR. THAT THERE IS AMY, AND NEXT TO HER IS RORY. IGNORE THE OTHERS.
WE HAVE NOT HAD—I'M SORRY, BUT WHAT ARE YOU DOING?
AH. THOUGHT AS MUCH. ANOTHER HOLOGRAM. SO WHAT IS IT THIS TIME? BATH TOWELS? LITTLE BLUE PILLS?
NOTHING OF THE SORT, DOCTOR! I AM INDEED A HARD-LIGHT HOLOGRAM, BUT I'M NOT ONE OF YOURS!
THERE ARE MANY OF US ON PHAYKE, A PLANET FILLED WITH HOLOGRAMS!
REALLY? SO, THAT'S WHY THE TARDIS BROUGHT US HERE!
IF YOU DON'T MIND, IMAGE, WE'RE KIND OF STUCK HERE FOR ABOUT THREE HOURS.
THREE HOURS? THAT IS A SHAME.
IT IS? WHY IS IT A SHAME?
BECAUSE IN AN HOUR, THEY WILL BE DESTROYING THIS PLANET.

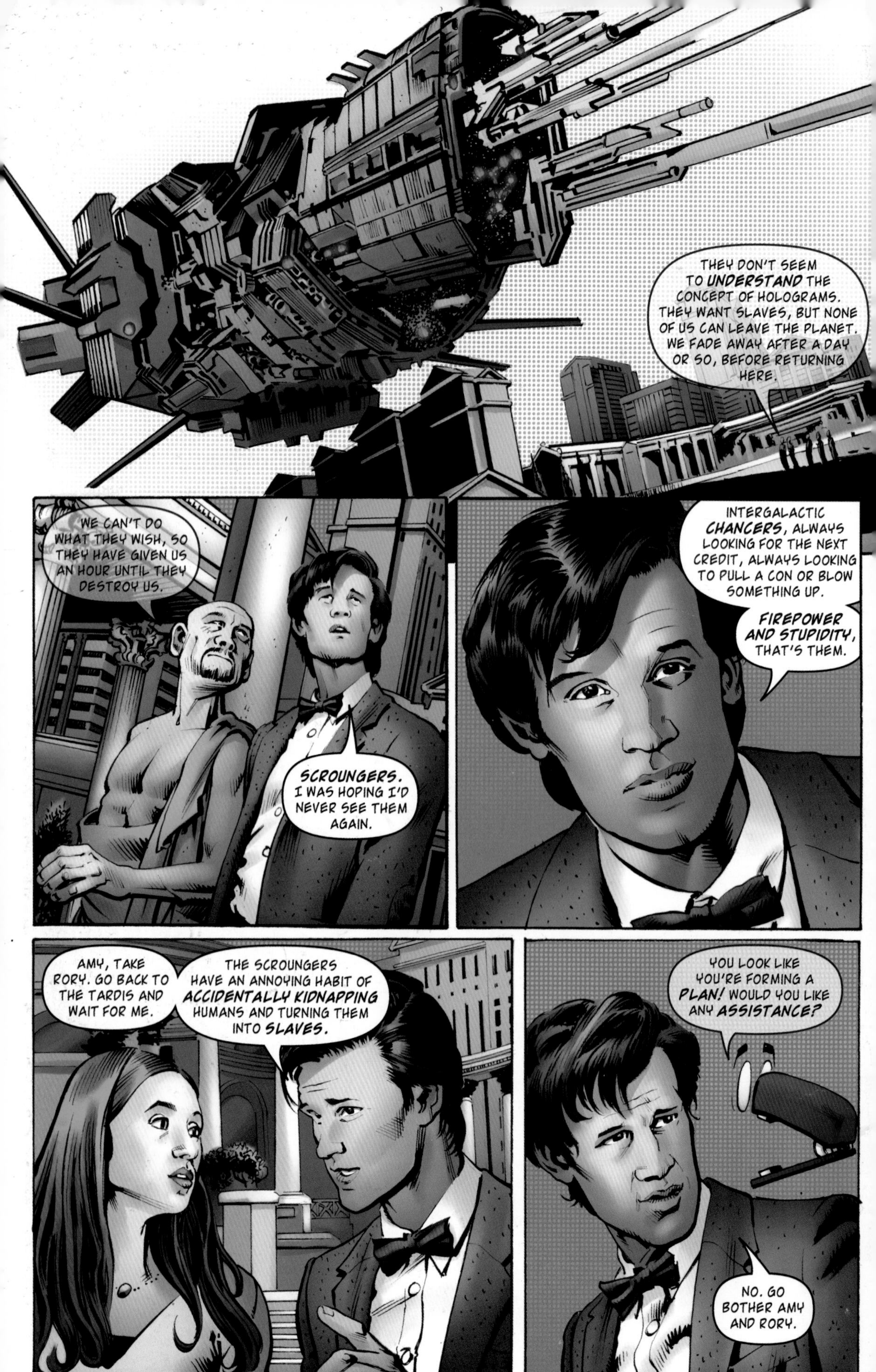
THEY DON'T SEEM TO UNDERSTAND THE CONCEPT OF HOLOGRAMS. THEY WANT SLAVES, BUT NONE OF US CAN LEAVE THE PLANET. WE FADE AWAY AFTER A DAY OR SO, BEFORE RETURNING HERE.
WE CAN'T DO WHAT THEY WISH, SO THEY HAVE GIVEN US AN HOUR UNTIL THEY DESTROY US.
SCROUNGERS. I WAS HOPING I'D NEVER SEE THEM AGAIN.
INTERGALACTIC CHANCERS, ALWAYS LOOKING FOR THE NEXT CREDIT, ALWAYS LOOKING TO PULL A CON OR BLOW SOMETHING UP.
FIREPOWER AND STUPIDITY, THAT'S THEM.
AMY, TAKE RORY. GO BACK TO THE TARDIS AND WAIT FOR ME.
THE SCROUNGERS HAVE AN ANNOYING HABIT OF ACCIDENTALLY KIDNAPPING HUMANS AND TURNING THEM INTO SLAVES.
YOU LOOK LIKE YOU'RE FORMING A PLAN! WOULD YOU LIKE ANY ASSISTANCE?
NO. GO BOTHER AMY AND RORY.

YOU SEEM TO BE HIDING IN THE TARDIS! WOULD YOU LIKE ANY ASSISTANCE?

THANK YOU, DOCTOR. THANK YOU SO MUCH.

QUICK, AMY, GET INSIDE. I HAVE A FEELING THAT THIS WHOLE PLANET IS A SPAM HOLOGRAM.

JUST LET ME IN, AND I'LL GET US OUT OF HERE.

LET YOU IN? WHAT HAPPENED TO YOUR KEY?

PUBLIC TELEPH
FREE
FOR USE OF
PUBLIC
& ASST
E IMM
E CAR
ALLC
PULL TO O

HE DOESN'T HAVE ONE BECAUSE HE ISN'T THE DOCTOR. HE'S PHISHING SPAM. YOU KNOW, THE ONES THAT CONTACT YOU, PRETENDING TO BE YOUR BANK, NEEDING YOUR PASSWORD.

RORY! YOU HURT ME—

ACTUALLY, THAT'LL HURT YOU.

CLUNK

NO MATTER HOW GOOD IT LOOKS ON THE SURFACE, LOOK UNDERNEATH AND IT'LL ALWAYS LOOK FAKE.

NOW. TARDIS. YOU. IN.

ALL RIGHT! WE'RE GOING!

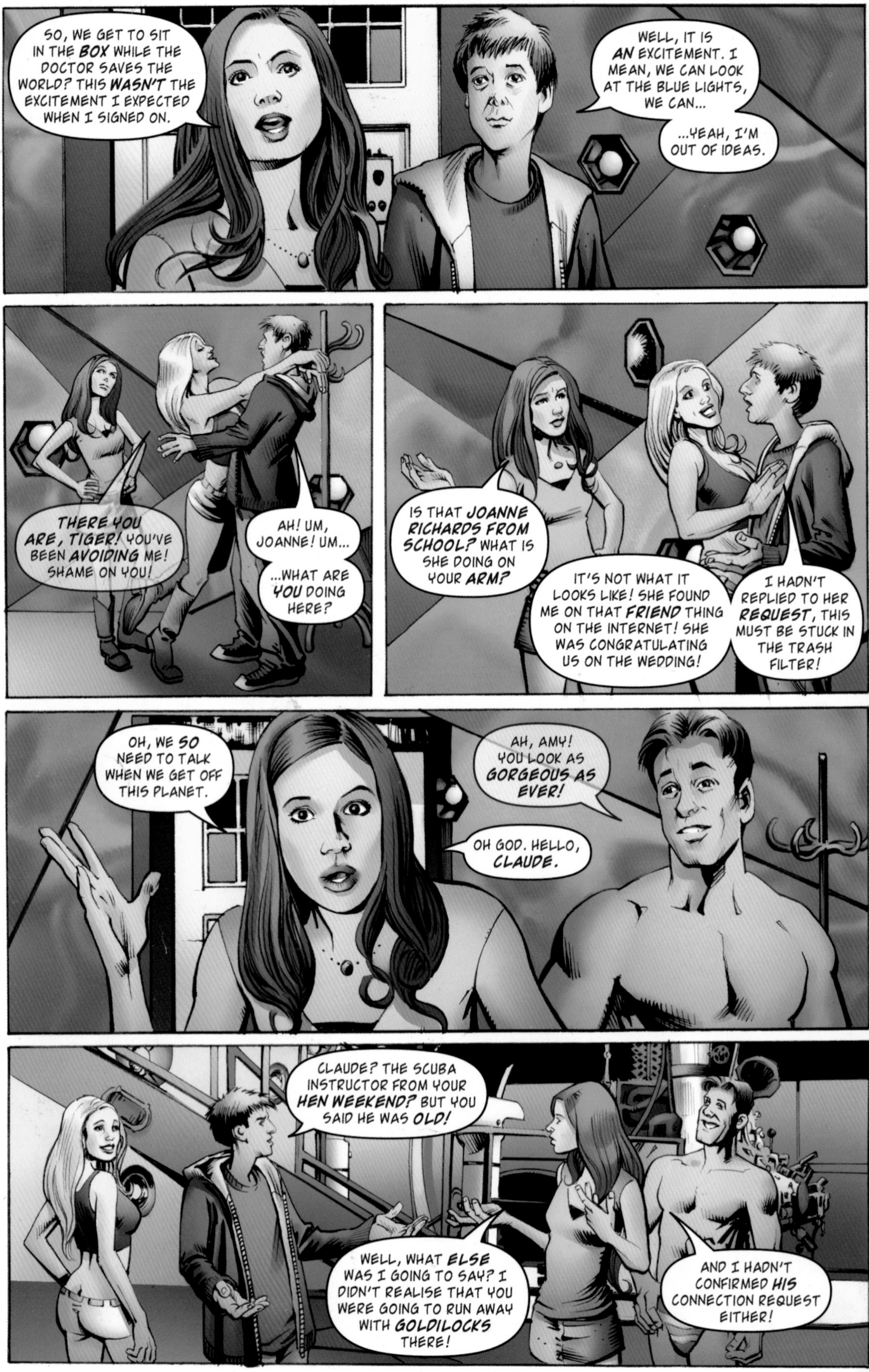
SO, WE GET TO SIT IN THE BOX WHILE THE DOCTOR SAVES THE WORLD? THIS WASN'T THE EXCITEMENT I EXPECTED WHEN I SIGNED ON.
WELL, IT IS AN EXCITEMENT. I MEAN, WE CAN LOOK AT THE BLUE LIGHTS, WE CAN...
...YEAH, I'M OUT OF IDEAS.
THERE YOU ARE, TIGER! YOU'VE BEEN AVOIDING ME! SHAME ON YOU!
AH! UM, JOANNE! UM...
...WHAT ARE YOU DOING HERE?
IS THAT JOANNE RICHARDS FROM SCHOOL? WHAT IS SHE DOING ON YOUR ARM?
IT'S NOT WHAT IT LOOKS LIKE! SHE FOUND ME ON THAT FRIEND THING ON THE INTERNET! SHE WAS CONGRATULATING US ON THE WEDDING!
I HADN'T REPLIED TO HER REQUEST, THIS MUST BE STUCK IN THE TRASH FILTER!
OH, WE SO NEED TO TALK WHEN WE GET OFF THIS PLANET.
AH, AMY! YOU LOOK AS GORGEOUS AS EVER!
OH GOD. HELLO, CLAUDE.
CLAUDE? THE SCUBA INSTRUCTOR FROM YOUR HEN WEEKEND? BUT YOU SAID HE WAS OLD!
WELL, WHAT ELSE WAS I GOING TO SAY? I DIDN'T REALISE THAT YOU WERE GOING TO RUN AWAY WITH GOLDILOCKS THERE!
AND I HADN'T CONFIRMED HIS CONNECTION REQUEST EITHER!

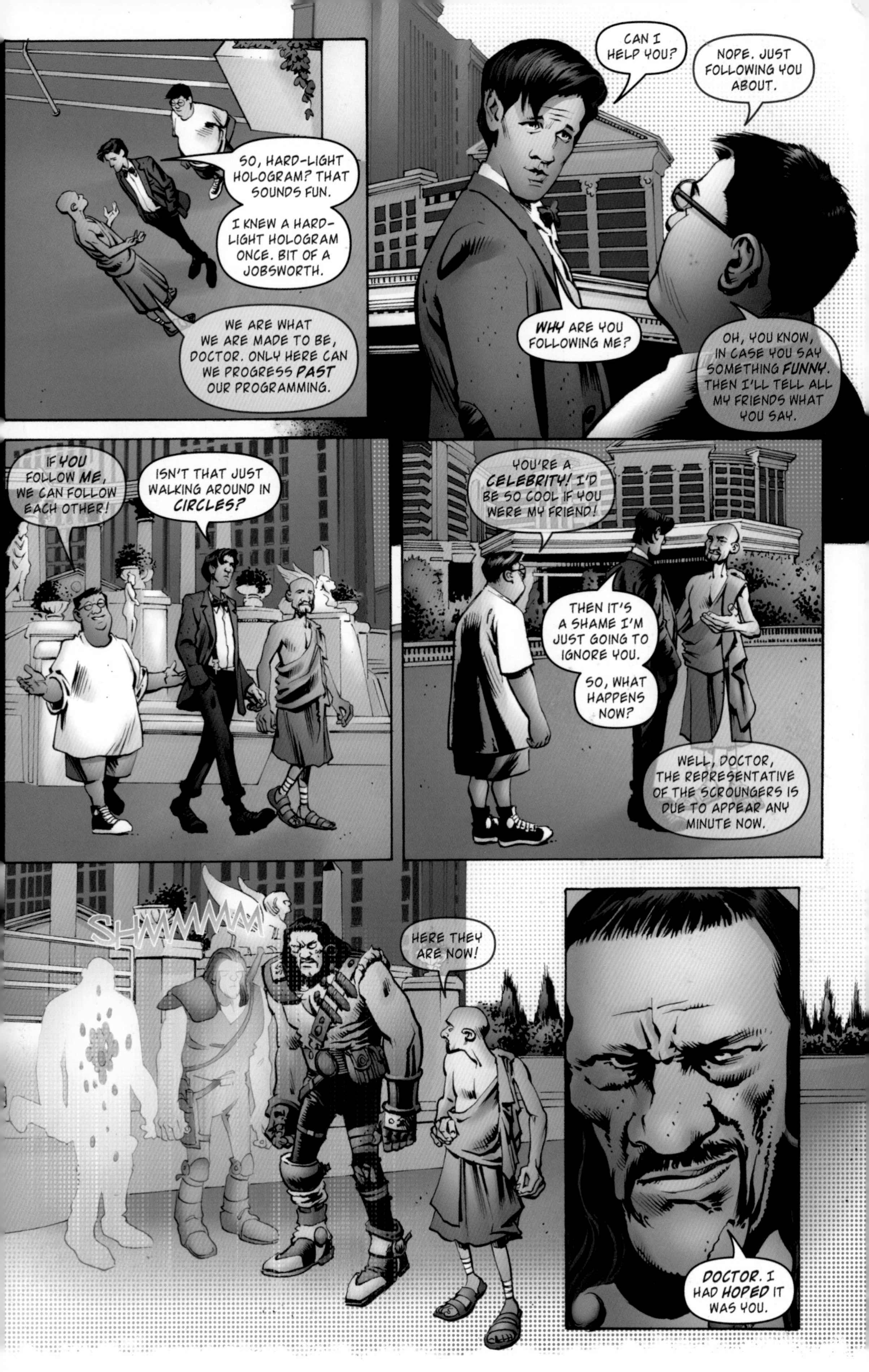
SO, HARD-LIGHT HOLOGRAM? THAT SOUNDS FUN.
I KNEW A HARD-LIGHT HOLOGRAM ONCE. BIT OF A JOBSWORTH.
WE ARE WHAT WE ARE MADE TO BE, DOCTOR. ONLY HERE CAN WE PROGRESS PAST OUR PROGRAMMING.
CAN I HELP YOU?
NOPE. JUST FOLLOWING YOU ABOUT.
WHY ARE YOU FOLLOWING ME?
OH, YOU KNOW, IN CASE YOU SAY SOMETHING FUNNY. THEN I'LL TELL ALL MY FRIENDS WHAT YOU SAY.
IF YOU FOLLOW ME, WE CAN FOLLOW EACH OTHER!
ISN'T THAT JUST WALKING AROUND IN CIRCLES?
YOU'RE A CELEBRITY! I'D BE SO COOL IF YOU WERE MY FRIEND!
THEN IT'S A SHAME I'M JUST GOING TO IGNORE YOU.
SO, WHAT HAPPENS NOW?
WELL, DOCTOR, THE REPRESENTATIVE OF THE SCROUNGERS IS DUE TO APPEAR ANY MINUTE NOW.
SHMMMM
HERE THEY ARE NOW!
DOCTOR. I HAD HOPED IT WAS YOU.

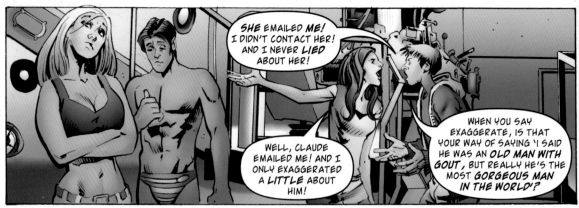

SHE EMAILED *ME*! I DIDN'T CONTACT HER! AND I NEVER *LIED* ABOUT HER!

WELL, CLAUDE EMAILED *ME*! AND I ONLY EXAGGERATED A *LITTLE* ABOUT HIM!

WHEN YOU SAY EXAGGERATE, IS THAT YOUR WAY OF SAYING 'I SAID HE WAS AN *OLD MAN WITH GOUT*, BUT REALLY HE'S THE *MOST GORGEOUS MAN IN THE WORLD*'?

DON'T BE SILLY! *YOU'RE* THE MOST GORGEOUS MAN IN THE WORLD!

THIS IS MADNESS. WE'RE ARGUING ABOUT TWO PEOPLE WHO WE NEVER EVEN CONTACTED IN THE FIRST PLACE!

UM, HELLO. LOOK, I'M REALLY *SORRY*, BUT I THINK WE'RE GOING TO HAVE TO *REFUSE* YOUR REQUESTS.

AMY? YOU WISH TO STAY WITH THIS MAN? YOU DO NOT WISH TO BE MY *FRIEND*?

YEAH, SORRY. I JUST DON'T THINK IT'D BE A GOOD IDEA.

IS THAT WHAT WE ARE TO YOU, RORY? *BAD IDEAS*? YOU DON'T WANT TO BE OUR *FRIENDS*? GREAT—

—WE'LL JUST HAVE TO *BLOCK* YOU.

THAT DOESN'T SOUND GOOD.

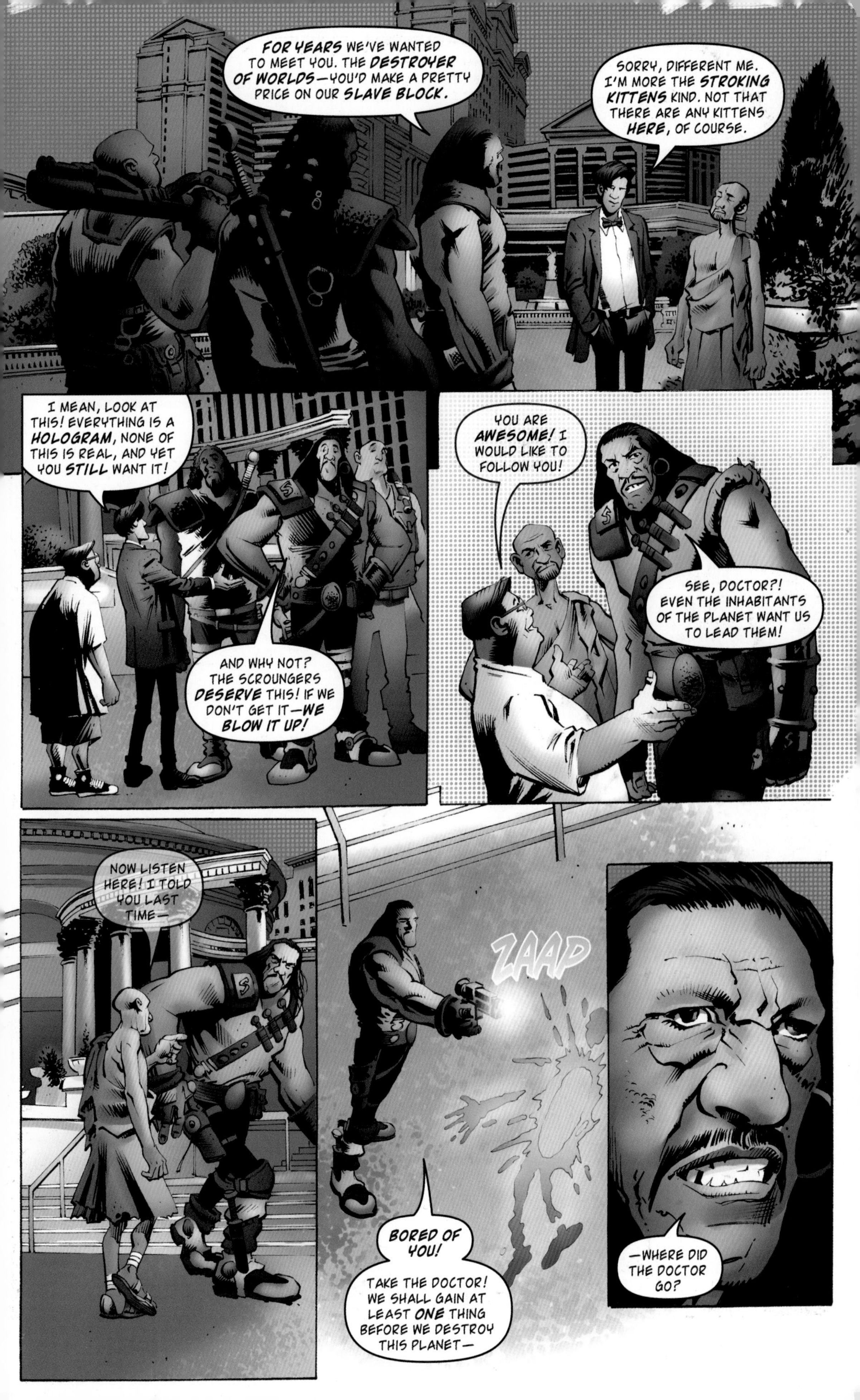
FOR YEARS WE'VE WANTED TO MEET YOU. THE DESTROYER OF WORLDS—YOU'D MAKE A PRETTY PRICE ON OUR SLAVE BLOCK.
SORRY, DIFFERENT ME. I'M MORE THE STROKING KITTENS KIND. NOT THAT THERE ARE ANY KITTENS HERE, OF COURSE.
I MEAN, LOOK AT THIS! EVERYTHING IS A HOLOGRAM, NONE OF THIS IS REAL, AND YET YOU STILL WANT IT!
AND WHY NOT? THE SCROUNGERS DESERVE THIS! IF WE DON'T GET IT—WE BLOW IT UP!
YOU ARE AWESOME! I WOULD LIKE TO FOLLOW YOU!
SEE, DOCTOR?! EVEN THE INHABITANTS OF THE PLANET WANT US TO LEAD THEM!
NOW LISTEN HERE! I TOLD YOU LAST TIME—
ZAAP
BORED OF YOU!
TAKE THE DOCTOR! WE SHALL GAIN AT LEAST ONE THING BEFORE WE DESTROY THIS PLANET—
—WHERE DID THE DOCTOR GO?

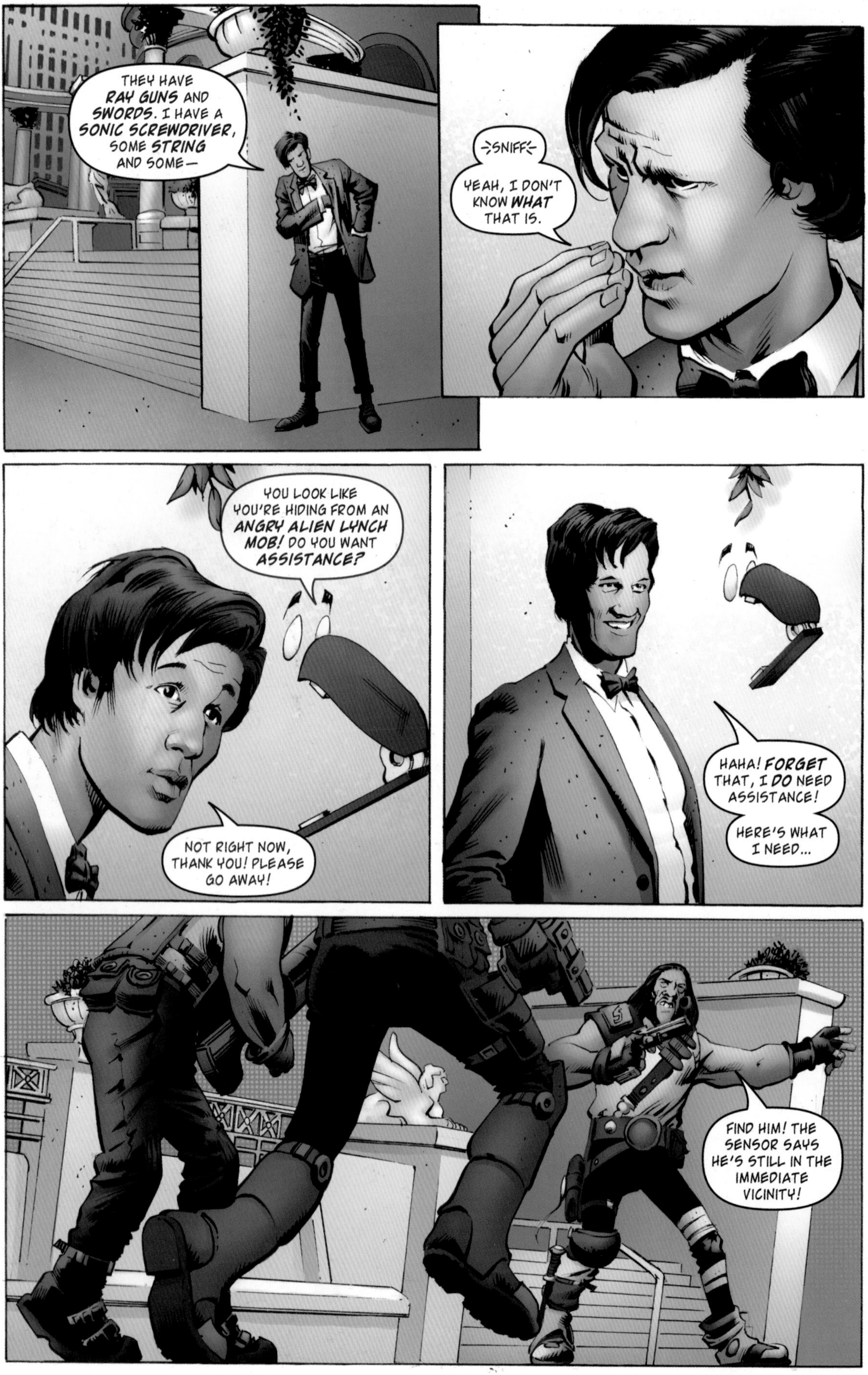
THEY HAVE RAY GUNS AND SWORDS. I HAVE A SONIC SCREWDRIVER, SOME STRING AND SOME—
SNIFF
YEAH, I DON'T KNOW WHAT THAT IS.
YOU LOOK LIKE YOU'RE HIDING FROM AN ANGRY ALIEN LYNCH MOB! DO YOU WANT ASSISTANCE?
NOT RIGHT NOW, THANK YOU! PLEASE GO AWAY!
HAHA! FORGET THAT, I DO NEED ASSISTANCE!
HERE'S WHAT I NEED...
FIND HIM! THE SENSOR SAYS HE'S STILL IN THE IMMEDIATE VICINITY!

AH, *THERE* YOU ARE! THOUGHT YOU'D WANDERED OFF!

DOCTOR! BAR US, YOU ARE THE ONLY LIFE FORM ON THIS PLANET! THERE IS NOWHERE TO HIDE!

OH, I DON'T WANT TO *HIDE* FROM YOU.

I'M HERE TO *HELP* YOU. YOU KNOW, *SHOULDERPADS FOREVER* AND ALL THAT.

TAKE HIM! CAPTURE THE DOCTOR!

WELL DONE, YOU! YOU REALLY *HAVE* THOUGHT THIS ALL OUT!

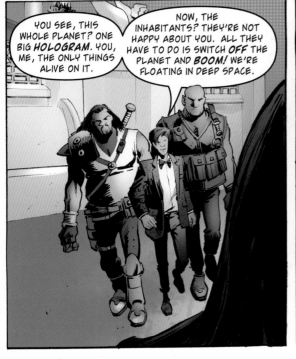

YOU SEE, THIS WHOLE PLANET? ONE BIG *HOLOGRAM.* YOU, ME, THE ONLY THINGS ALIVE ON IT.

NOW, THE INHABITANTS? THEY'RE NOT HAPPY ABOUT YOU. ALL THEY HAVE TO DO IS SWITCH *OFF* THE PLANET AND *BOOM!* WE'RE FLOATING IN DEEP SPACE.

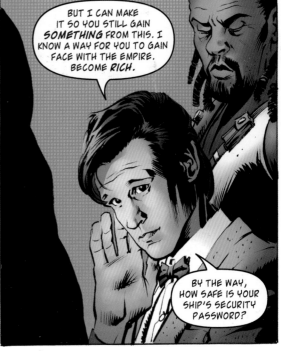

BUT I CAN MAKE IT SO YOU STILL GAIN *SOMETHING* FROM THIS. I KNOW A WAY FOR YOU TO GAIN FACE WITH THE EMPIRE. BECOME *RICH.*

BY THE WAY, HOW SAFE IS YOUR SHIP'S SECURITY PASSWORD?

17

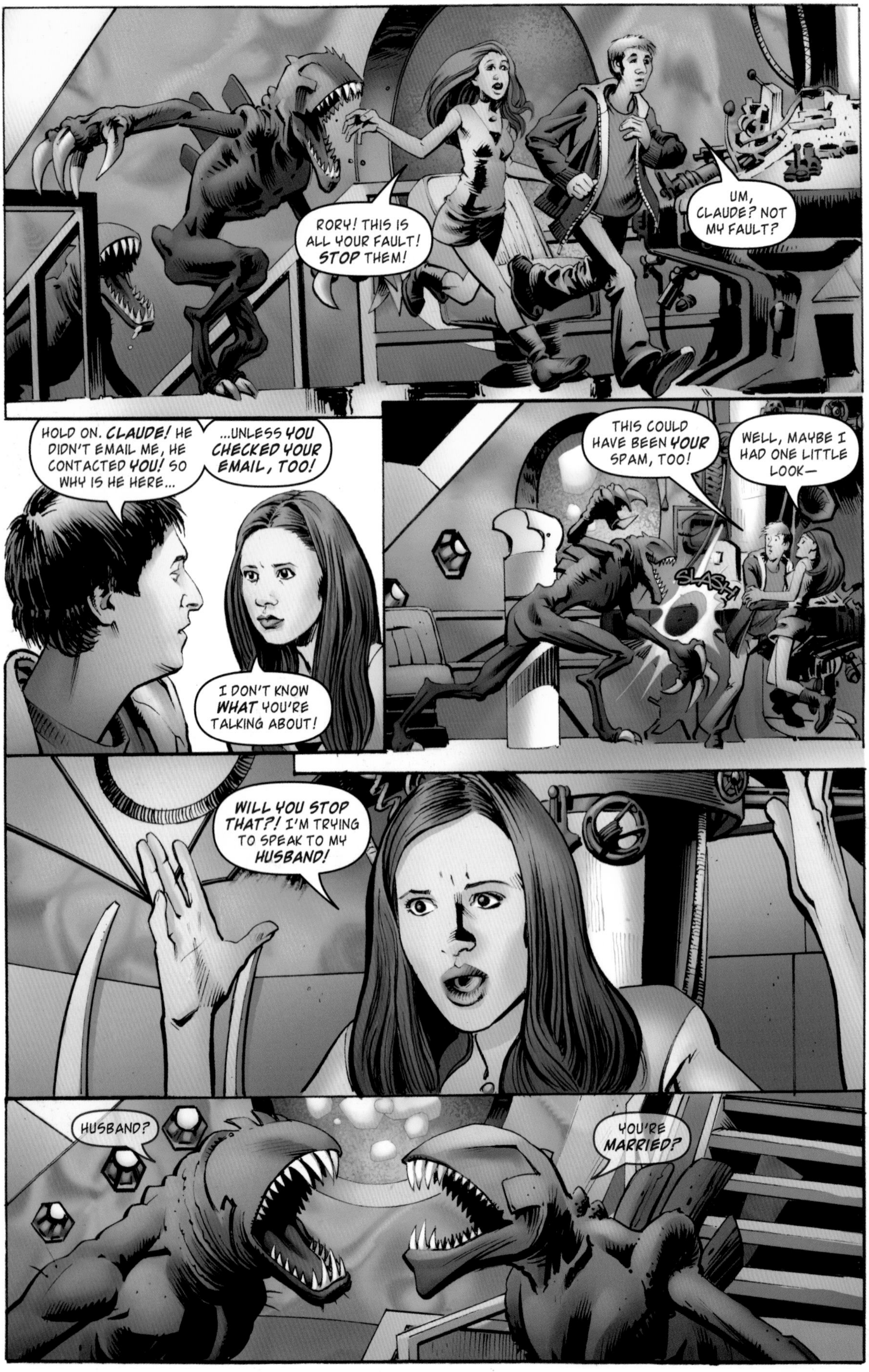
RORY! THIS IS ALL YOUR FAULT! STOP THEM!
UM, CLAUDE? NOT MY FAULT?
HOLD ON. CLAUDE! HE DIDN'T EMAIL ME, HE CONTACTED YOU! SO WHY IS HE HERE...
...UNLESS YOU CHECKED YOUR EMAIL, TOO!
I DON'T KNOW WHAT YOU'RE TALKING ABOUT!
THIS COULD HAVE BEEN YOUR SPAM, TOO!
WELL, MAYBE I HAD ONE LITTLE LOOK—
SLASH
WILL YOU STOP THAT?! I'M TRYING TO SPEAK TO MY HUSBAND!
HUSBAND?
YOU'RE MARRIED?

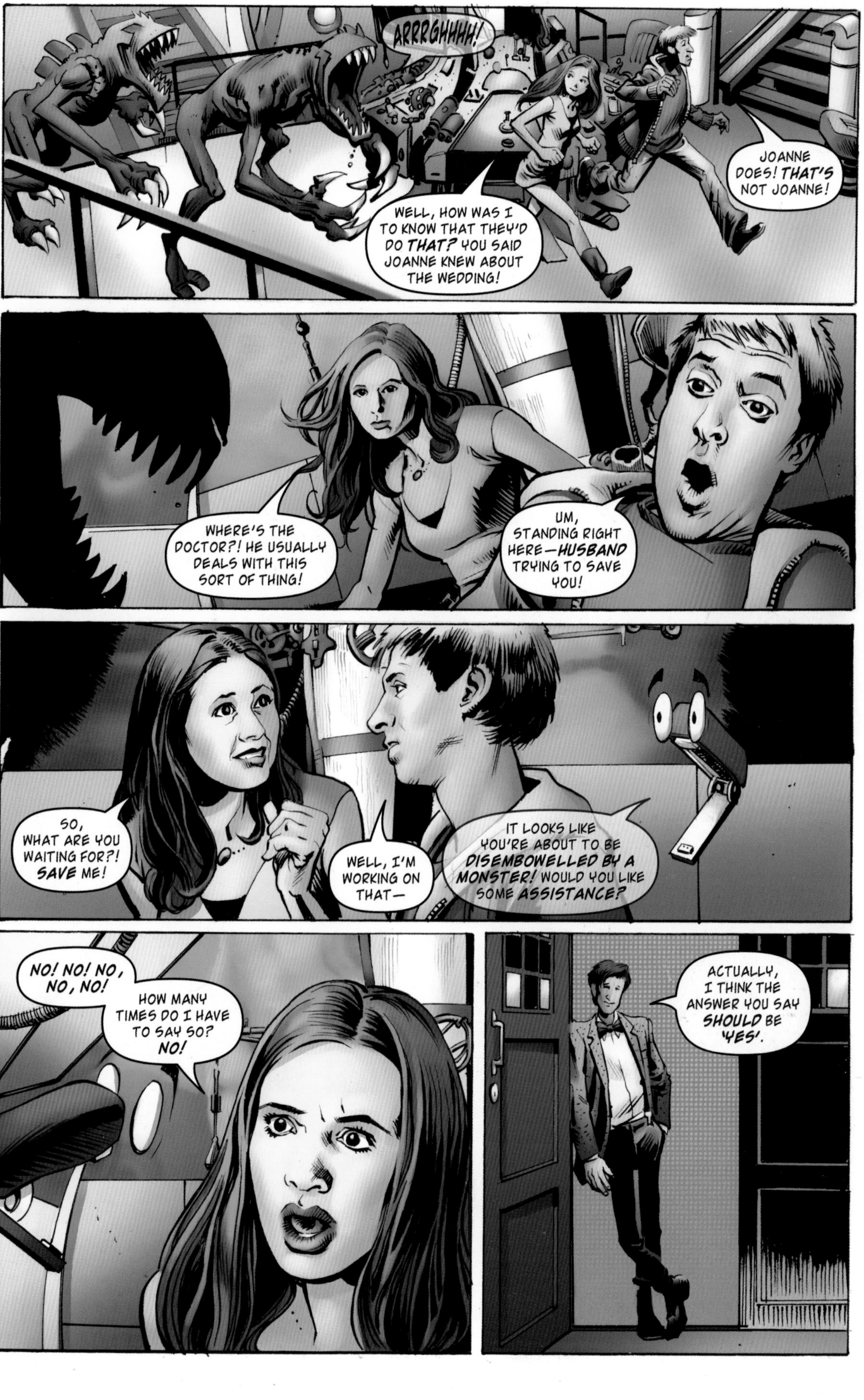
ARRRGHHHH!
WELL, HOW WAS I TO KNOW THAT THEY'D DO THAT? YOU SAID JOANNE KNEW ABOUT THE WEDDING!
JOANNE DOES! THAT'S NOT JOANNE!
WHERE'S THE DOCTOR?! HE USUALLY DEALS WITH THIS SORT OF THING!
UM, STANDING RIGHT HERE—HUSBAND TRYING TO SAVE YOU!
SO, WHAT ARE YOU WAITING FOR?! SAVE ME!
WELL, I'M WORKING ON THAT—
IT LOOKS LIKE YOU'RE ABOUT TO BE DISEMBOWELLED BY A MONSTER! WOULD YOU LIKE SOME ASSISTANCE?
NO! NO! NO, NO, NO!
HOW MANY TIMES DO I HAVE TO SAY SO? NO!
ACTUALLY, I THINK THE ANSWER YOU SAY SHOULD BE 'YES'.

DOCTOR! YES! YES! YES!
HELP ME, LITTLE STAPLER!
OKIE-DOKIE! HERE WE GO!
CLAUDE! JOANNE! THESE TWO HUMANS HAVE TREATED YOU SO BADLY—THEY DIDN'T TELL YOU OF THEIR LOVE, THEIR MARRIAGE!
I DID TELL HIM! I MEAN, HE KNEW I WAS ON MY HEN WEEKEND!
AND JOANNE KNEW ABOUT IT WHEN SHE CONTACTED ME!
SHH! THIS IS THE GOOD BIT!
I DO LIKE A HAPPY ENDING.
TWO LOST LOVES, ALONE IN THE UNIVERSE, BUT LOOK! YOU HAVE SO MUCH IN COMMON! IGNORE THEM, CONCENTRATE ON YOU!
WOULD YOU CONFIRM MY FRIENDLY REQUEST?
MY STATUS IS CHANGING FROM 'COMPLICATED' TO 'HOPEFUL'. OH YES, CLAUDE! YES!
AND 'FIN'! FADE OUT, BRING UP THE SOUNDTRACK!

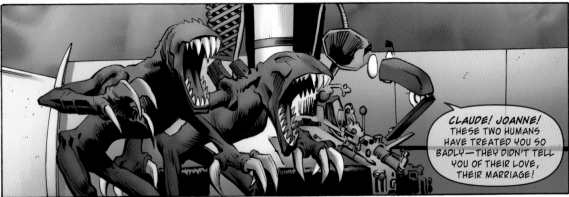

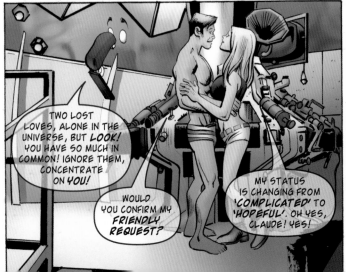

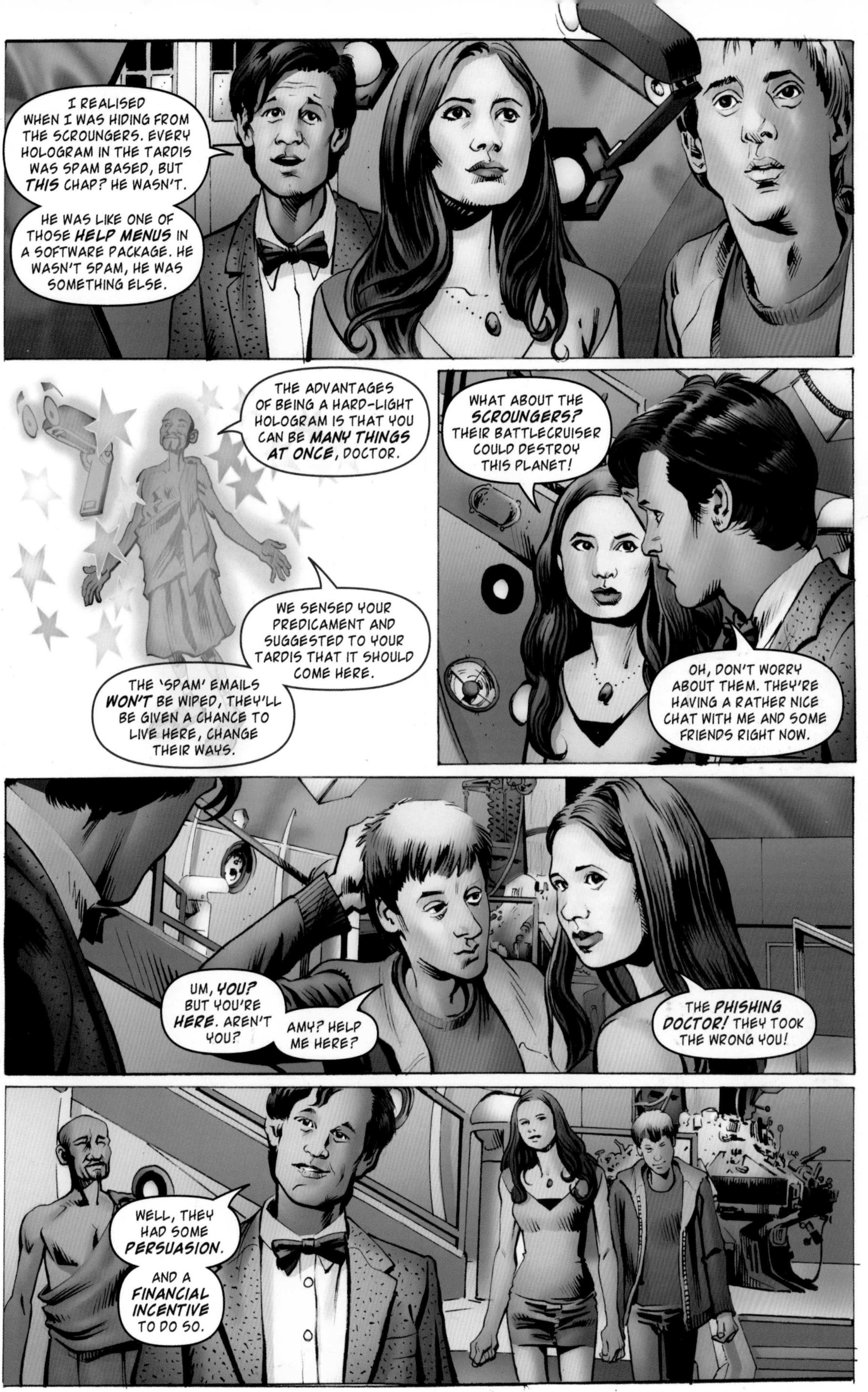
I REALISED WHEN I WAS HIDING FROM THE SCROUNGERS. EVERY HOLOGRAM IN THE TARDIS WAS SPAM BASED, BUT THIS CHAP? HE WASN'T.
HE WAS LIKE ONE OF THOSE HELP MENUS IN A SOFTWARE PACKAGE. HE WASN'T SPAM, HE WAS SOMETHING ELSE.
THE ADVANTAGES OF BEING A HARD-LIGHT HOLOGRAM IS THAT YOU CAN BE MANY THINGS AT ONCE, DOCTOR.
WE SENSED YOUR PREDICAMENT AND SUGGESTED TO YOUR TARDIS THAT IT SHOULD COME HERE.
THE 'SPAM' EMAILS WON'T BE WIPED, THEY'LL BE GIVEN A CHANCE TO LIVE HERE, CHANGE THEIR WAYS.
WHAT ABOUT THE SCROUNGERS? THEIR BATTLECRUISER COULD DESTROY THIS PLANET!
OH, DON'T WORRY ABOUT THEM. THEY'RE HAVING A RATHER NICE CHAT WITH ME AND SOME FRIENDS RIGHT NOW.
UM, YOU? BUT YOU'RE HERE. AREN'T YOU?
AMY? HELP ME HERE?
THE PHISHING DOCTOR! THEY TOOK THE WRONG YOU!
WELL, THEY HAD SOME PERSUASION.
AND A FINANCIAL INCENTIVE TO DO SO.

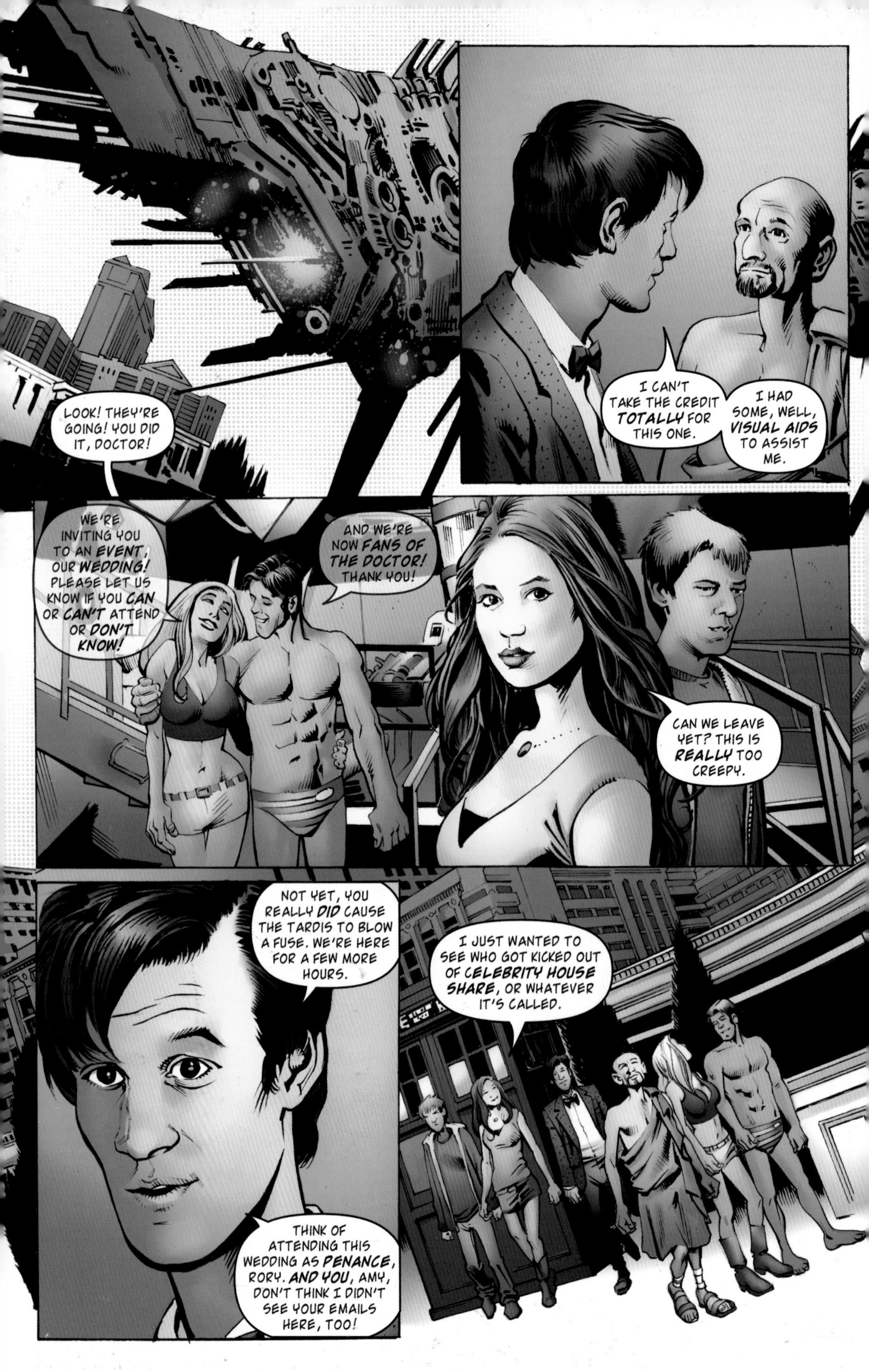

LOOK! THEY'RE GOING! YOU DID IT, DOCTOR!
I CAN'T TAKE THE CREDIT TOTALLY FOR THIS ONE.
I HAD SOME, WELL, VISUAL AIDS TO ASSIST ME.
WE'RE INVITING YOU TO AN EVENT, OUR WEDDING! PLEASE LET US KNOW IF YOU CAN OR CAN'T ATTEND OR DON'T KNOW!
AND WE'RE NOW FANS OF THE DOCTOR! THANK YOU!
CAN WE LEAVE YET? THIS IS REALLY TOO CREEPY.
NOT YET, YOU REALLY DID CAUSE THE TARDIS TO BLOW A FUSE. WE'RE HERE FOR A FEW MORE HOURS.
THINK OF ATTENDING THIS WEDDING AS PENANCE, RORY. AND YOU, AMY, DON'T THINK I DIDN'T SEE YOUR EMAILS HERE, TOO!
I JUST WANTED TO SEE WHO GOT KICKED OUT OF CELEBRITY HOUSE SHARE, OR WHATEVER IT'S CALLED.

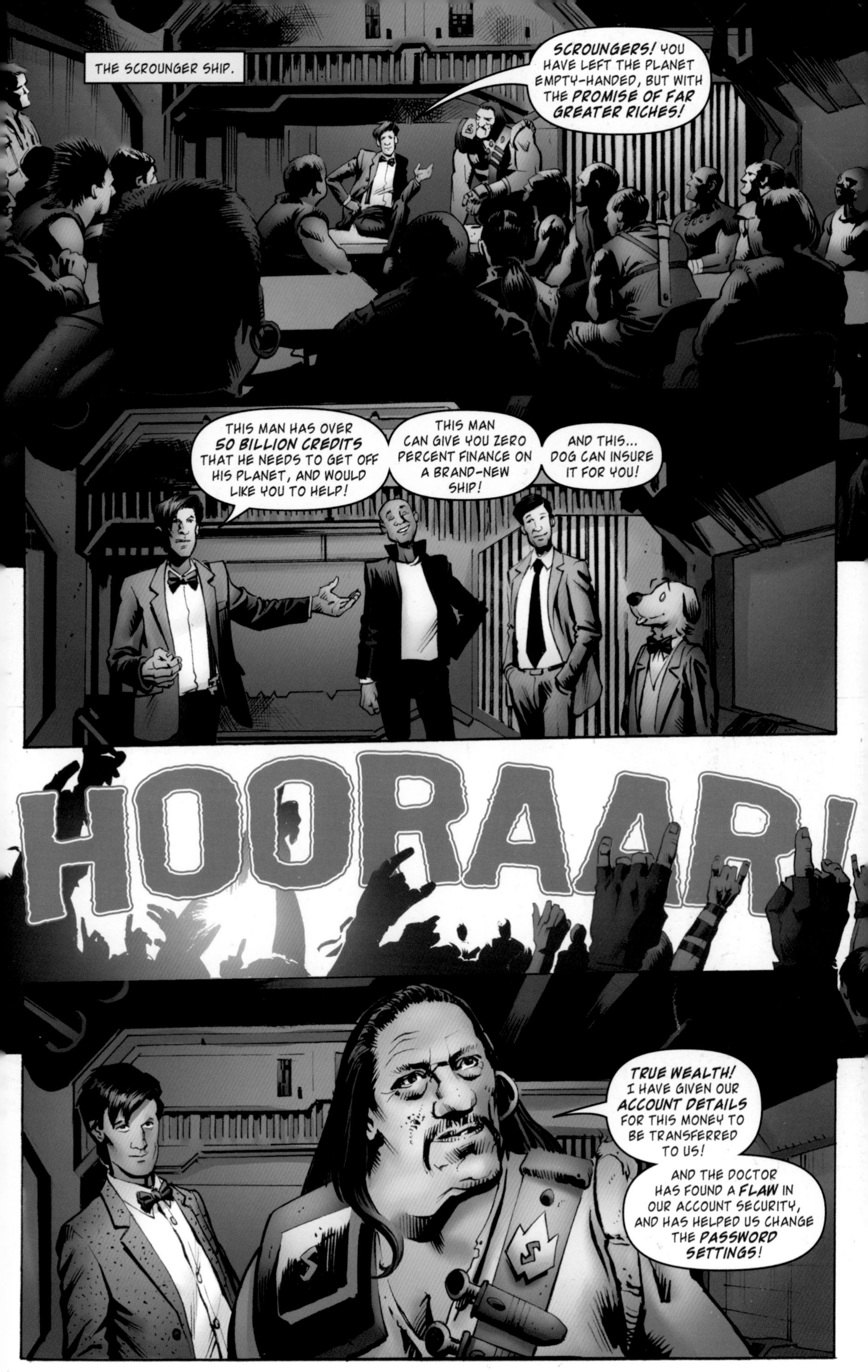
THE SCROUNGER SHIP.
SCROUNGERS! YOU HAVE LEFT THE PLANET EMPTY-HANDED, BUT WITH THE PROMISE OF FAR GREATER RICHES!
THIS MAN HAS OVER 50 BILLION CREDITS THAT HE NEEDS TO GET OFF HIS PLANET, AND WOULD LIKE YOU TO HELP!
THIS MAN CAN GIVE YOU ZERO PERCENT FINANCE ON A BRAND-NEW SHIP!
AND THIS... DOG CAN INSURE IT FOR YOU!
HOORAAR!
TRUE WEALTH! I HAVE GIVEN OUR ACCOUNT DETAILS FOR THIS MONEY TO BE TRANSFERRED TO US!
AND THE DOCTOR HAS FOUND A FLAW IN OUR ACCOUNT SECURITY, AND HAS HELPED US CHANGE THE PASSWORD SETTINGS!

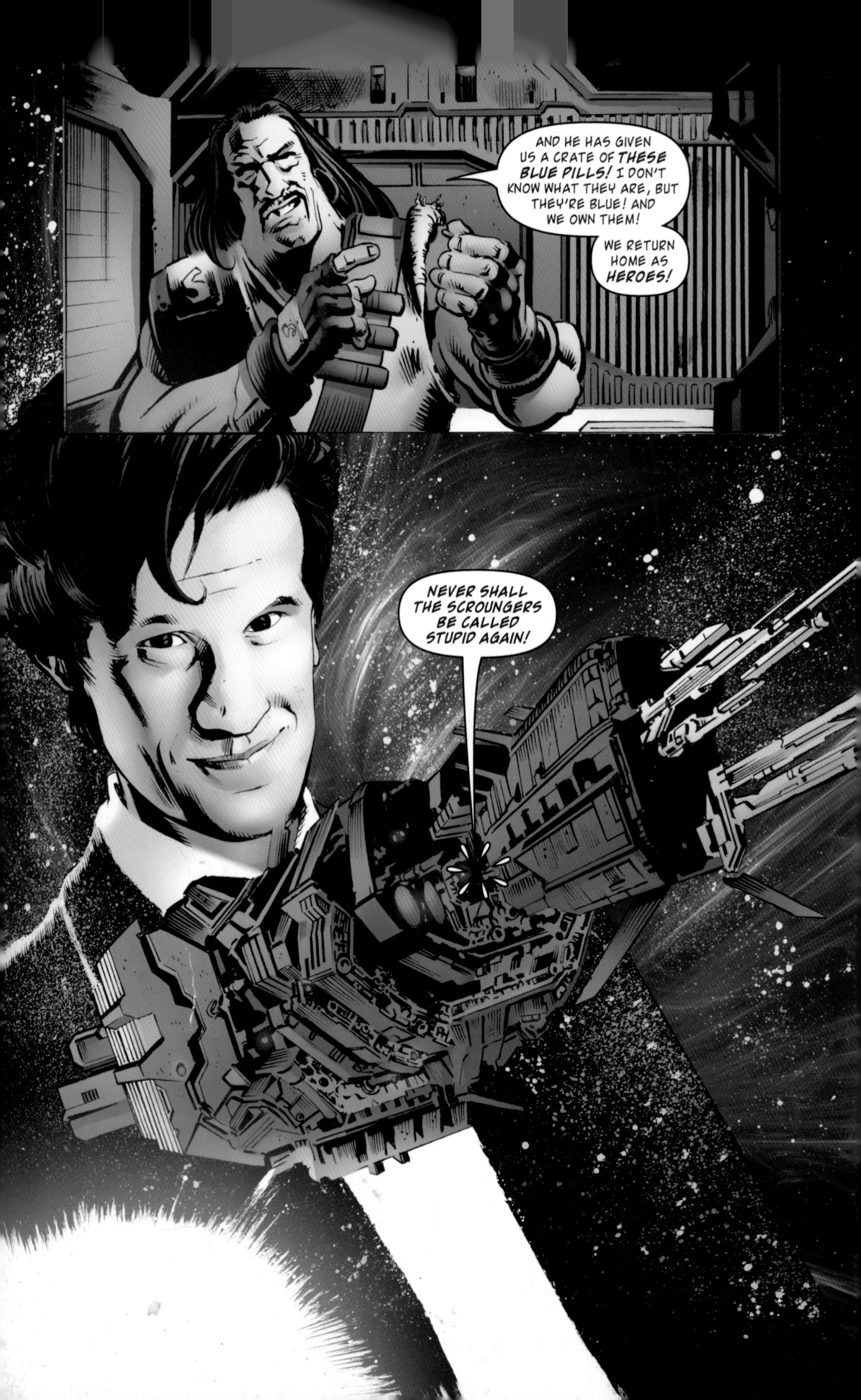
AND HE HAS GIVEN US A CRATE OF THESE BLUE PILLS! I DON'T KNOW WHAT THEY ARE, BUT THEY'RE BLUE! AND WE OWN THEM!
WE RETURN HOME AS HEROES!
NEVER SHALL THE SCROUNGERS BE CALLED STUPID AGAIN!

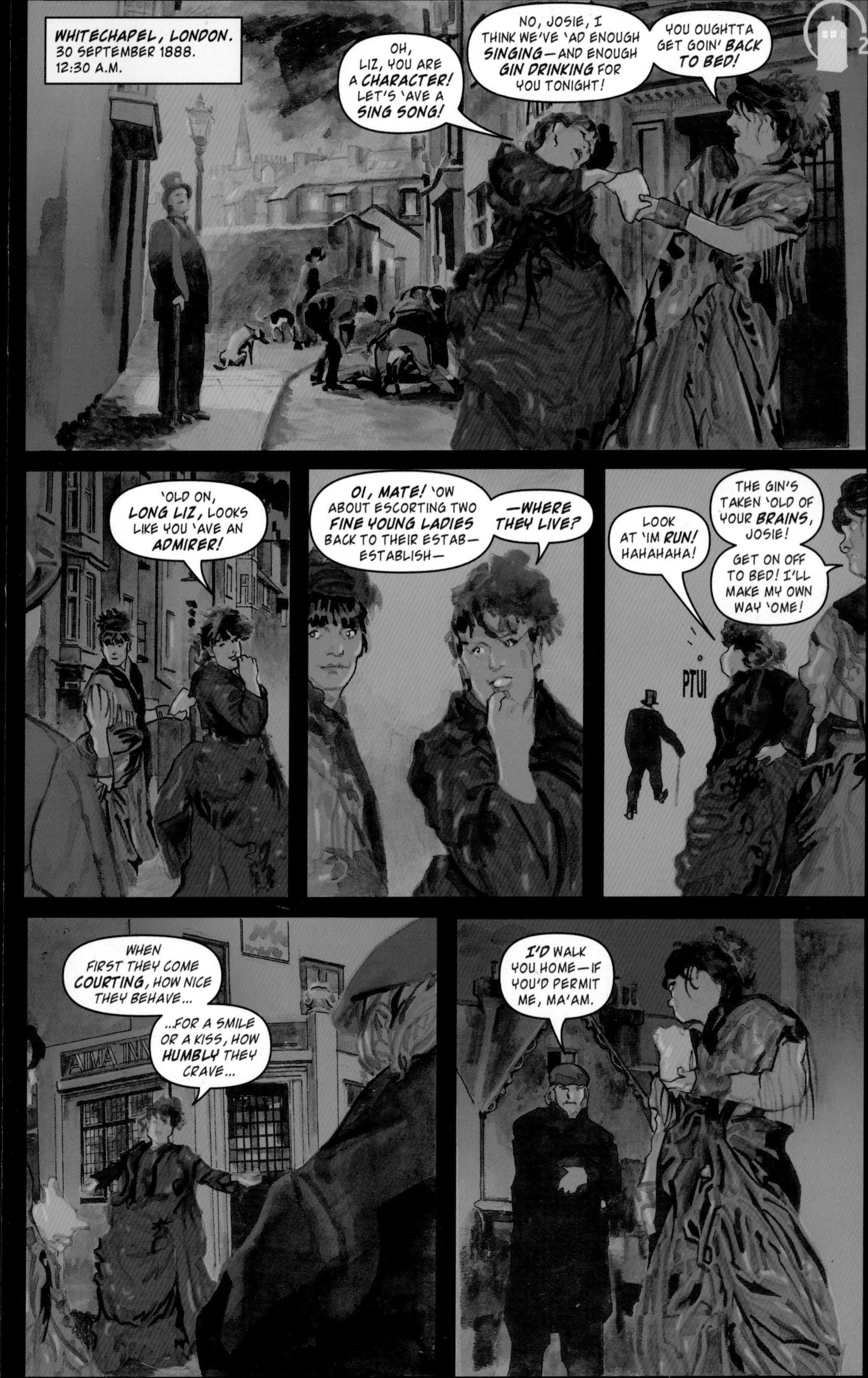
WHITECHAPEL, LONDON. 30 SEPTEMBER 1888. 12:30 A.M.
OH, LIZ, YOU ARE A CHARACTER! LET'S 'AVE A SING SONG!
NO, JOSIE, I THINK WE'VE 'AD ENOUGH SINGING—AND ENOUGH GIN DRINKING FOR YOU TONIGHT!
YOU OUGHTTA GET GOIN' BACK TO BED!
'OLD ON, LONG LIZ, LOOKS LIKE YOU 'AVE AN ADMIRER!
OI, MATE! 'OW ABOUT ESCORTING TWO FINE YOUNG LADIES BACK TO THEIR ESTAB-ESTABLISH—
—WHERE THEY LIVE?
LOOK AT 'IM RUN! HAHAHAHA!
PTUI
THE GIN'S TAKEN 'OLD OF YOUR BRAINS, JOSIE!
GET ON OFF TO BED! I'LL MAKE MY OWN WAY 'OME!
WHEN FIRST THEY COME COURTING, HOW NICE THEY BEHAVE...
...FOR A SMILE OR A KISS, HOW HUMBLY THEY CRAVE...
I'D WALK YOU HOME—IF YOU'D PERMIT ME, MA'AM.

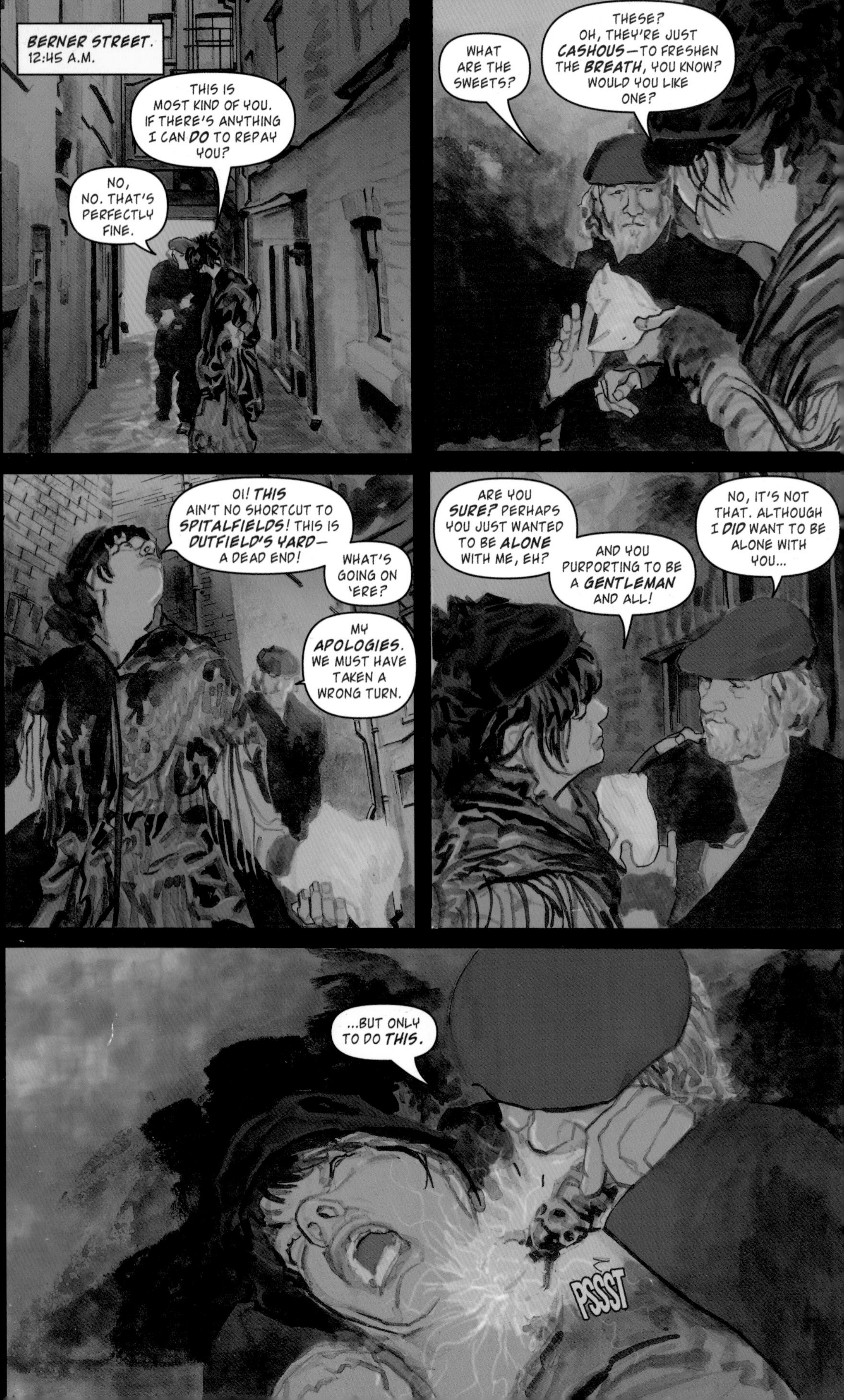

BERNER STREET. 12:45 A.M.
THIS IS MOST KIND OF YOU. IF THERE'S ANYTHING I CAN DO TO REPAY YOU?
NO, NO. THAT'S PERFECTLY FINE.
WHAT ARE THE SWEETS?
THESE? OH, THEY'RE JUST CASHOUS—TO FRESHEN THE BREATH, YOU KNOW? WOULD YOU LIKE ONE?
OI! THIS AIN'T NO SHORTCUT TO SPITALFIELDS! THIS IS DUTFIELD'S YARD—A DEAD END!
WHAT'S GOING ON 'ERE?
MY APOLOGIES. WE MUST HAVE TAKEN A WRONG TURN.
ARE YOU SURE? PERHAPS YOU JUST WANTED TO BE ALONE WITH ME, EH?
AND YOU PURPORTING TO BE A GENTLEMAN AND ALL!
NO, IT'S NOT THAT. ALTHOUGH I DID WANT TO BE ALONE WITH YOU...
...BUT ONLY TO DO THIS.
PSSST

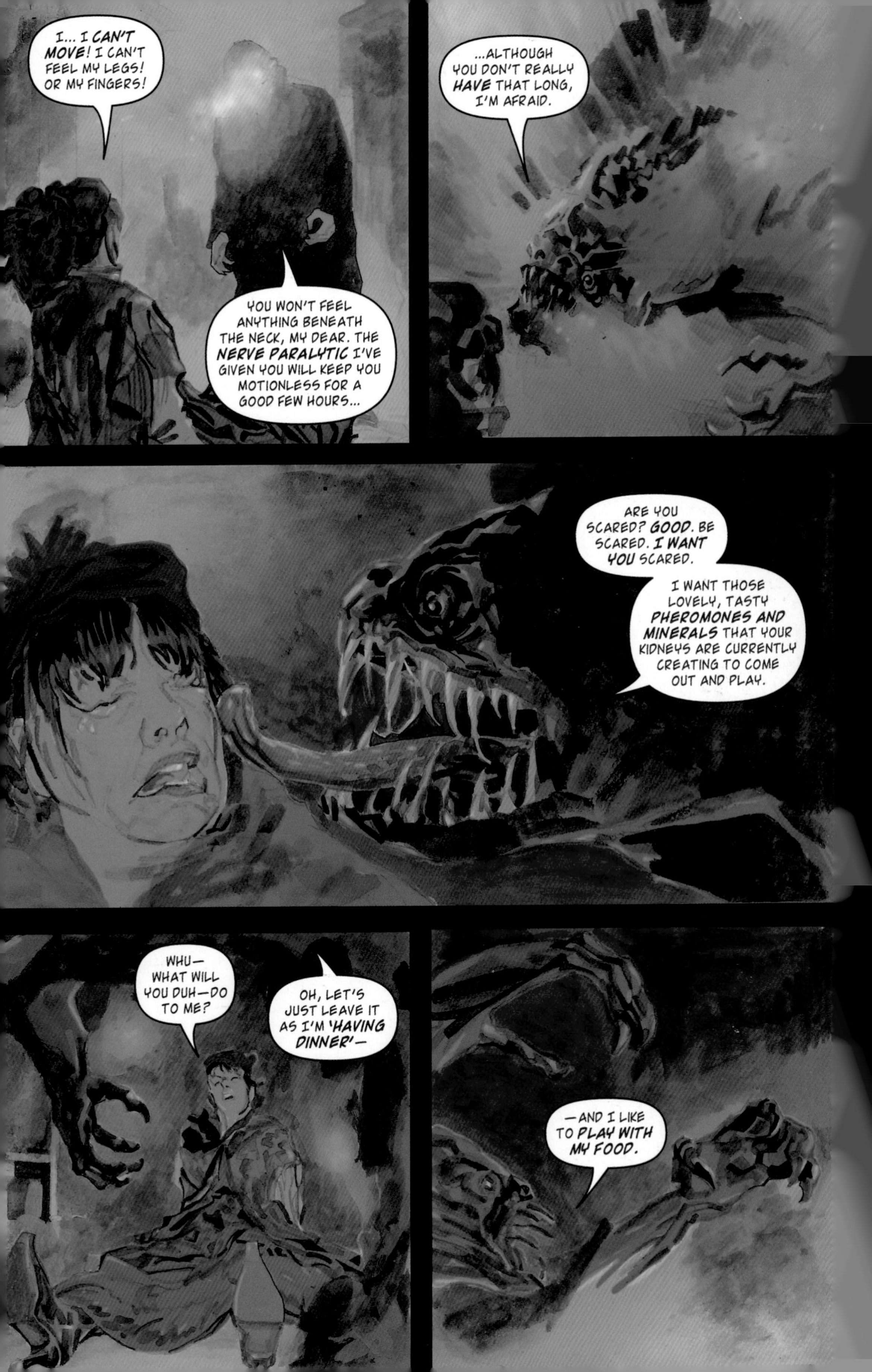
I... I CAN'T MOVE! I CAN'T FEEL MY LEGS! OR MY FINGERS!
YOU WON'T FEEL ANYTHING BENEATH THE NECK, MY DEAR. THE NERVE PARALYTIC I'VE GIVEN YOU WILL KEEP YOU MOTIONLESS FOR A GOOD FEW HOURS...
...ALTHOUGH YOU DON'T REALLY HAVE THAT LONG, I'M AFRAID.
ARE YOU SCARED? GOOD. BE SCARED. I WANT YOU SCARED.
I WANT THOSE LOVELY, TASTY PHEROMONES AND MINERALS THAT YOUR KIDNEYS ARE CURRENTLY CREATING TO COME OUT AND PLAY.
WHU— WHAT WILL YOU DUH—DO TO ME?
OH, LET'S JUST LEAVE IT AS I'M 'HAVING DINNER'—
—AND I LIKE TO PLAY WITH MY FOOD.

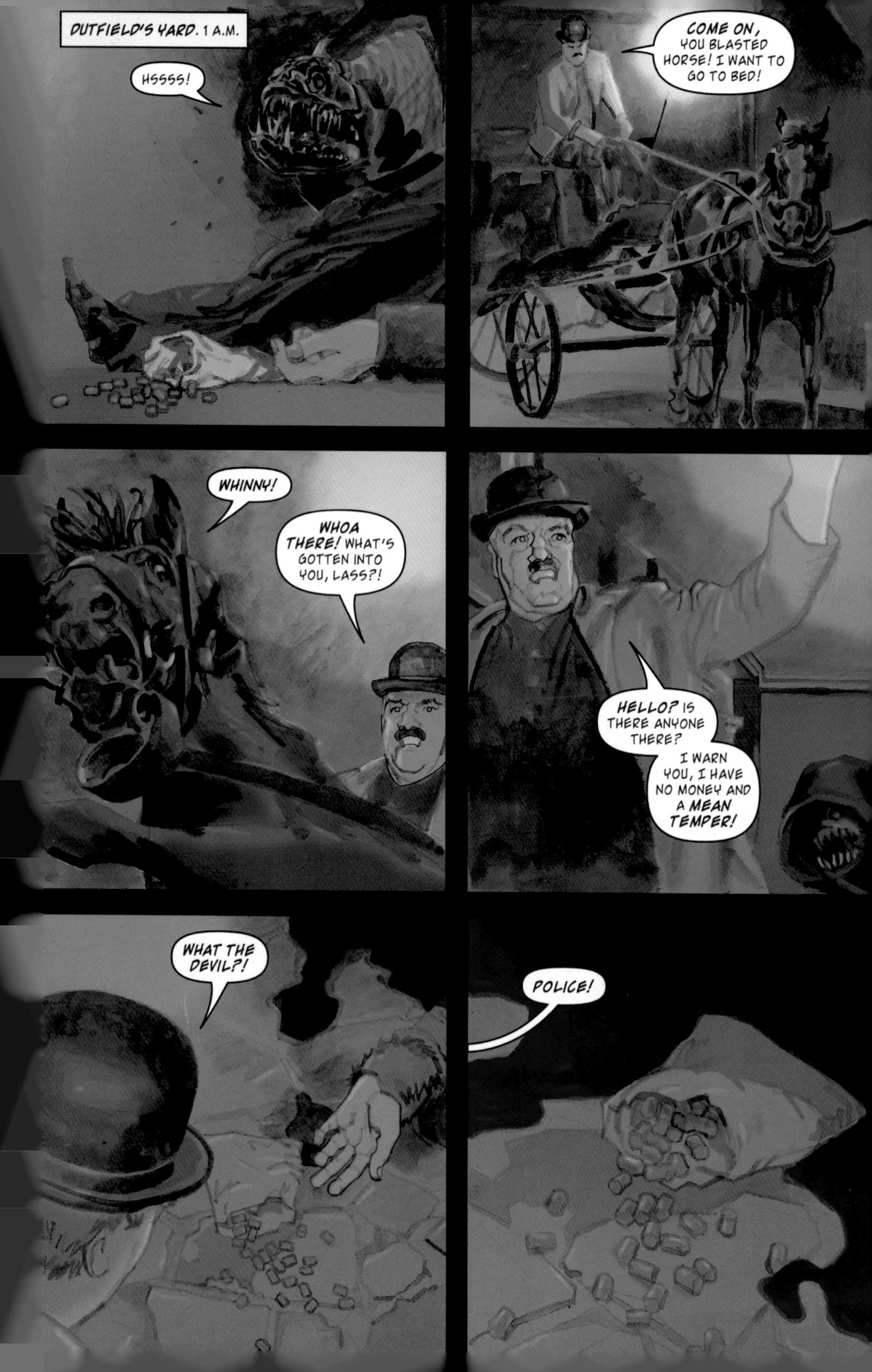
DUTFIELD'S YARD. 1 A.M.
HSSSS!
COME ON, YOU BLASTED HORSE! I WANT TO GO TO BED!
WHINNY!
WHOA THERE! WHAT'S GOTTEN INTO YOU, LASS?!
HELLO? IS THERE ANYONE THERE?
I WARN YOU, I HAVE NO MONEY AND A MEAN TEMPER!
WHAT THE DEVIL?!
POLICE!

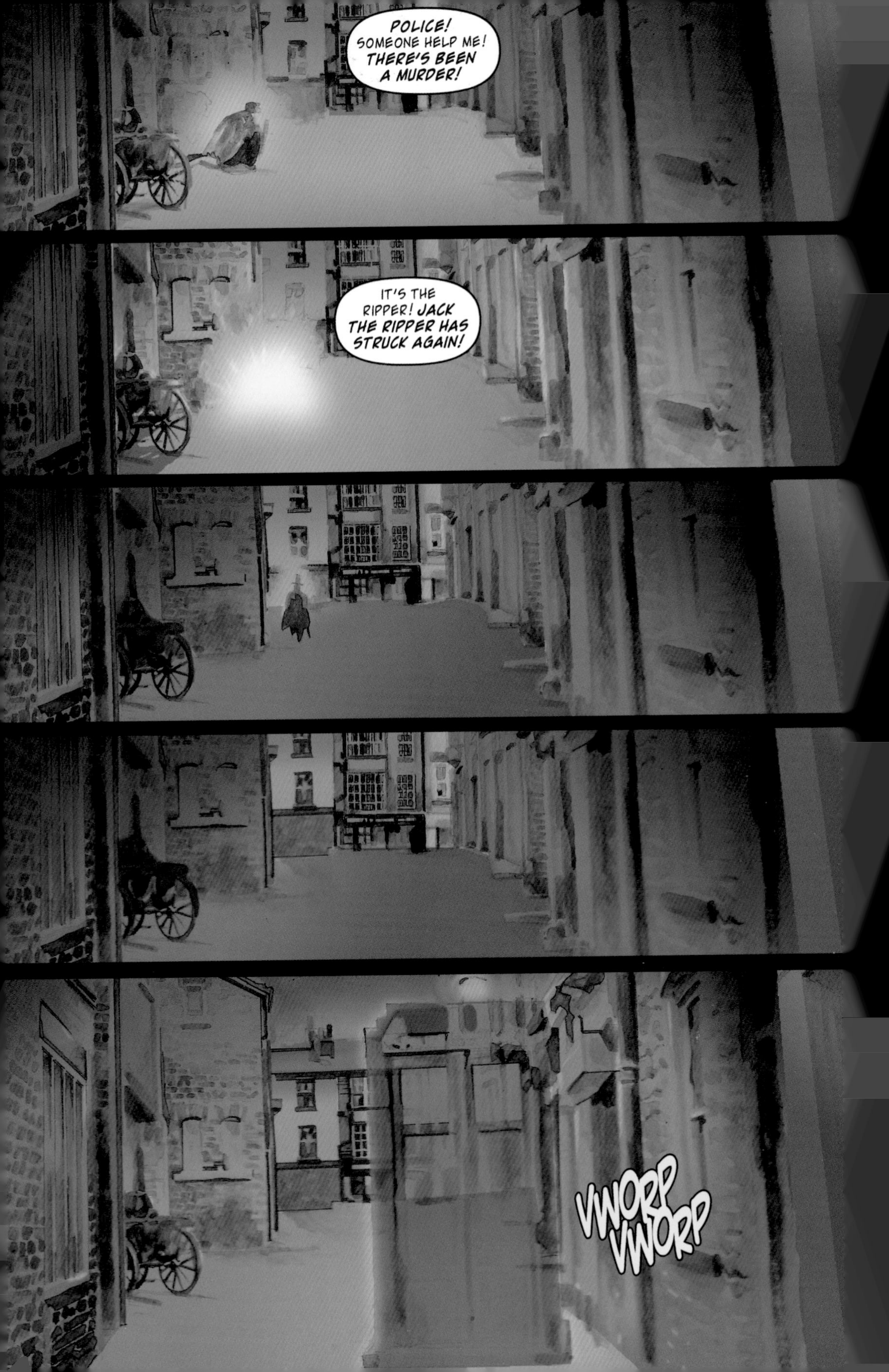
POLICE! SOMEONE HELP ME! THERE'S BEEN A MURDER!
IT'S THE RIPPER! JACK THE RIPPER HAS STRUCK AGAIN!
VWORP VWORP

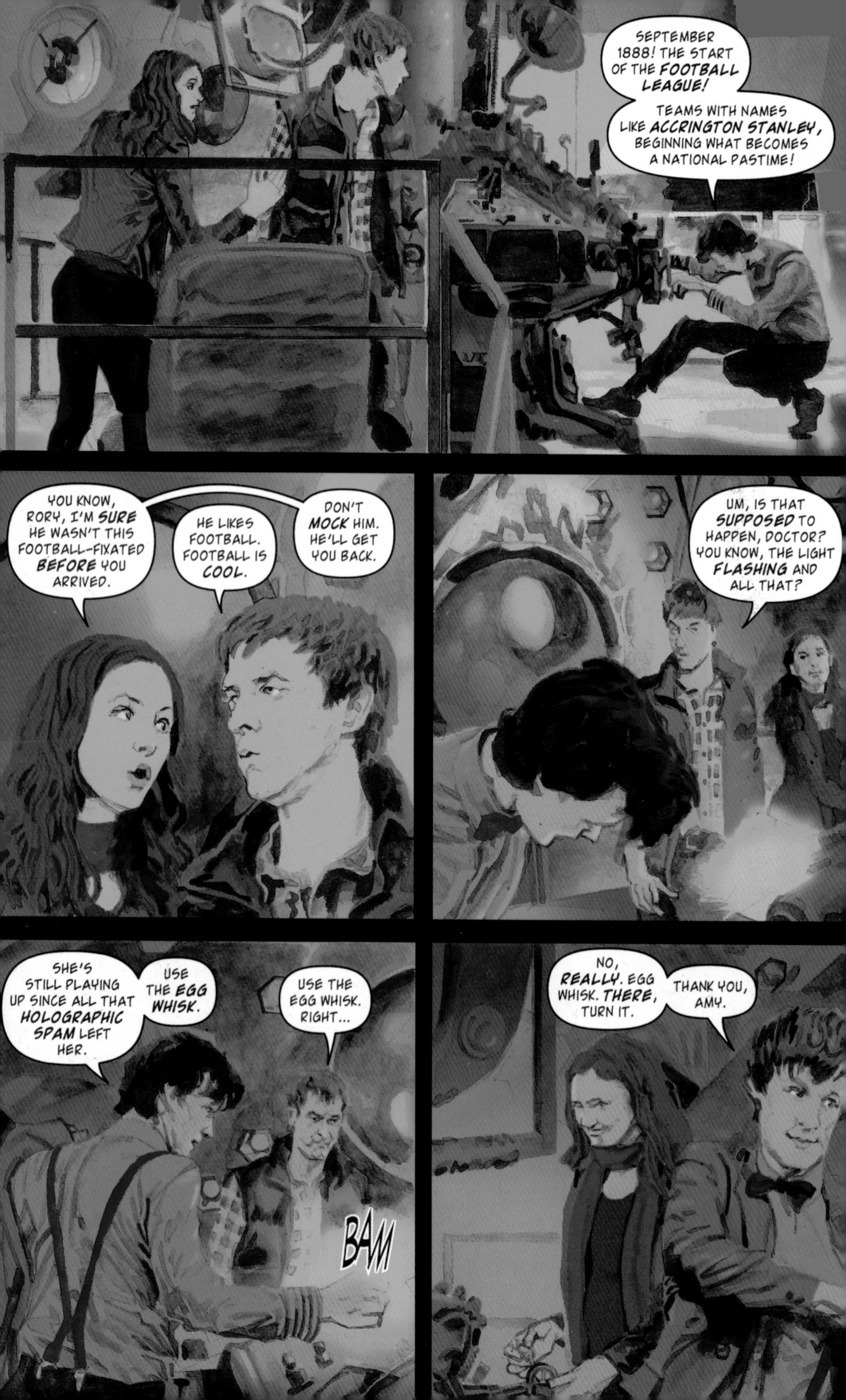

SEPTEMBER 1888! THE START OF THE FOOTBALL LEAGUE!
TEAMS WITH NAMES LIKE ACCRINGTON STANLEY, BEGINNING WHAT BECOMES A NATIONAL PASTIME!
YOU KNOW, RORY, I'M SURE HE WASN'T THIS FOOTBALL-FIXATED BEFORE YOU ARRIVED.
HE LIKES FOOTBALL. FOOTBALL IS COOL.
DON'T MOCK HIM. HE'LL GET YOU BACK.
UM, IS THAT SUPPOSED TO HAPPEN, DOCTOR? YOU KNOW, THE LIGHT FLASHING AND ALL THAT?
SHE'S STILL PLAYING UP SINCE ALL THAT HOLOGRAPHIC SPAM LEFT HER.
USE THE EGG WHISK.
USE THE EGG WHISK. RIGHT...
BAM
NO, REALLY. EGG WHISK. THERE, TURN IT.
THANK YOU, AMY.

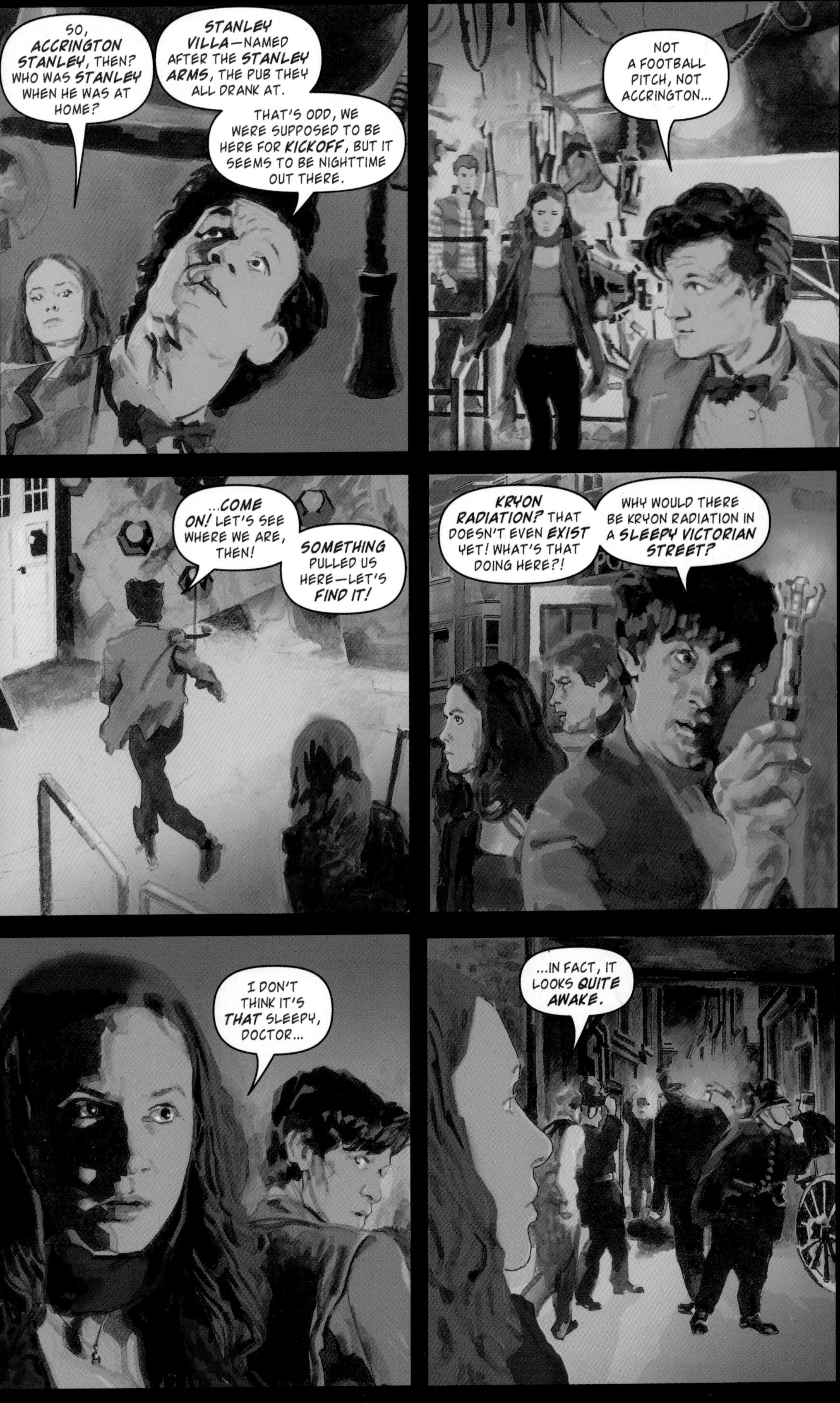
SO, ACCRINGTON STANLEY, THEN? WHO WAS STANLEY WHEN HE WAS AT HOME?
STANLEY VILLA—NAMED AFTER THE STANLEY ARMS, THE PUB THEY ALL DRANK AT.
THAT'S ODD, WE WERE SUPPOSED TO BE HERE FOR KICKOFF, BUT IT SEEMS TO BE NIGHTTIME OUT THERE.
NOT A FOOTBALL PITCH, NOT ACCRINGTON...
...COME ON! LET'S SEE WHERE WE ARE, THEN!
SOMETHING PULLED US HERE—LET'S FIND IT!
KRYON RADIATION? THAT DOESN'T EVEN EXIST YET! WHAT'S THAT DOING HERE?!
WHY WOULD THERE BE KRYON RADIATION IN A SLEEPY VICTORIAN STREET?
I DON'T THINK IT'S THAT SLEEPY, DOCTOR...
...IN FACT, IT LOOKS QUITE AWAKE.

SORRY, SIR, GONNA HAVE TO **STOP** YOU THERE. THERE'S BEEN AN INCIDENT.

I CAN TELL THAT. ALL THE **RUNNING AROUND** REALLY GIVES IT AWAY.

HELLO, I'M THE **DOCTOR**.

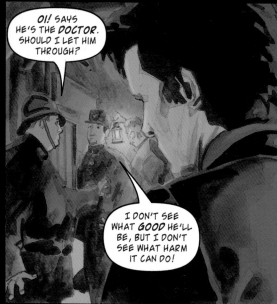

OI! SAYS HE'S THE **DOCTOR**. SHOULD I LET HIM THROUGH?

I DON'T SEE WHAT **GOOD** HE'LL BE, BUT I DON'T SEE WHAT HARM IT CAN DO!

HMM. HER THROAT WAS CUT. SHE DIED PRETTY MUCH INSTANTLY, I RECKON.

WHAT DO **YOU** THINK, RORY?

UM, **WHY** ARE YOU ASKING ME? **YOU'RE** THE DOCTOR HERE!

YES, BUT YOU'RE THE **NURSE**. AND YOU'VE BEEN PRACTISING MEDICINE FAR MORE **RECENTLY** THAN I HAVE. **WHAT DO YOU SEE?**

WELL, SHE'S **DEAD**, WE CAN SEE THAT. THE WOUND WAS MADE BY SOMETHING **SHARP**—

—OF **COURSE** IT WAS, RORY, THAT'S A **STUPID** STATEMENT.

THERE'S A FUNNY **SMELL**...

BREATH MINTS. THEY'RE IN HER HAND. NO, SOMETHING ELSE... ALMOST LIKE THERE **SHOULD** BE A SMELL, BUT THERE ISN'T.

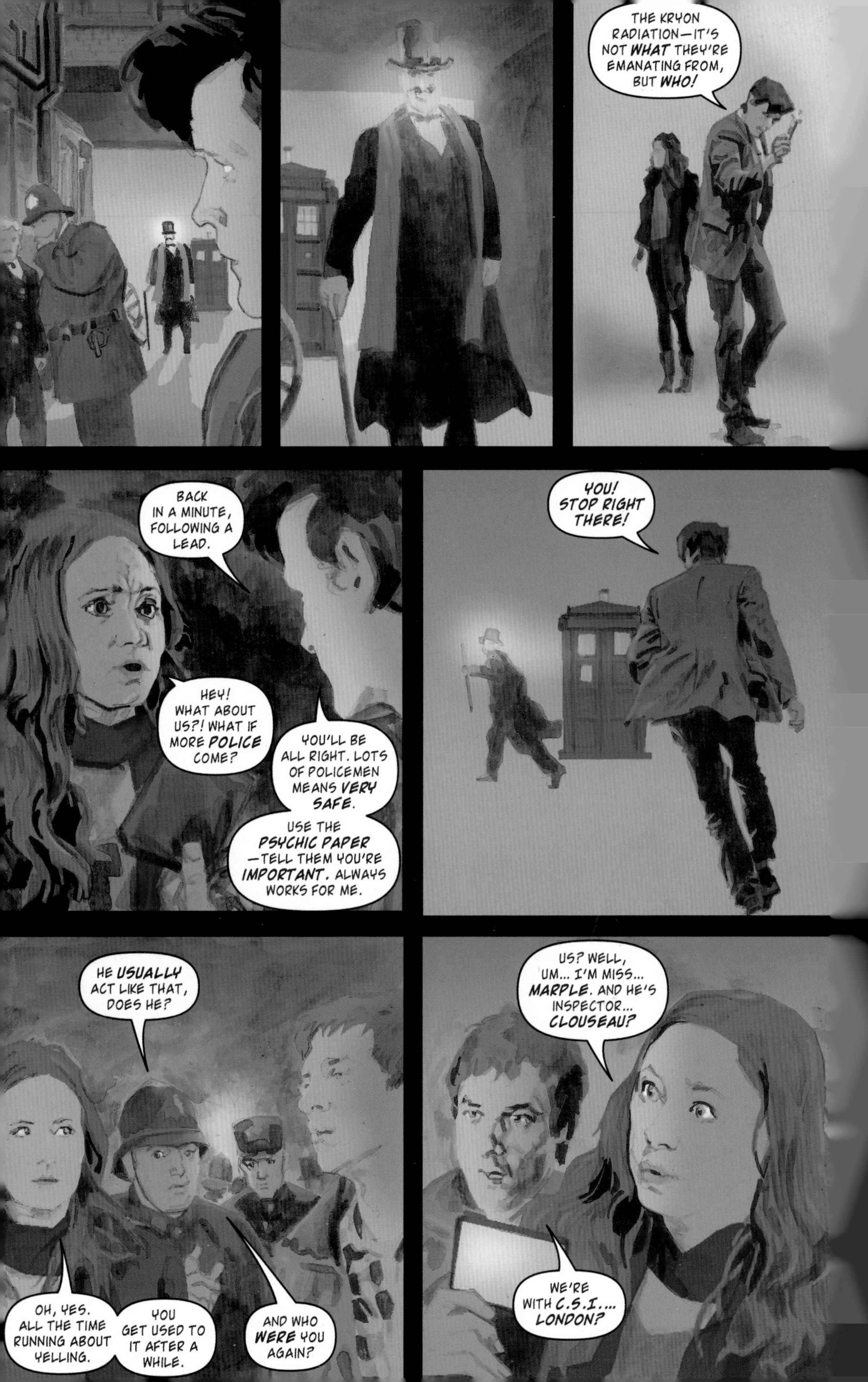
THE KRYON RADIATION—IT'S NOT WHAT THEY'RE EMANATING FROM, BUT WHO!
BACK IN A MINUTE, FOLLOWING A LEAD.
HEY! WHAT ABOUT US?! WHAT IF MORE POLICE COME?
YOU'LL BE ALL RIGHT. LOTS OF POLICEMEN MEANS VERY SAFE.
USE THE PSYCHIC PAPER —TELL THEM YOU'RE IMPORTANT. ALWAYS WORKS FOR ME.
YOU! STOP RIGHT THERE!
HE USUALLY ACT LIKE THAT, DOES HE?
OH, YES. ALL THE TIME RUNNING ABOUT YELLING.
YOU GET USED TO IT AFTER A WHILE.
AND WHO WERE YOU AGAIN?
US? WELL, UM... I'M MISS... MARPLE. AND HE'S INSPECTOR... CLOUSEAU?
WE'RE WITH C.S.I.... LONDON?

I JUST WANT TO **TALK!**

WHY DON'T PEOPLE WANT TO **STOP AND TALK** ANYMORE?

YOU SEEM TO HAVE A LOT OF **KRYON RADIATION.** AND THAT'S A BIT STRANGE AS IT COMES FROM THE **MATRUA NEBULA.**

I WAS JUST WONDERING IF YOU COULD—

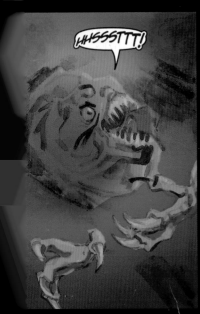

HHSSSTTT!

SWISH

WHOOPS!

FINGERS ALL THERE? GOOD.

COME BACK!

YES, BECAUSE OF **COURSE** A **REPTILE KILLER** IS GOING TO LISTEN TO YOU.

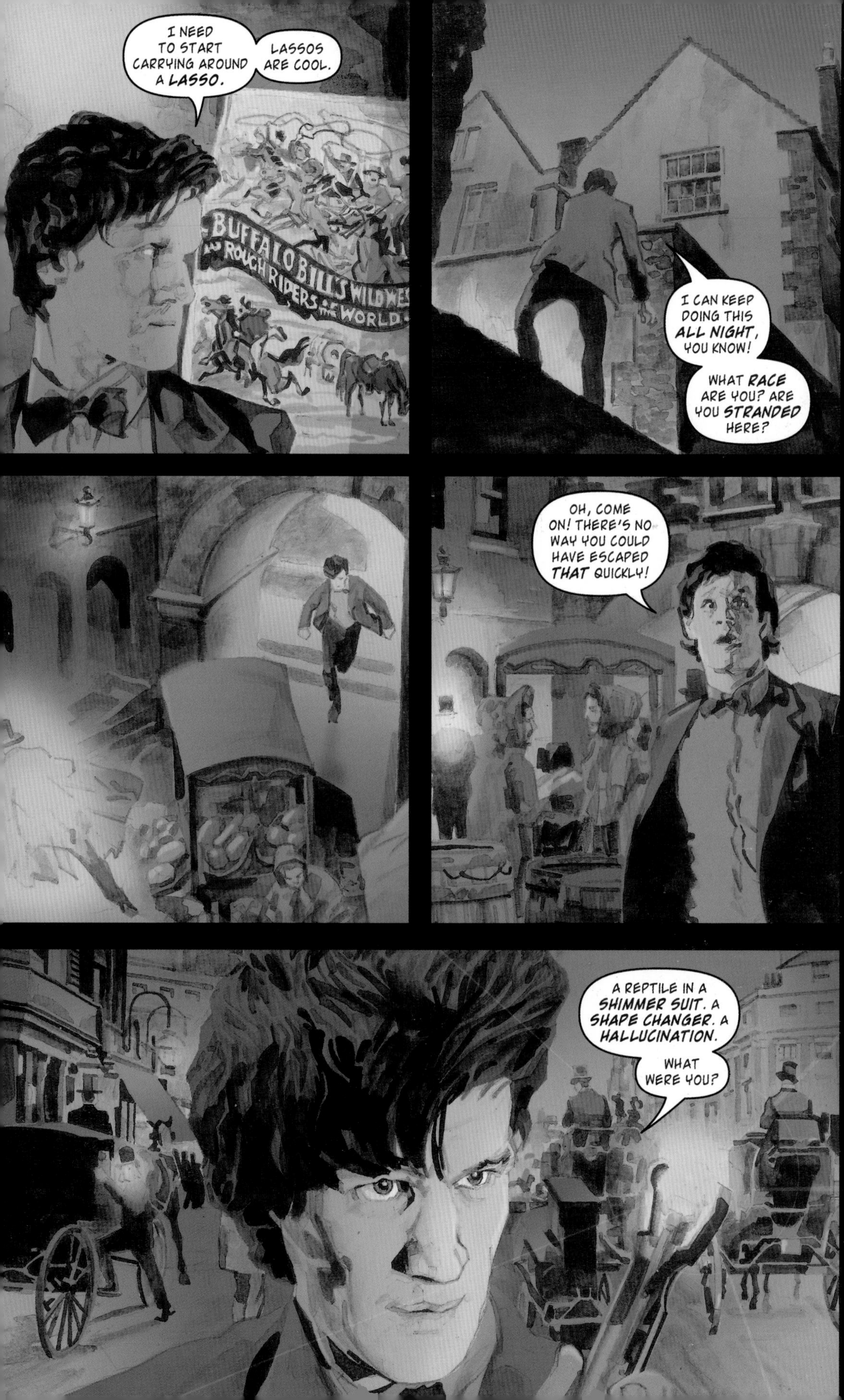
I NEED TO START CARRYING AROUND A LASSO.
LASSOS ARE COOL.
BUFFALO BILL'S WILD WEST AND ROUGH RIDERS OF THE WORLD
I CAN KEEP DOING THIS ALL NIGHT, YOU KNOW!
WHAT RACE ARE YOU? ARE YOU STRANDED HERE?
OH, COME ON! THERE'S NO WAY YOU COULD HAVE ESCAPED THAT QUICKLY!
A REPTILE IN A SHIMMER SUIT. A SHAPE CHANGER. A HALLUCINATION.
WHAT WERE YOU?

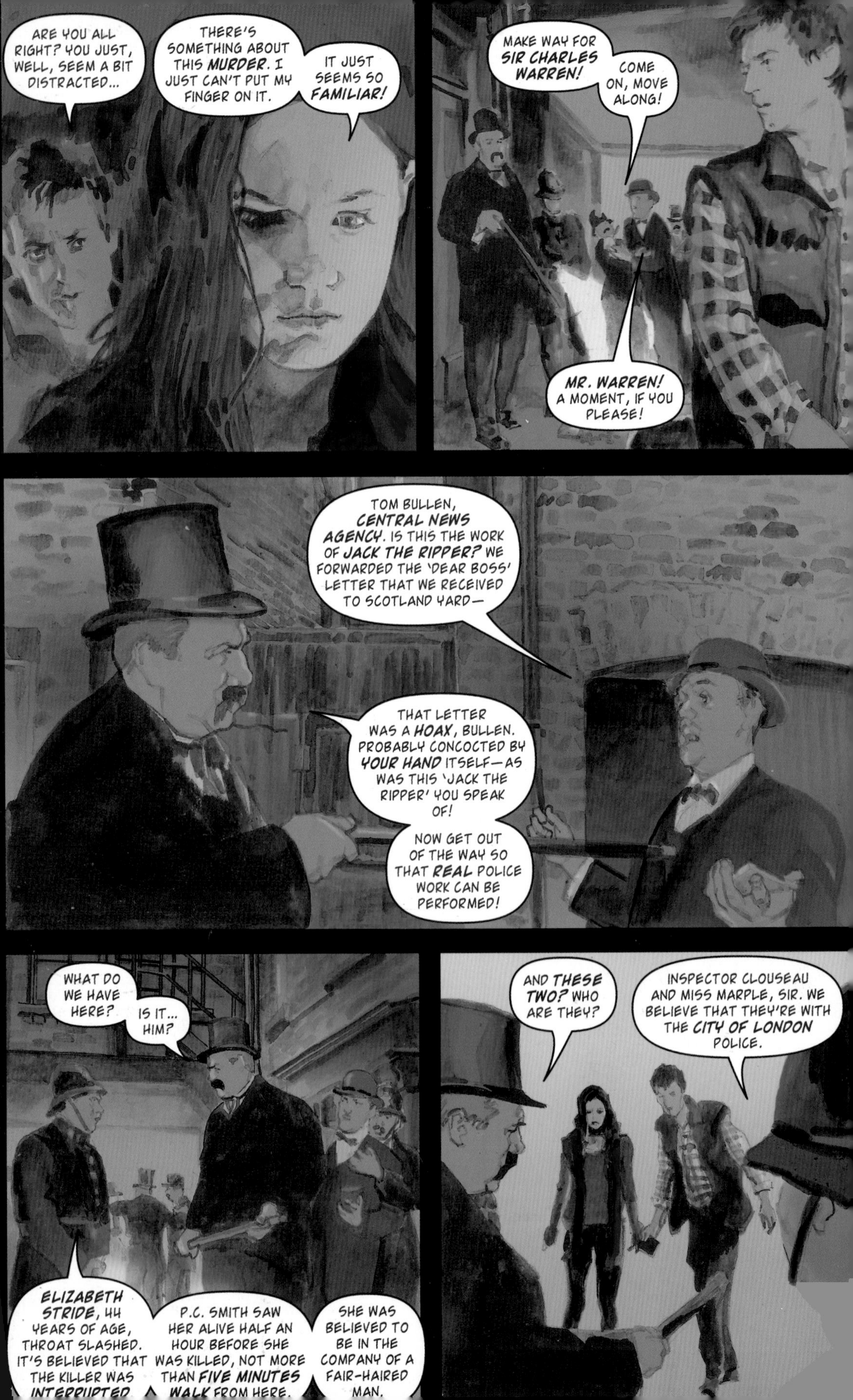

ARE YOU ALL RIGHT? YOU JUST, WELL, SEEM A BIT DISTRACTED...
THERE'S SOMETHING ABOUT THIS MURDER. I JUST CAN'T PUT MY FINGER ON IT.
IT JUST SEEMS SO FAMILIAR!
MAKE WAY FOR SIR CHARLES WARREN!
COME ON, MOVE ALONG!
MR. WARREN! A MOMENT, IF YOU PLEASE!
TOM BULLEN, CENTRAL NEWS AGENCY. IS THIS THE WORK OF JACK THE RIPPER? WE FORWARDED THE 'DEAR BOSS' LETTER THAT WE RECEIVED TO SCOTLAND YARD—
THAT LETTER WAS A HOAX, BULLEN. PROBABLY CONCOCTED BY YOUR HAND ITSELF—AS WAS THIS 'JACK THE RIPPER' YOU SPEAK OF!
NOW GET OUT OF THE WAY SO THAT REAL POLICE WORK CAN BE PERFORMED!
WHAT DO WE HAVE HERE?
IS IT... HIM?
ELIZABETH STRIDE, 44 YEARS OF AGE, THROAT SLASHED. IT'S BELIEVED THAT THE KILLER WAS INTERRUPTED.
P.C. SMITH SAW HER ALIVE HALF AN HOUR BEFORE SHE WAS KILLED, NOT MORE THAN FIVE MINUTES WALK FROM HERE.
SHE WAS BELIEVED TO BE IN THE COMPANY OF A FAIR-HAIRED MAN.
AND THESE TWO? WHO ARE THEY?
INSPECTOR CLOUSEAU AND MISS MARPLE, SIR. WE BELIEVE THAT THEY'RE WITH THE CITY OF LONDON POLICE.

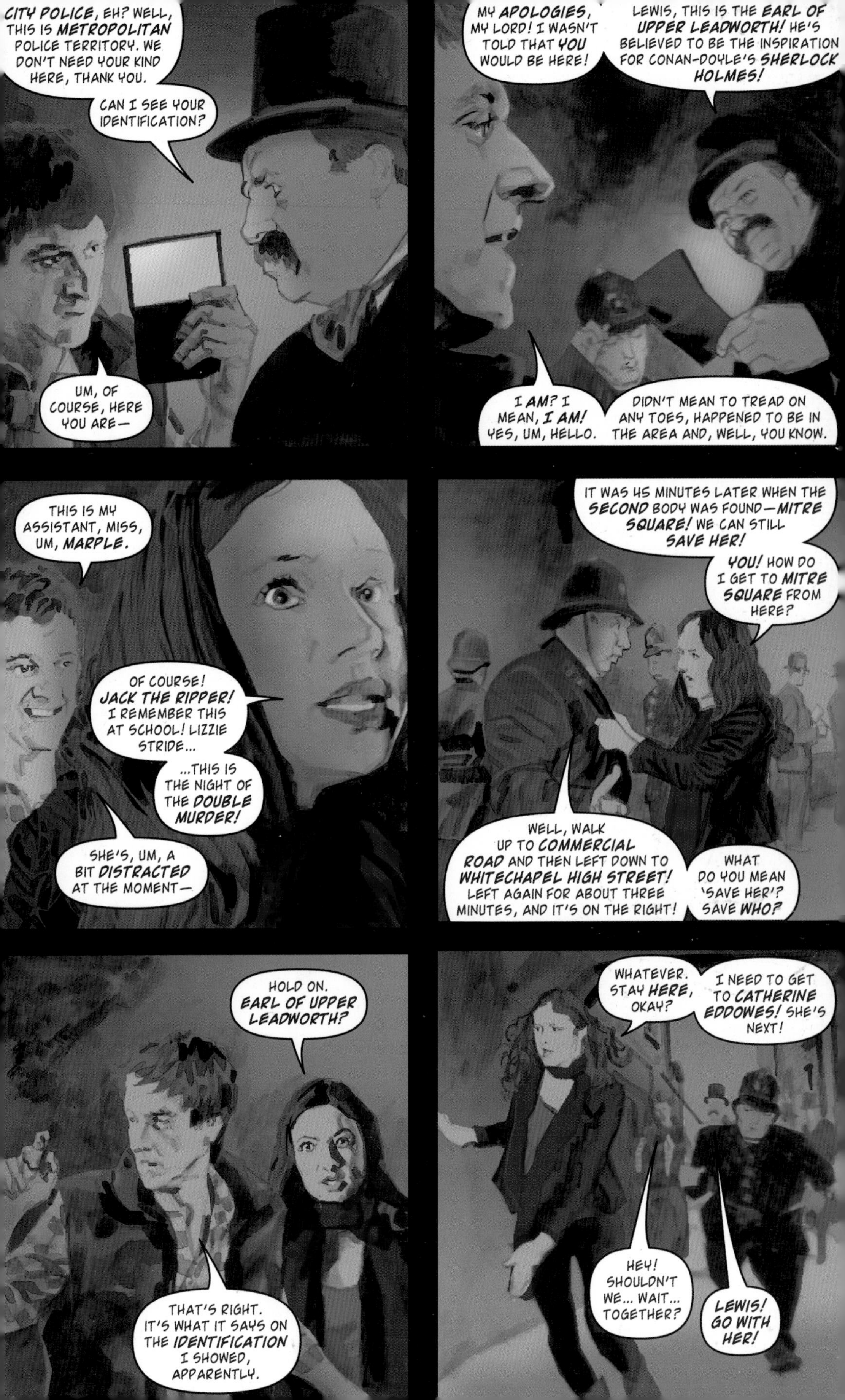
CITY POLICE, EH? WELL, THIS IS METROPOLITAN POLICE TERRITORY. WE DON'T NEED YOUR KIND HERE, THANK YOU.
CAN I SEE YOUR IDENTIFICATION?
UM, OF COURSE, HERE YOU ARE—
MY APOLOGIES, MY LORD! I WASN'T TOLD THAT YOU WOULD BE HERE!
LEWIS, THIS IS THE EARL OF UPPER LEADWORTH! HE'S BELIEVED TO BE THE INSPIRATION FOR CONAN-DOYLE'S SHERLOCK HOLMES!
I AM? I MEAN, I AM! YES, UM, HELLO.
DIDN'T MEAN TO TREAD ON ANY TOES, HAPPENED TO BE IN THE AREA AND, WELL, YOU KNOW.
THIS IS MY ASSISTANT, MISS, UM, MARPLE.
OF COURSE! JACK THE RIPPER! I REMEMBER THIS AT SCHOOL! LIZZIE STRIDE...
...THIS IS THE NIGHT OF THE DOUBLE MURDER!
SHE'S, UM, A BIT DISTRACTED AT THE MOMENT—
IT WAS 45 MINUTES LATER WHEN THE SECOND BODY WAS FOUND—MITRE SQUARE! WE CAN STILL SAVE HER!
YOU! HOW DO I GET TO MITRE SQUARE FROM HERE?
WELL, WALK UP TO COMMERCIAL ROAD AND THEN LEFT DOWN TO WHITECHAPEL HIGH STREET! LEFT AGAIN FOR ABOUT THREE MINUTES, AND IT'S ON THE RIGHT!
WHAT DO YOU MEAN 'SAVE HER'? SAVE WHO?
HOLD ON. EARL OF UPPER LEADWORTH?
THAT'S RIGHT. IT'S WHAT IT SAYS ON THE IDENTIFICATION I SHOWED, APPARENTLY.
WHATEVER. STAY HERE, OKAY?
I NEED TO GET TO CATHERINE EDDOWES! SHE'S NEXT!
HEY! SHOULDN'T WE... WAIT... TOGETHER?
LEWIS! GO WITH HER!

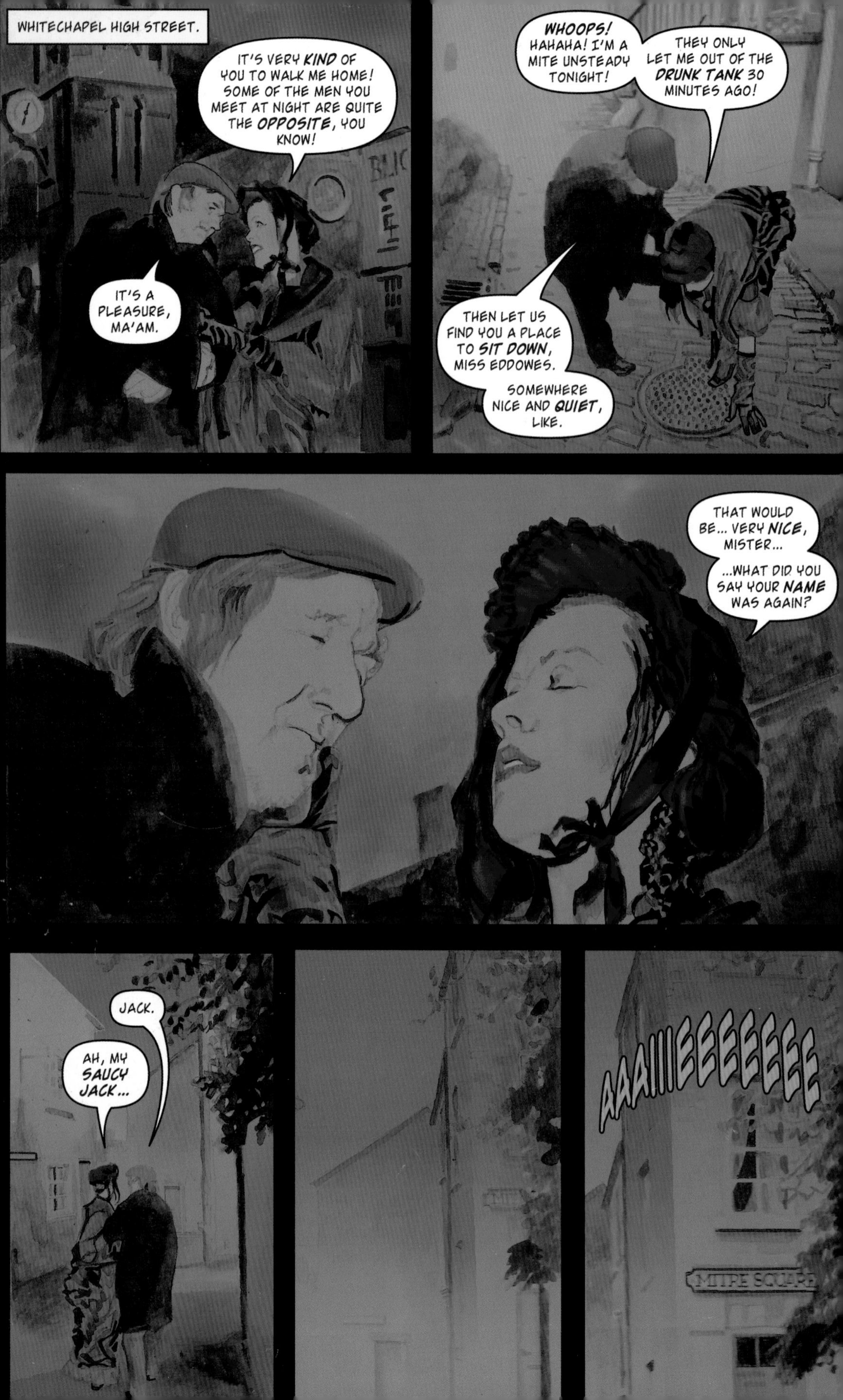
WHITECHAPEL HIGH STREET.
IT'S VERY KIND OF YOU TO WALK ME HOME! SOME OF THE MEN YOU MEET AT NIGHT ARE QUITE THE OPPOSITE, YOU KNOW!
IT'S A PLEASURE, MA'AM.
WHOOPS! HAHAHA! I'M A MITE UNSTEADY TONIGHT!
THEY ONLY LET ME OUT OF THE DRUNK TANK 30 MINUTES AGO!
THEN LET US FIND YOU A PLACE TO SIT DOWN, MISS EDDOWES.
SOMEWHERE NICE AND QUIET, LIKE.
THAT WOULD BE... VERY NICE, MISTER...
...WHAT DID YOU SAY YOUR NAME WAS AGAIN?
JACK.
AH, MY SAUCY JACK...
AAAIIIEEEEEEE
MITRE SQUARE

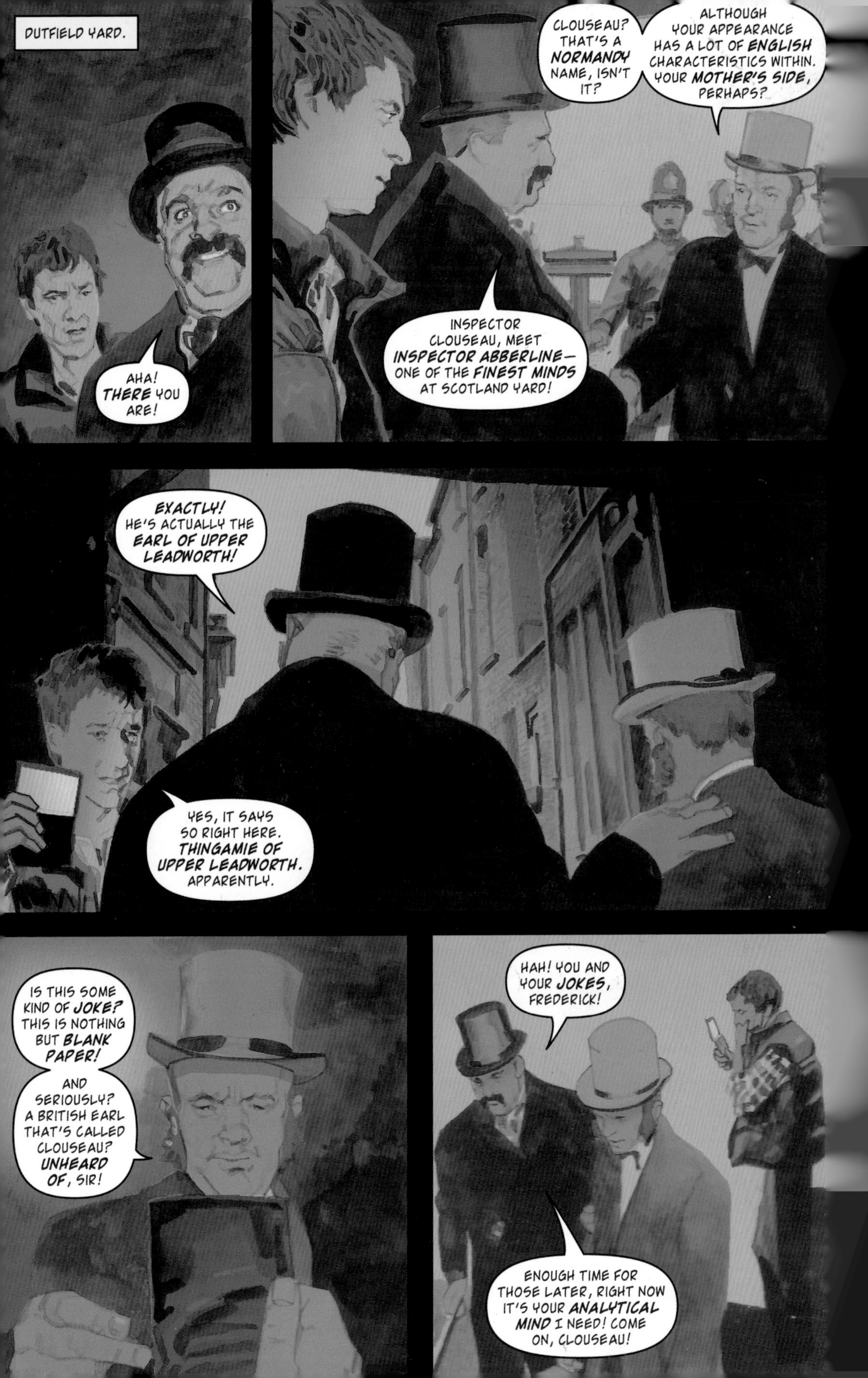
DUTFIELD YARD.
AHA! THERE YOU ARE!
CLOUSEAU? THAT'S A NORMANDY NAME, ISN'T IT?
ALTHOUGH YOUR APPEARANCE HAS A LOT OF ENGLISH CHARACTERISTICS WITHIN. YOUR MOTHER'S SIDE, PERHAPS?
INSPECTOR CLOUSEAU, MEET INSPECTOR ABBERLINE— ONE OF THE FINEST MINDS AT SCOTLAND YARD!
EXACTLY! HE'S ACTUALLY THE EARL OF UPPER LEADWORTH!
YES, IT SAYS SO RIGHT HERE. THINGAMIE OF UPPER LEADWORTH. APPARENTLY.
IS THIS SOME KIND OF JOKE? THIS IS NOTHING BUT BLANK PAPER!
AND SERIOUSLY? A BRITISH EARL THAT'S CALLED CLOUSEAU? UNHEARD OF, SIR!
HAH! YOU AND YOUR JOKES, FREDERICK!
ENOUGH TIME FOR THOSE LATER, RIGHT NOW IT'S YOUR ANALYTICAL MIND I NEED! COME ON, CLOUSEAU!

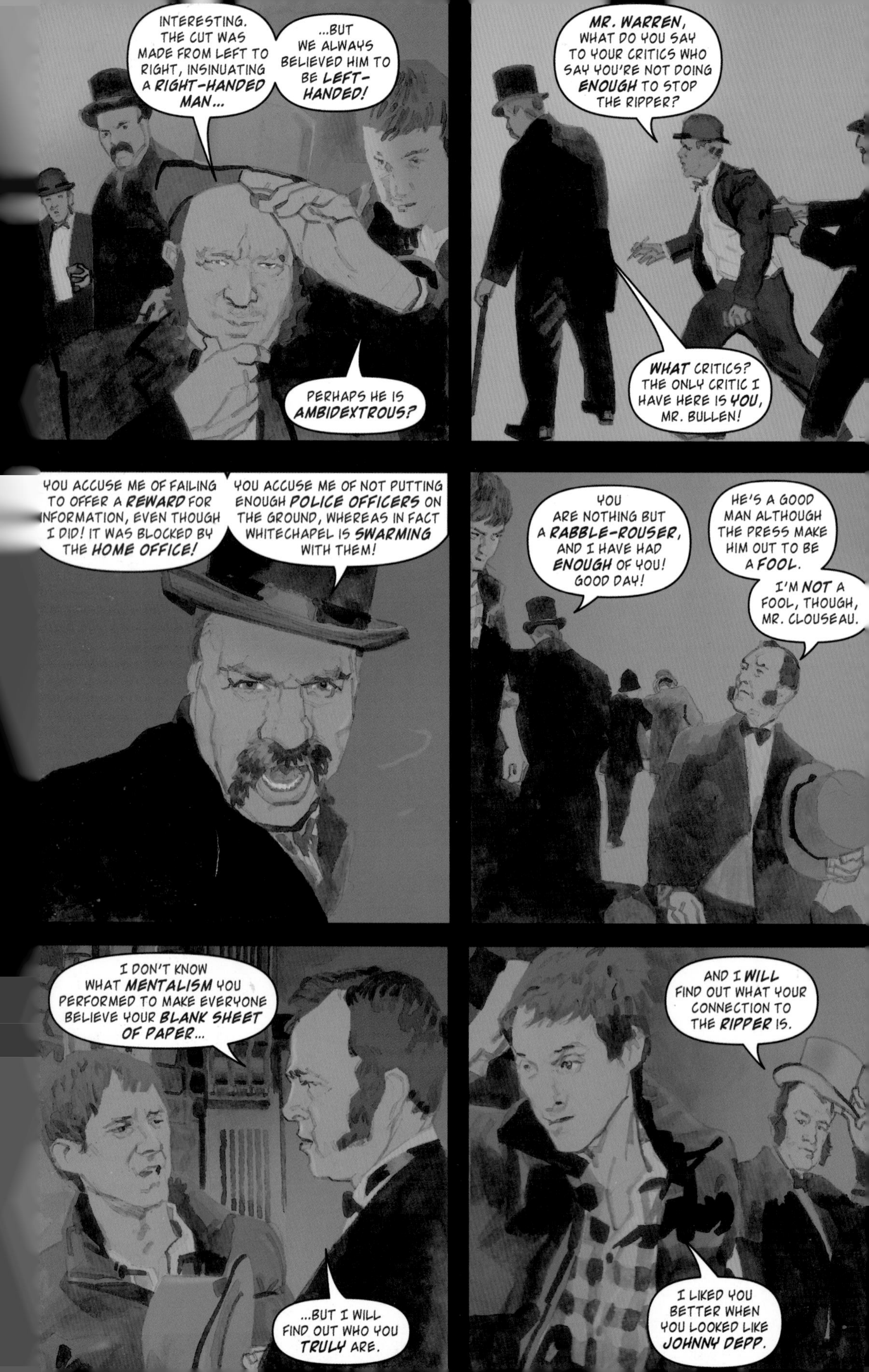
INTERESTING. THE CUT WAS MADE FROM LEFT TO RIGHT, INSINUATING A RIGHT-HANDED MAN...
...BUT WE ALWAYS BELIEVED HIM TO BE LEFT-HANDED!
PERHAPS HE IS AMBIDEXTROUS?
MR. WARREN, WHAT DO YOU SAY TO YOUR CRITICS WHO SAY YOU'RE NOT DOING ENOUGH TO STOP THE RIPPER?
WHAT CRITICS? THE ONLY CRITIC I HAVE HERE IS YOU, MR. BULLEN!
YOU ACCUSE ME OF FAILING TO OFFER A REWARD FOR INFORMATION, EVEN THOUGH I DID! IT WAS BLOCKED BY THE HOME OFFICE!
YOU ACCUSE ME OF NOT PUTTING ENOUGH POLICE OFFICERS ON THE GROUND, WHEREAS IN FACT WHITECHAPEL IS SWARMING WITH THEM!
YOU ARE NOTHING BUT A RABBLE-ROUSER, AND I HAVE HAD ENOUGH OF YOU! GOOD DAY!
HE'S A GOOD MAN ALTHOUGH THE PRESS MAKE HIM OUT TO BE A FOOL.
I'M NOT A FOOL, THOUGH, MR. CLOUSEAU.
I DON'T KNOW WHAT MENTALISM YOU PERFORMED TO MAKE EVERYONE BELIEVE YOUR BLANK SHEET OF PAPER...
...BUT I WILL FIND OUT WHO YOU TRULY ARE.
AND I WILL FIND OUT WHAT YOUR CONNECTION TO THE RIPPER IS.
I LIKED YOU BETTER WHEN YOU LOOKED LIKE JOHNNY DEPP.

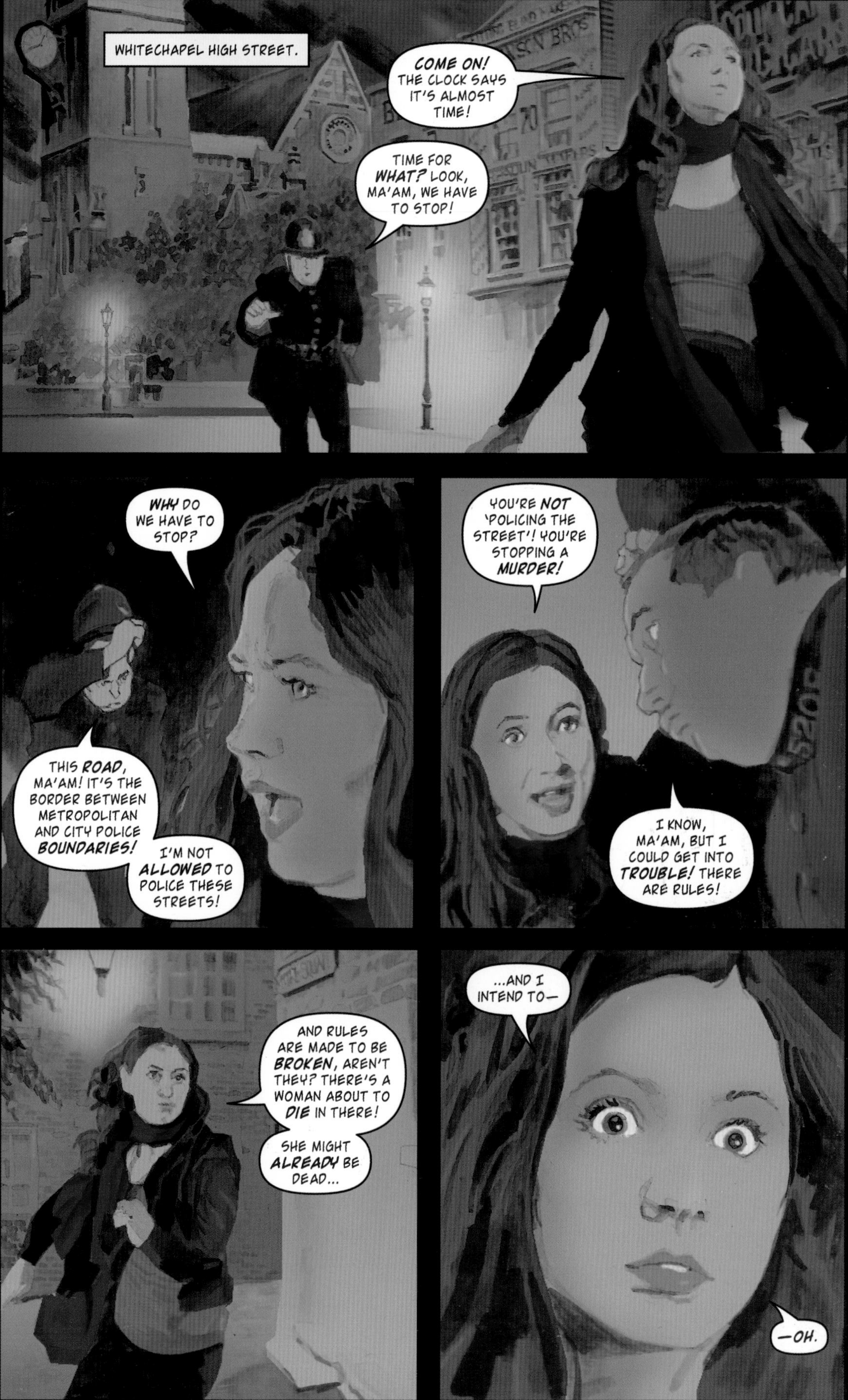
WHITECHAPEL HIGH STREET.
COME ON! THE CLOCK SAYS IT'S ALMOST TIME!
TIME FOR WHAT? LOOK, MA'AM, WE HAVE TO STOP!
WHY DO WE HAVE TO STOP?
THIS ROAD, MA'AM! IT'S THE BORDER BETWEEN METROPOLITAN AND CITY POLICE BOUNDARIES!
I'M NOT ALLOWED TO POLICE THESE STREETS!
YOU'RE NOT 'POLICING THE STREET'! YOU'RE STOPPING A MURDER!
I KNOW, MA'AM, BUT I COULD GET INTO TROUBLE! THERE ARE RULES!
AND RULES ARE MADE TO BE BROKEN, AREN'T THEY? THERE'S A WOMAN ABOUT TO DIE IN THERE!
SHE MIGHT ALREADY BE DEAD...
...AND I INTEND TO—
—OH.

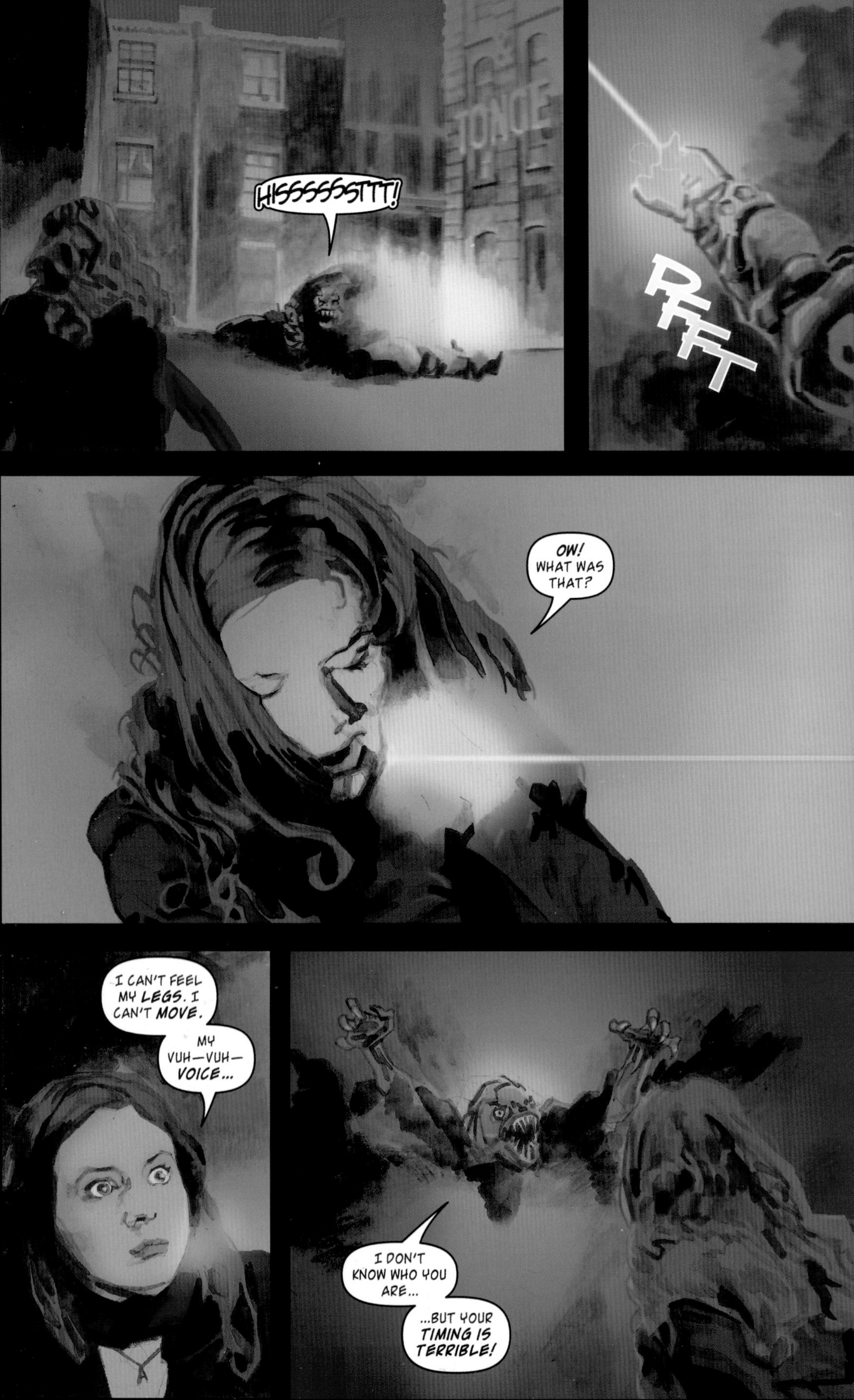
HISSSSSSSTTT!
PFFT
OW! WHAT WAS THAT?
I CAN'T FEEL MY LEGS. I CAN'T MOVE.
MY VUH—VUH—VOICE...
I DON'T KNOW WHO YOU ARE...
...BUT YOUR TIMING IS TERRIBLE!

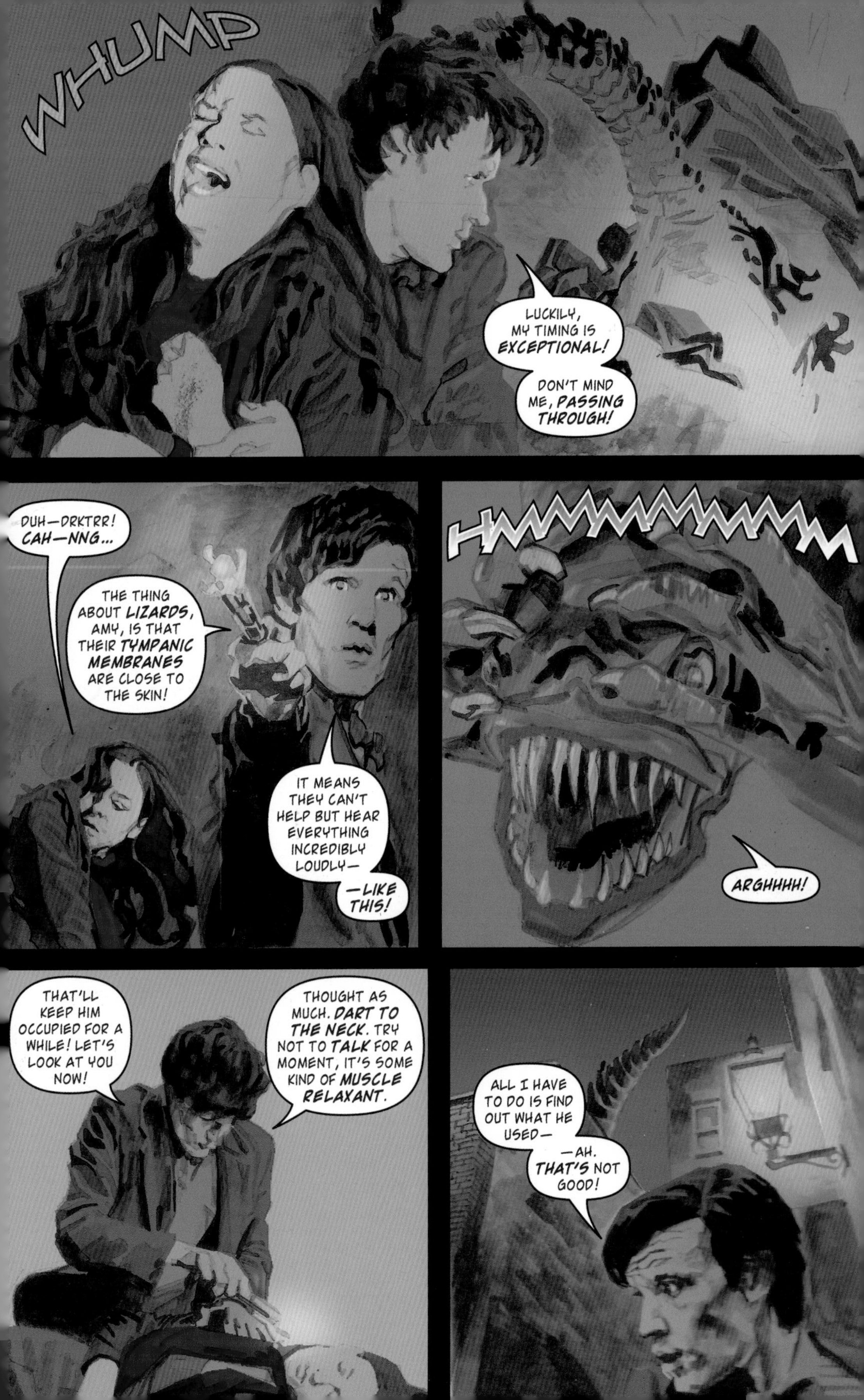
WHUMP
LUCKILY, MY TIMING IS EXCEPTIONAL!
DON'T MIND ME, PASSING THROUGH!
DUH—DRKTRR! CAH—NNG...
THE THING ABOUT LIZARDS, AMY, IS THAT THEIR TYMPANIC MEMBRANES ARE CLOSE TO THE SKIN!
IT MEANS THEY CAN'T HELP BUT HEAR EVERYTHING INCREDIBLY LOUDLY—
—LIKE THIS!
HWWWWWWWWWWM
ARGHHHH!
THAT'LL KEEP HIM OCCUPIED FOR A WHILE! LET'S LOOK AT YOU NOW!
THOUGHT AS MUCH. DART TO THE NECK. TRY NOT TO TALK FOR A MOMENT, IT'S SOME KIND OF MUSCLE RELAXANT.
ALL I HAVE TO DO IS FIND OUT WHAT HE USED—
—AH. THAT'S NOT GOOD!

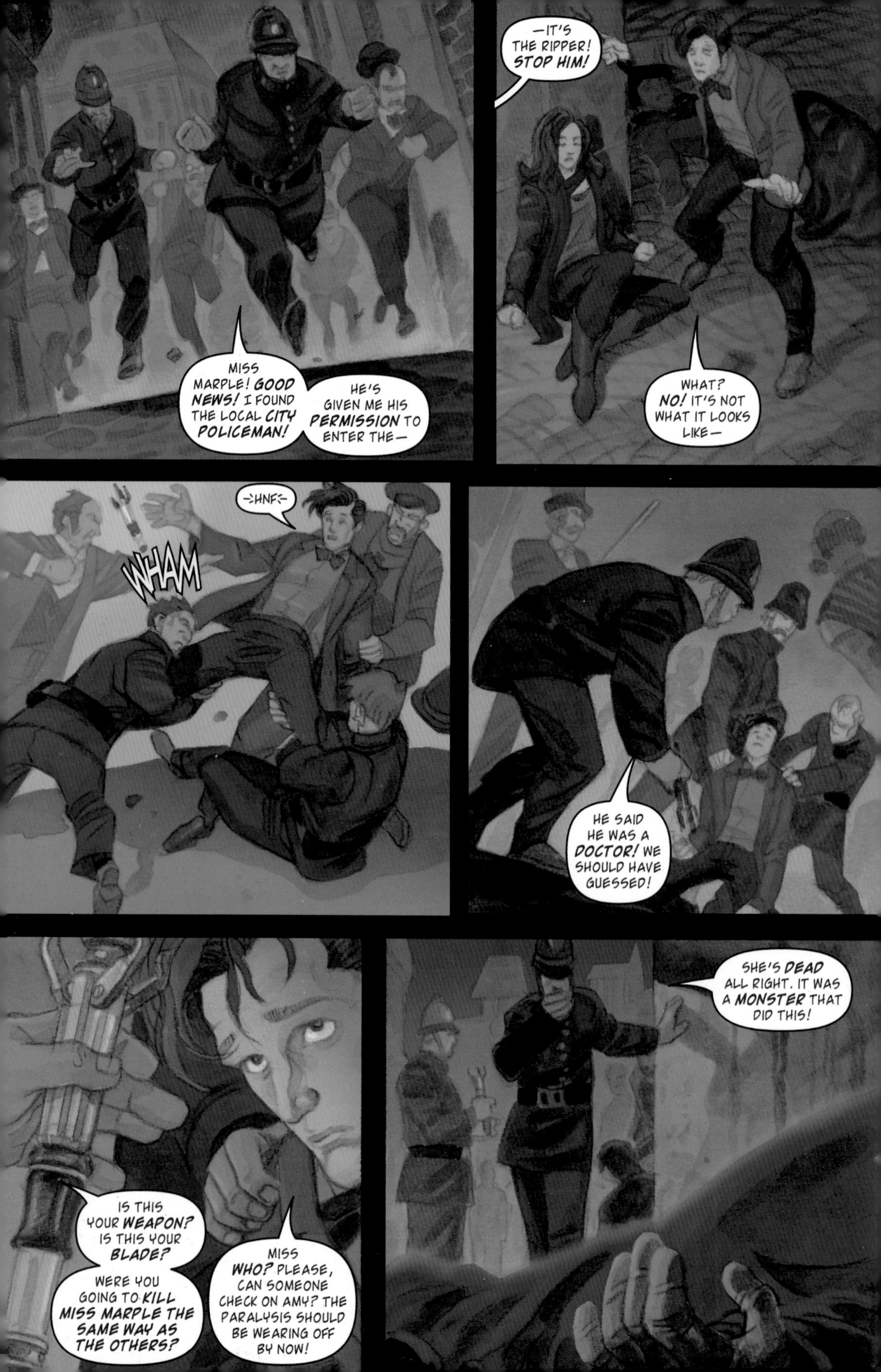
MISS MARPLE! GOOD NEWS! I FOUND THE LOCAL CITY POLICEMAN!
HE'S GIVEN ME HIS PERMISSION TO ENTER THE—
—IT'S THE RIPPER! STOP HIM!
WHAT? NO! IT'S NOT WHAT IT LOOKS LIKE—
HNF
WHAM
HE SAID HE WAS A DOCTOR! WE SHOULD HAVE GUESSED!
IS THIS YOUR WEAPON? IS THIS YOUR BLADE?
WERE YOU GOING TO KILL MISS MARPLE THE SAME WAY AS THE OTHERS?
MISS WHO? PLEASE, CAN SOMEONE CHECK ON AMY? THE PARALYSIS SHOULD BE WEARING OFF BY NOW!
SHE'S DEAD ALL RIGHT. IT WAS A MONSTER THAT DID THIS!

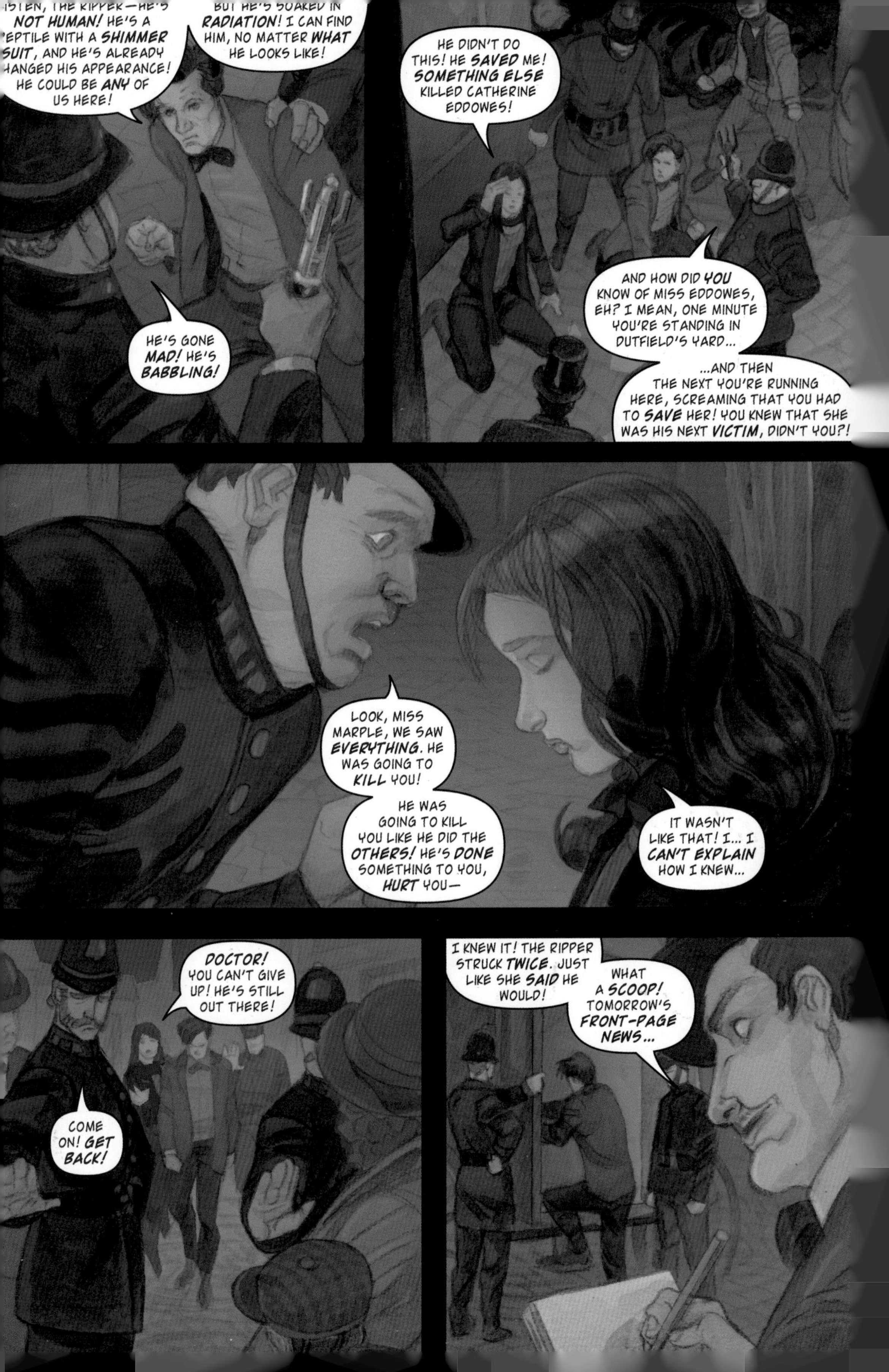
ISTEN, THE RIPPER—HE'S NOT HUMAN! HE'S A EPTILE WITH A SHIMMER SUIT, AND HE'S ALREADY HANGED HIS APPEARANCE! HE COULD BE ANY OF US HERE!
BUT HE'S SOAKED IN RADIATION! I CAN FIND HIM, NO MATTER WHAT HE LOOKS LIKE!
HE'S GONE MAD! HE'S BABBLING!
HE DIDN'T DO THIS! HE SAVED ME! SOMETHING ELSE KILLED CATHERINE EDDOWES!
AND HOW DID YOU KNOW OF MISS EDDOWES, EH? I MEAN, ONE MINUTE YOU'RE STANDING IN DUTFIELD'S YARD...
...AND THEN THE NEXT YOU'RE RUNNING HERE, SCREAMING THAT YOU HAD TO SAVE HER! YOU KNEW THAT SHE WAS HIS NEXT VICTIM, DIDN'T YOU?!
LOOK, MISS MARPLE, WE SAW EVERYTHING. HE WAS GOING TO KILL YOU!
HE WAS GOING TO KILL YOU LIKE HE DID THE OTHERS! HE'S DONE SOMETHING TO YOU, HURT YOU—
IT WASN'T LIKE THAT! I... I CAN'T EXPLAIN HOW I KNEW...
DOCTOR! YOU CAN'T GIVE UP! HE'S STILL OUT THERE!
COME ON! GET BACK!
I KNEW IT! THE RIPPER STRUCK TWICE. JUST LIKE SHE SAID HE WOULD!
WHAT A SCOOP! TOMORROW'S FRONT-PAGE NEWS...

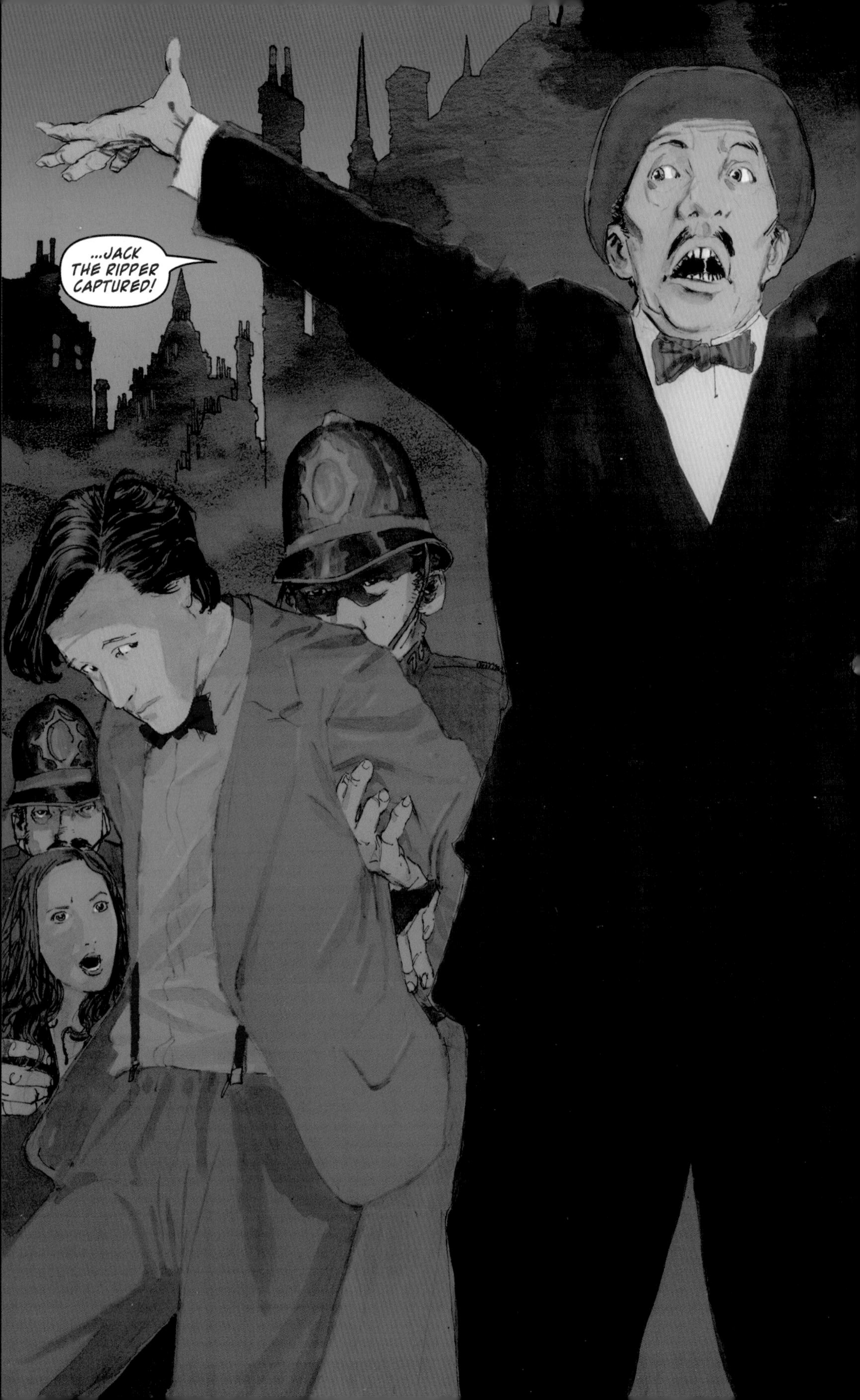
...JACK THE RIPPER CAPTURED!

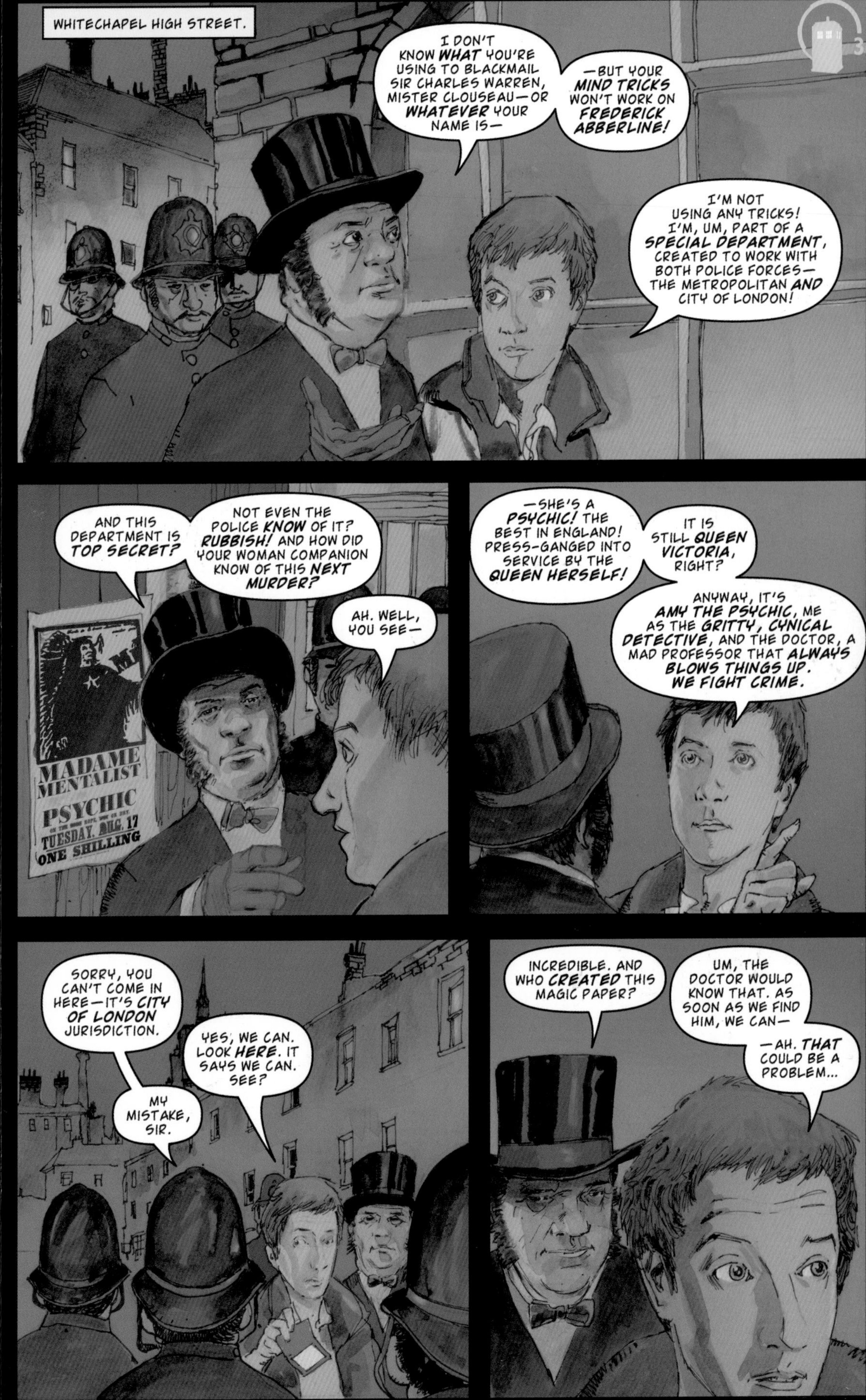
WHITECHAPEL HIGH STREET.
I DON'T KNOW WHAT YOU'RE USING TO BLACKMAIL SIR CHARLES WARREN, MISTER CLOUSEAU—OR WHATEVER YOUR NAME IS—
—BUT YOUR MIND TRICKS WON'T WORK ON FREDERICK ABBERLINE!
I'M NOT USING ANY TRICKS! I'M, UM, PART OF A SPECIAL DEPARTMENT, CREATED TO WORK WITH BOTH POLICE FORCES—THE METROPOLITAN AND CITY OF LONDON!
AND THIS DEPARTMENT IS TOP SECRET?
NOT EVEN THE POLICE KNOW OF IT? RUBBISH! AND HOW DID YOUR WOMAN COMPANION KNOW OF THIS NEXT MURDER?
AH. WELL, YOU SEE—
MADAME MENTALIST
PSYCHIC
TUESDAY, AUG. 17
ONE SHILLING
—SHE'S A PSYCHIC! THE BEST IN ENGLAND! PRESS-GANGED INTO SERVICE BY THE QUEEN HERSELF!
IT IS STILL QUEEN VICTORIA, RIGHT?
ANYWAY, IT'S AMY THE PSYCHIC, ME AS THE GRITTY, CYNICAL DETECTIVE, AND THE DOCTOR, A MAD PROFESSOR THAT ALWAYS BLOWS THINGS UP. WE FIGHT CRIME.
SORRY, YOU CAN'T COME IN HERE—IT'S CITY OF LONDON JURISDICTION.
YES, WE CAN. LOOK HERE. IT SAYS WE CAN. SEE?
MY MISTAKE, SIR.
INCREDIBLE. AND WHO CREATED THIS MAGIC PAPER?
UM, THE DOCTOR WOULD KNOW THAT. AS SOON AS WE FIND HIM, WE CAN—
—AH. THAT COULD BE A PROBLEM...

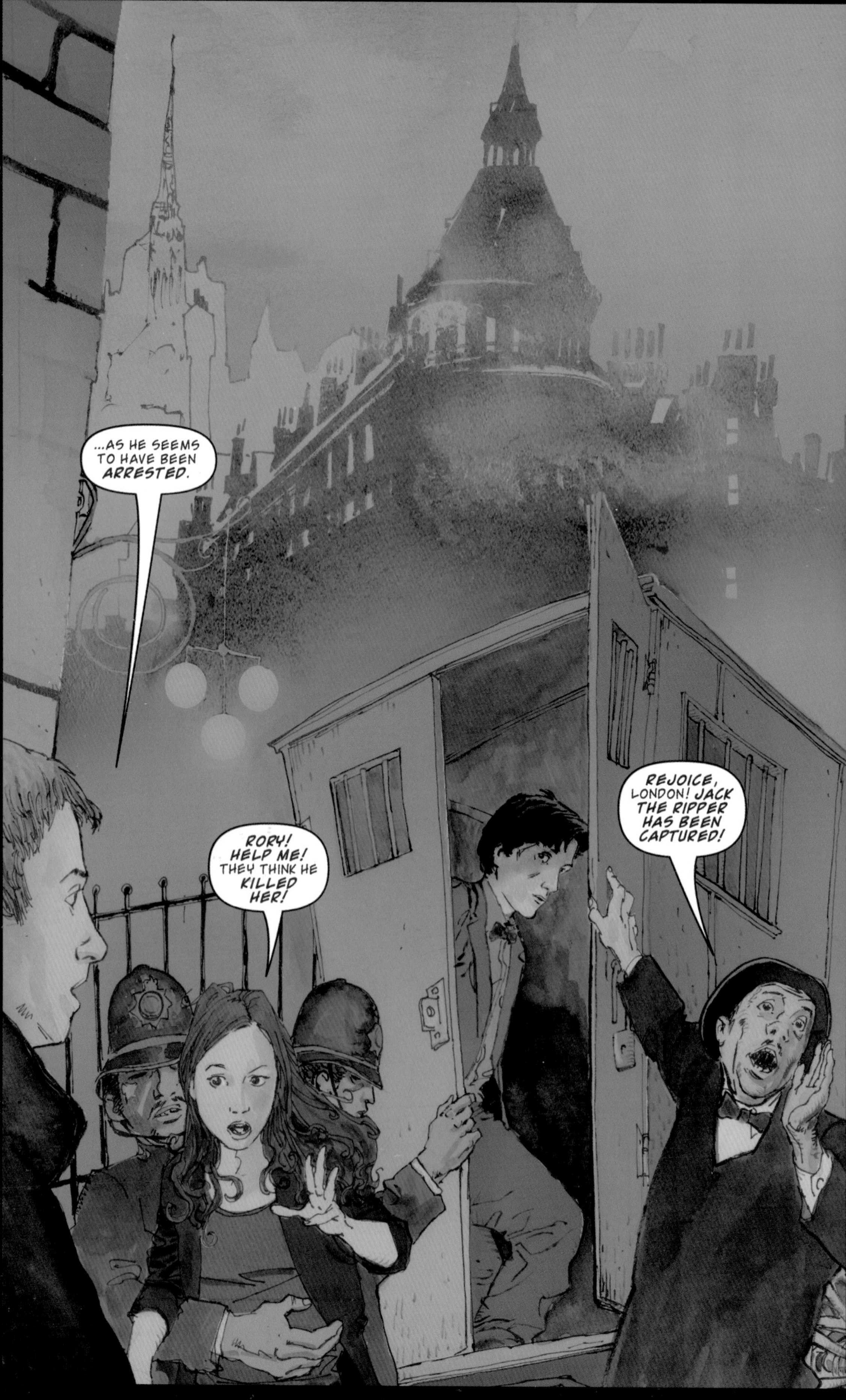
...AS HE SEEMS TO HAVE BEEN ARRESTED.
RORY! HELP ME! THEY THINK HE KILLED HER!
REJOICE, LONDON! JACK THE RIPPER HAS BEEN CAPTURED!

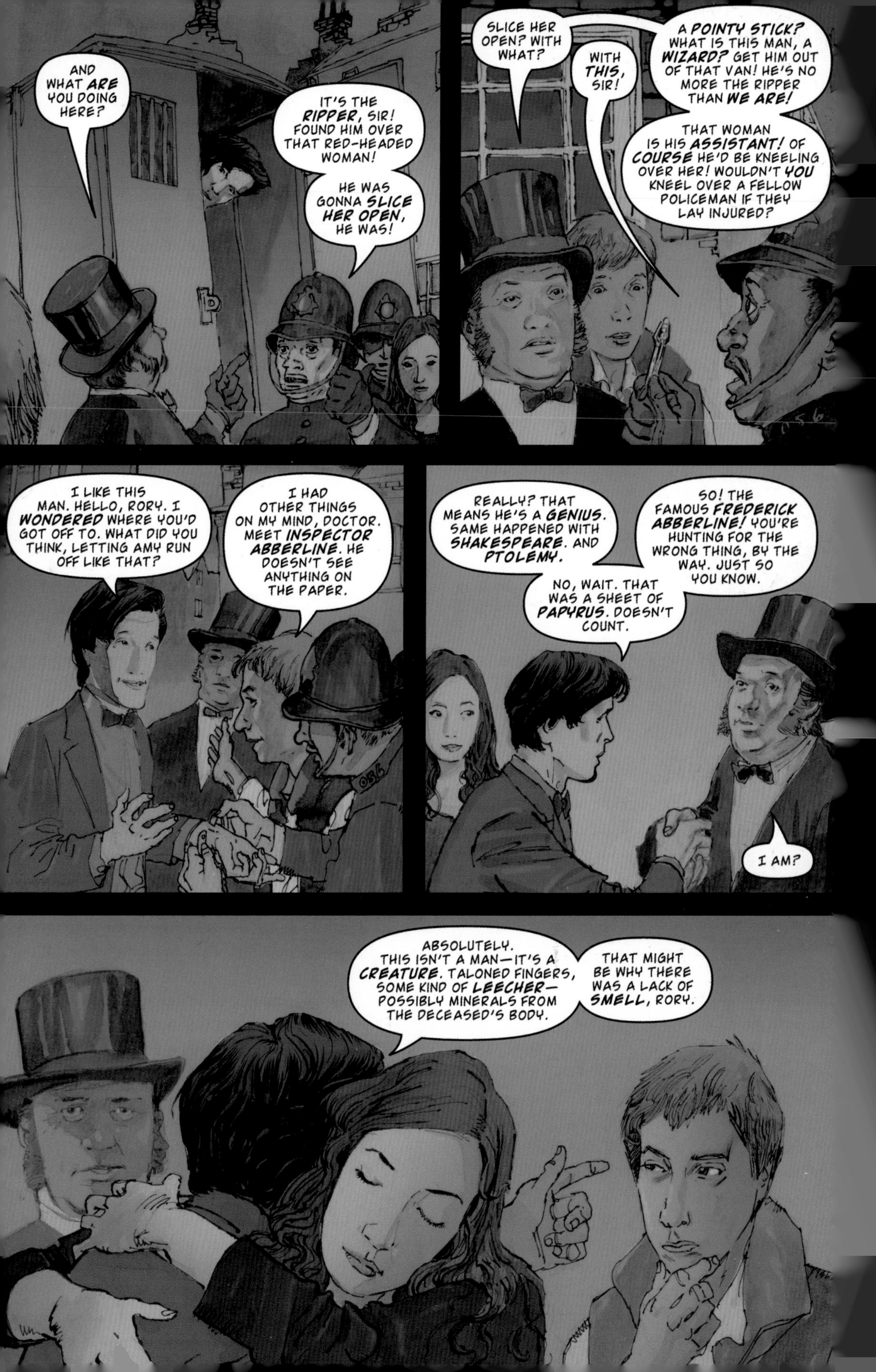
AND WHAT ARE YOU DOING HERE?
IT'S THE RIPPER, SIR! FOUND HIM OVER THAT RED-HEADED WOMAN!
HE WAS GONNA SLICE HER OPEN, HE WAS!
SLICE HER OPEN? WITH WHAT?
WITH THIS, SIR!
A POINTY STICK? WHAT IS THIS MAN, A WIZARD? GET HIM OUT OF THAT VAN! HE'S NO MORE THE RIPPER THAN WE ARE!
THAT WOMAN IS HIS ASSISTANT! OF COURSE HE'D BE KNEELING OVER HER! WOULDN'T YOU KNEEL OVER A FELLOW POLICEMAN IF THEY LAY INJURED?
I LIKE THIS MAN. HELLO, RORY. I WONDERED WHERE YOU'D GOT OFF TO. WHAT DID YOU THINK, LETTING AMY RUN OFF LIKE THAT?
I HAD OTHER THINGS ON MY MIND, DOCTOR. MEET INSPECTOR ABBERLINE. HE DOESN'T SEE ANYTHING ON THE PAPER.
REALLY? THAT MEANS HE'S A GENIUS. SAME HAPPENED WITH SHAKESPEARE. AND PTOLEMY.
NO, WAIT. THAT WAS A SHEET OF PAPYRUS. DOESN'T COUNT.
SO! THE FAMOUS FREDERICK ABBERLINE! YOU'RE HUNTING FOR THE WRONG THING, BY THE WAY. JUST SO YOU KNOW.
I AM?
ABSOLUTELY. THIS ISN'T A MAN—IT'S A CREATURE. TALONED FINGERS, SOME KIND OF LEECHER—POSSIBLY MINERALS FROM THE DECEASED'S BODY.
THAT MIGHT BE WHY THERE WAS A LACK OF SMELL, RORY.

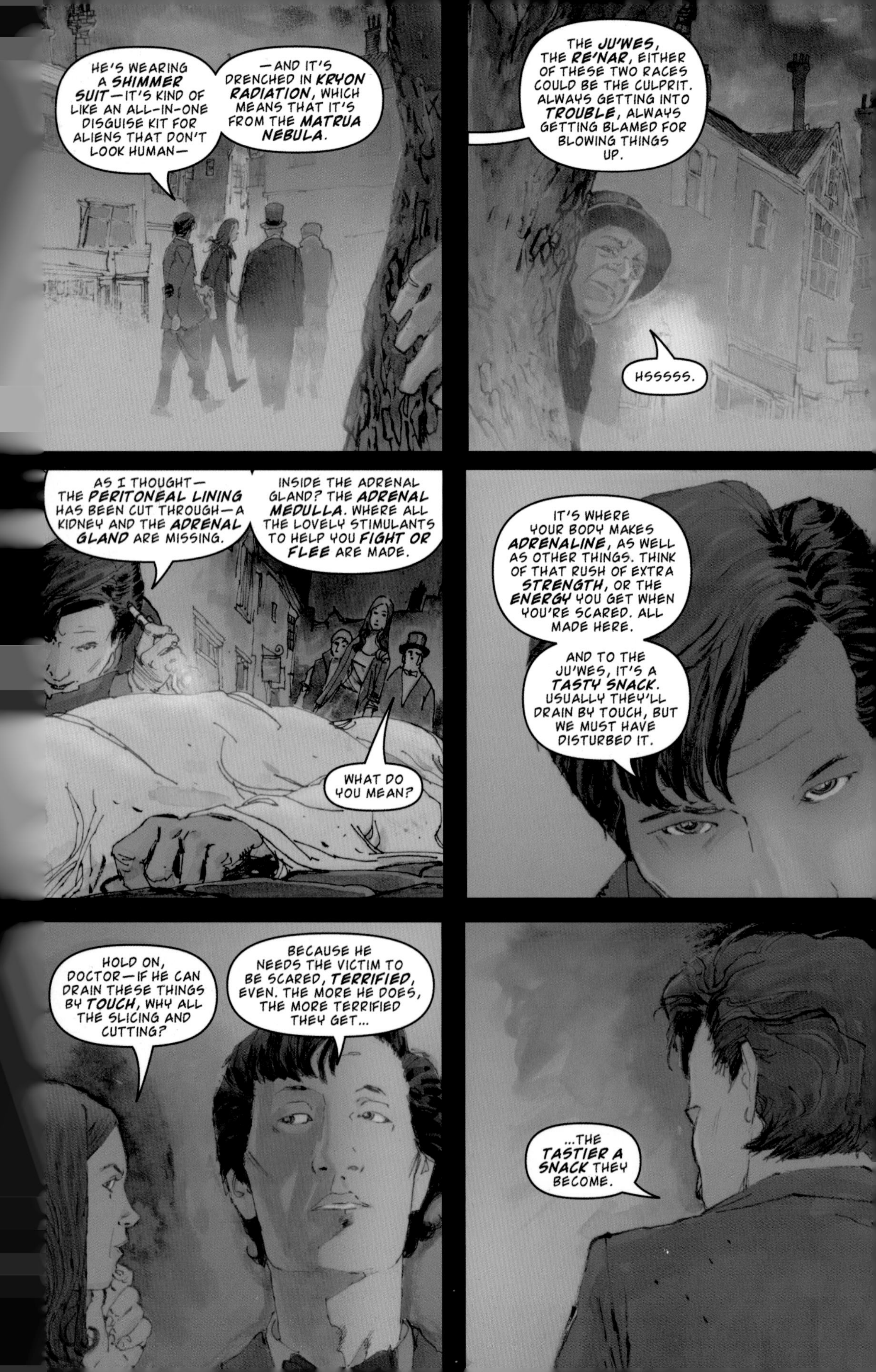
HE'S WEARING A SHIMMER SUIT—IT'S KIND OF LIKE AN ALL-IN-ONE DISGUISE KIT FOR ALIENS THAT DON'T LOOK HUMAN—
—AND IT'S DRENCHED IN KRYON RADIATION, WHICH MEANS THAT IT'S FROM THE MATRUA NEBULA.
THE JU'WES, THE RE'NAR, EITHER OF THESE TWO RACES COULD BE THE CULPRIT. ALWAYS GETTING INTO TROUBLE, ALWAYS GETTING BLAMED FOR BLOWING THINGS UP.
HSSSSS.
AS I THOUGHT—THE PERITONEAL LINING HAS BEEN CUT THROUGH—A KIDNEY AND THE ADRENAL GLAND ARE MISSING.
INSIDE THE ADRENAL GLAND? THE ADRENAL MEDULLA. WHERE ALL THE LOVELY STIMULANTS TO HELP YOU FIGHT OR FLEE ARE MADE.
WHAT DO YOU MEAN?
IT'S WHERE YOUR BODY MAKES ADRENALINE, AS WELL AS OTHER THINGS. THINK OF THAT RUSH OF EXTRA STRENGTH, OR THE ENERGY YOU GET WHEN YOU'RE SCARED. ALL MADE HERE.
AND TO THE JU'WES, IT'S A TASTY SNACK. USUALLY THEY'LL DRAIN BY TOUCH, BUT WE MUST HAVE DISTURBED IT.
HOLD ON, DOCTOR—IF HE CAN DRAIN THESE THINGS BY TOUCH, WHY ALL THE SLICING AND CUTTING?
BECAUSE HE NEEDS THE VICTIM TO BE SCARED, TERRIFIED, EVEN. THE MORE HE DOES, THE MORE TERRIFIED THEY GET...
...THE TASTIER A SNACK THEY BECOME.

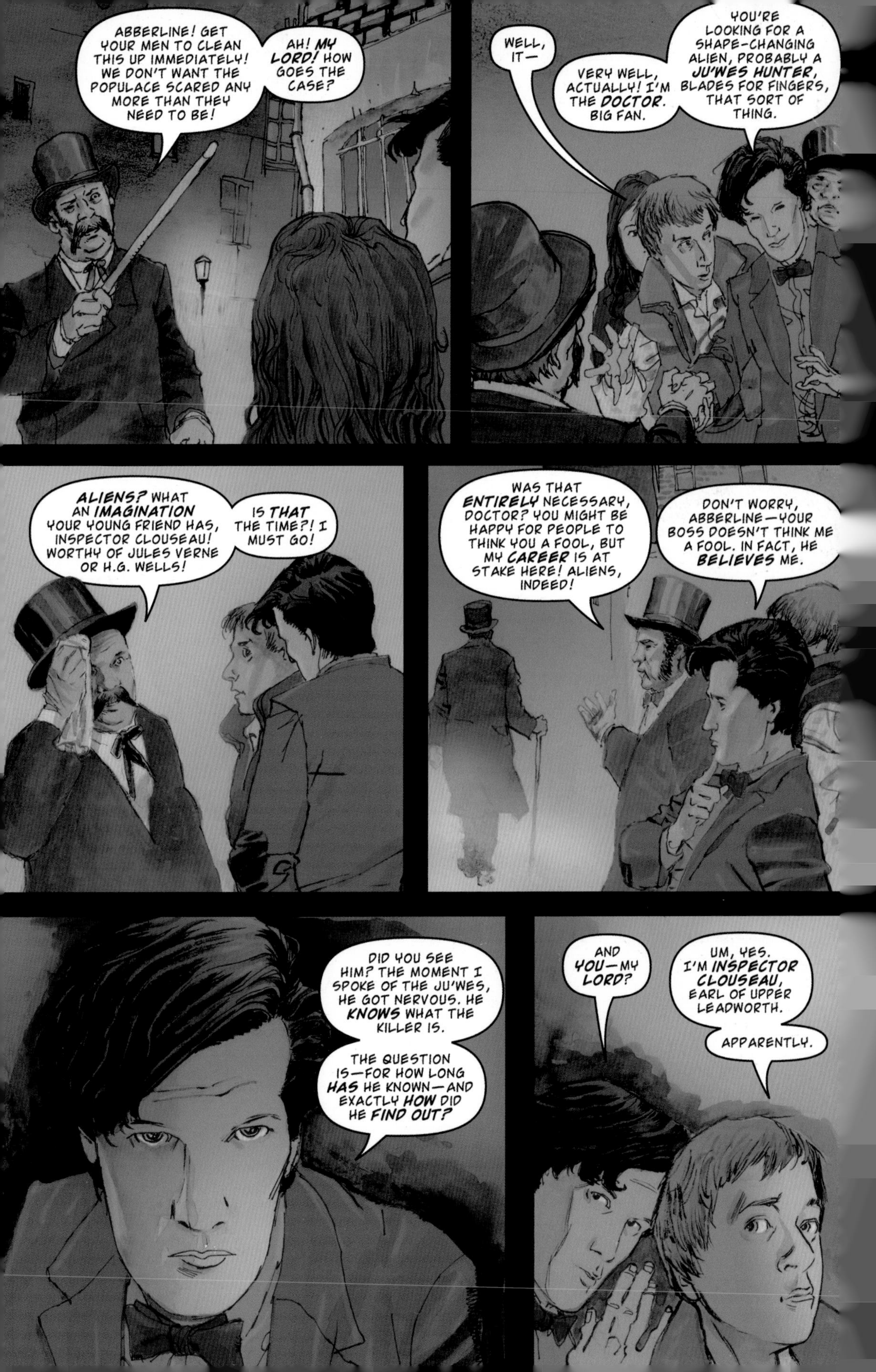
ABBERLINE! GET YOUR MEN TO CLEAN THIS UP IMMEDIATELY! WE DON'T WANT THE POPULACE SCARED ANY MORE THAN THEY NEED TO BE!
AH! MY LORD! HOW GOES THE CASE?
WELL, IT—
VERY WELL, ACTUALLY! I'M THE DOCTOR. BIG FAN.
YOU'RE LOOKING FOR A SHAPE-CHANGING ALIEN, PROBABLY A JU'WES HUNTER, BLADES FOR FINGERS, THAT SORT OF THING.
ALIENS? WHAT AN IMAGINATION YOUR YOUNG FRIEND HAS, INSPECTOR CLOUSEAU! WORTHY OF JULES VERNE OR H.G. WELLS!
IS THAT THE TIME?! I MUST GO!
WAS THAT ENTIRELY NECESSARY, DOCTOR? YOU MIGHT BE HAPPY FOR PEOPLE TO THINK YOU A FOOL, BUT MY CAREER IS AT STAKE HERE! ALIENS, INDEED!
DON'T WORRY, ABBERLINE—YOUR BOSS DOESN'T THINK ME A FOOL. IN FACT, HE BELIEVES ME.
DID YOU SEE HIM? THE MOMENT I SPOKE OF THE JU'WES, HE GOT NERVOUS. HE KNOWS WHAT THE KILLER IS.
THE QUESTION IS—FOR HOW LONG HAS HE KNOWN—AND EXACTLY HOW DID HE FIND OUT?
AND YOU—MY LORD?
UM, YES. I'M INSPECTOR CLOUSEAU, EARL OF UPPER LEADWORTH.
APPARENTLY.

GOULSTEN STREET. 3AM.

♫ THEY CALLED HER OLD NELLY, FOR THAT'S WHO SHE WAS... ♫

CLATTER

...WHAT WAS THAT?

WHO'S IN HERE? I *WARN YOU*, I'M AN OFFICER OF THE LAW, SO NO FUNNY BUSINESS.

GOOD GOD!

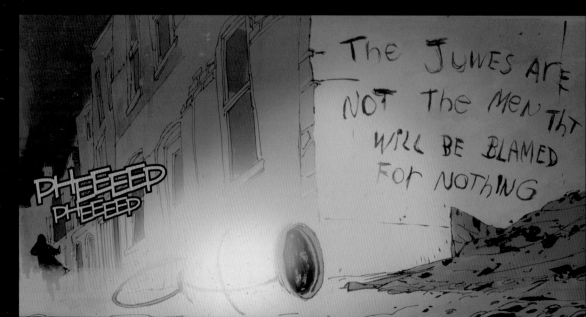

The JUWES ARE NOT THE MEN THT WILL BE BLAMED FOR NOTHING

PHEEEED PHEEEED

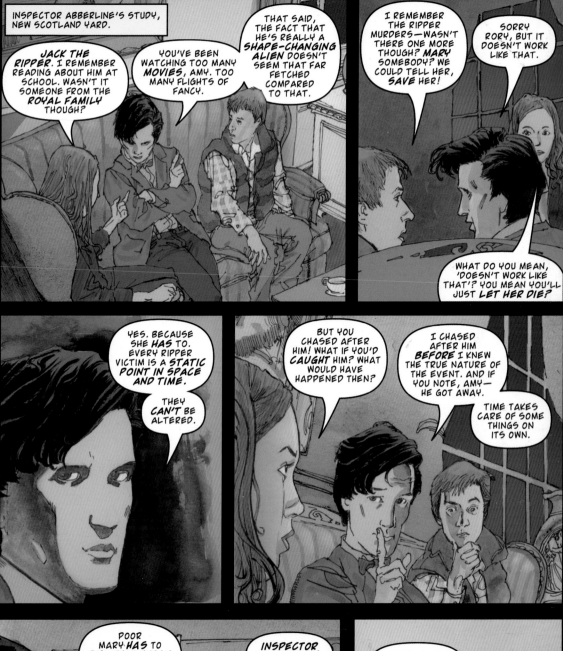

INSPECTOR ABBERLINE'S STUDY, NEW SCOTLAND YARD.

JACK THE RIPPER. I REMEMBER READING ABOUT HIM AT SCHOOL. WASN'T IT SOMEONE FROM THE ROYAL FAMILY THOUGH?

YOU'VE BEEN WATCHING TOO MANY MOVIES, AMY. TOO MANY FLIGHTS OF FANCY.

THAT SAID, THE FACT THAT HE'S REALLY A SHAPE-CHANGING ALIEN DOESN'T SEEM THAT FAR FETCHED COMPARED TO THAT.

I REMEMBER THE RIPPER MURDERS—WASN'T THERE ONE MORE THOUGH? MARY SOMEBODY? WE COULD TELL HER, SAVE HER!

SORRY RORY, BUT IT DOESN'T WORK LIKE THAT.

WHAT DO YOU MEAN, 'DOESN'T WORK LIKE THAT'? YOU MEAN YOU'LL JUST LET HER DIE?

YES. BECAUSE SHE HAS TO. EVERY RIPPER VICTIM IS A STATIC POINT IN SPACE AND TIME.

THEY CAN'T BE ALTERED.

BUT YOU CHASED AFTER HIM! WHAT IF YOU'D CAUGHT HIM? WHAT WOULD HAVE HAPPENED THEN?

I CHASED AFTER HIM BEFORE I KNEW THE TRUE NATURE OF THE EVENT. AND IF YOU NOTE, AMY— HE GOT AWAY.

TIME TAKES CARE OF SOME THINGS ON ITS OWN.

POOR MARY HAS TO DIE—THAT MUCH I KNOW. BUT SHE WAS THE RIPPER'S LAST VICTIM.

WHICH MEANS THAT AFTER HE KILLS HER—HE'S MINE.

INSPECTOR CLOUSEAU! COME QUICK!

WE'VE FOUND A CLUE—AND A MESSAGE FROM THE RIPPER!

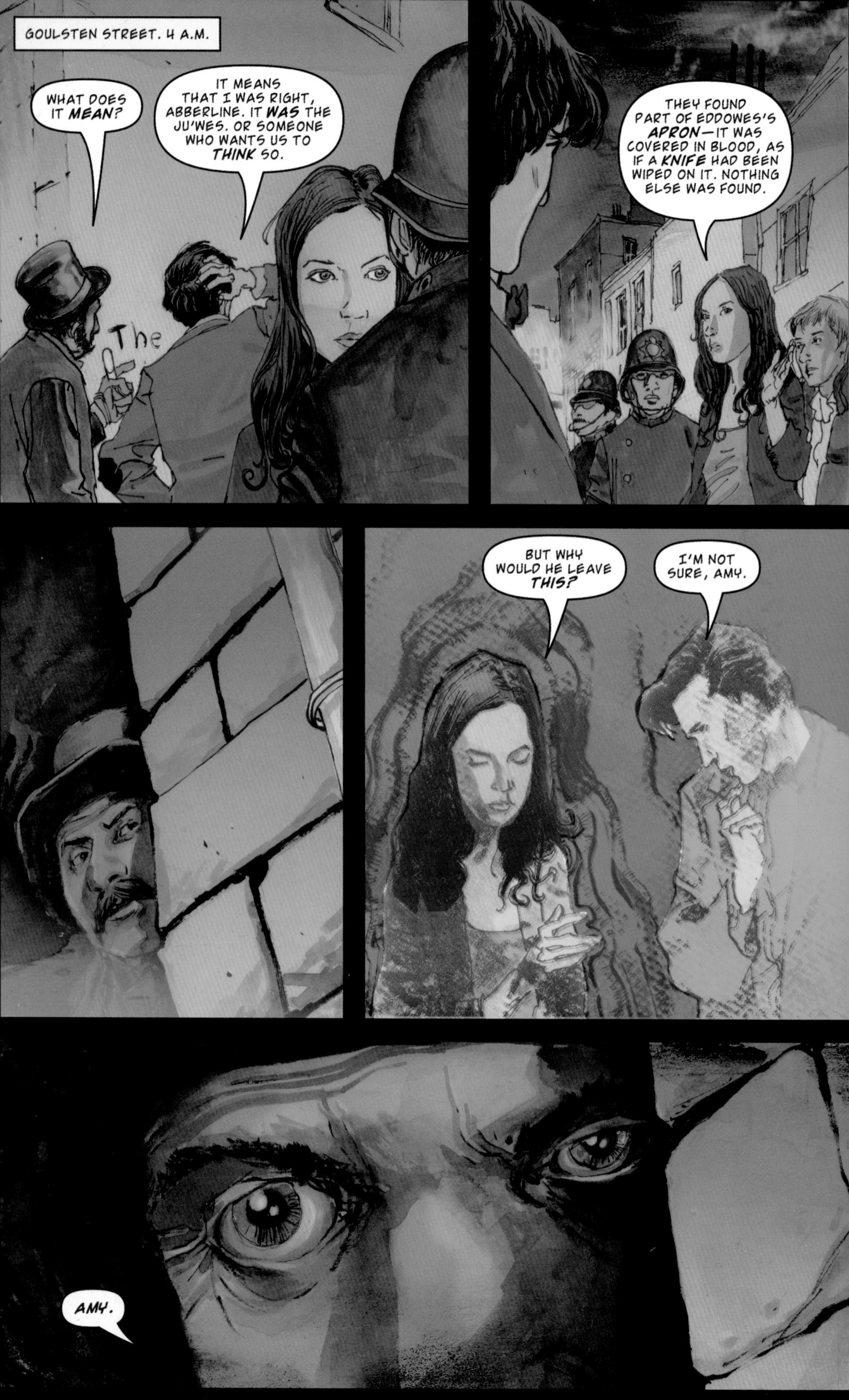
GOULSTEN STREET. 4 A.M.
WHAT DOES IT MEAN?
IT MEANS THAT I WAS RIGHT, ABBERLINE. IT WAS THE JU'WES. OR SOMEONE WHO WANTS US TO THINK SO.
The
THEY FOUND PART OF EDDOWES'S APRON—IT WAS COVERED IN BLOOD, AS IF A KNIFE HAD BEEN WIPED ON IT. NOTHING ELSE WAS FOUND.
BUT WHY WOULD HE LEAVE THIS?
I'M NOT SURE, AMY.
AMY.

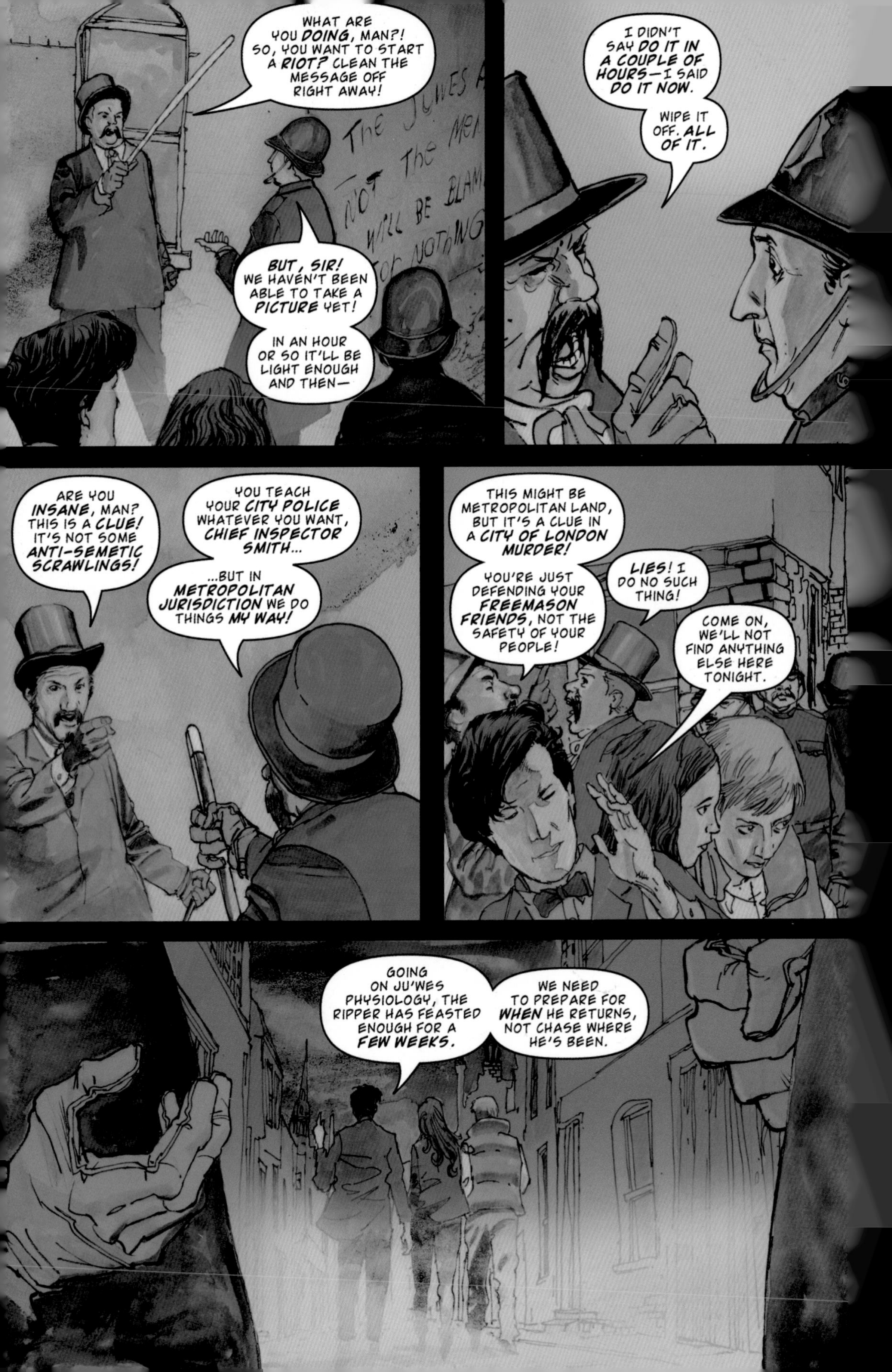
WHAT ARE YOU DOING, MAN?! SO, YOU WANT TO START A RIOT? CLEAN THE MESSAGE OFF RIGHT AWAY!
The Juwes A... Not The Men... Will be Blam... for nothing
BUT, SIR! WE HAVEN'T BEEN ABLE TO TAKE A PICTURE YET!
IN AN HOUR OR SO IT'LL BE LIGHT ENOUGH AND THEN—
I DIDN'T SAY DO IT IN A COUPLE OF HOURS—I SAID DO IT NOW.
WIPE IT OFF. ALL OF IT.
ARE YOU INSANE, MAN? THIS IS A CLUE! IT'S NOT SOME ANTI-SEMETIC SCRAWLINGS!
YOU TEACH YOUR CITY POLICE WHATEVER YOU WANT, CHIEF INSPECTOR SMITH...
...BUT IN METROPOLITAN JURISDICTION WE DO THINGS MY WAY!
THIS MIGHT BE METROPOLITAN LAND, BUT IT'S A CLUE IN A CITY OF LONDON MURDER!
YOU'RE JUST DEFENDING YOUR FREEMASON FRIENDS, NOT THE SAFETY OF YOUR PEOPLE!
LIES! I DO NO SUCH THING!
COME ON, WE'LL NOT FIND ANYTHING ELSE HERE TONIGHT.
GOING ON JU'WES PHYSIOLOGY, THE RIPPER HAS FEASTED ENOUGH FOR A FEW WEEKS.
WE NEED TO PREPARE FOR WHEN HE RETURNS, NOT CHASE WHERE HE'S BEEN.

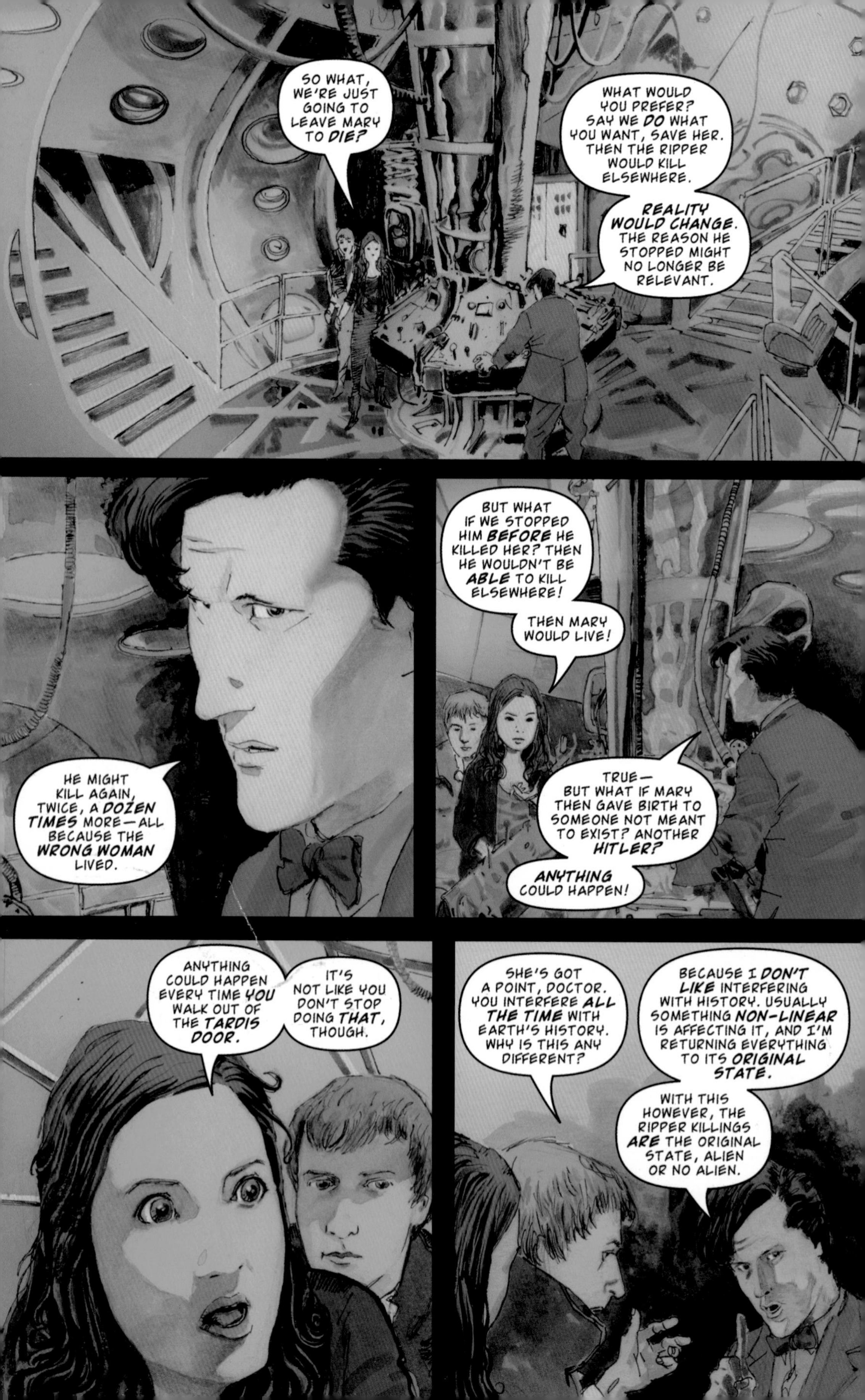

SO WHAT, WE'RE JUST GOING TO LEAVE MARY TO DIE?
WHAT WOULD YOU PREFER? SAY WE DO WHAT YOU WANT, SAVE HER. THEN THE RIPPER WOULD KILL ELSEWHERE.
REALITY WOULD CHANGE. THE REASON HE STOPPED MIGHT NO LONGER BE RELEVANT.
HE MIGHT KILL AGAIN, TWICE, A DOZEN TIMES MORE—ALL BECAUSE THE WRONG WOMAN LIVED.
BUT WHAT IF WE STOPPED HIM BEFORE HE KILLED HER? THEN HE WOULDN'T BE ABLE TO KILL ELSEWHERE!
THEN MARY WOULD LIVE!
TRUE— BUT WHAT IF MARY THEN GAVE BIRTH TO SOMEONE NOT MEANT TO EXIST? ANOTHER HITLER?
ANYTHING COULD HAPPEN!
ANYTHING COULD HAPPEN EVERY TIME YOU WALK OUT OF THE TARDIS DOOR.
IT'S NOT LIKE YOU DON'T STOP DOING THAT, THOUGH.
SHE'S GOT A POINT, DOCTOR. YOU INTERFERE ALL THE TIME WITH EARTH'S HISTORY. WHY IS THIS ANY DIFFERENT?
BECAUSE I DON'T LIKE INTERFERING WITH HISTORY. USUALLY SOMETHING NON-LINEAR IS AFFECTING IT, AND I'M RETURNING EVERYTHING TO ITS ORIGINAL STATE.
WITH THIS HOWEVER, THE RIPPER KILLINGS ARE THE ORIGINAL STATE, ALIEN OR NO ALIEN.

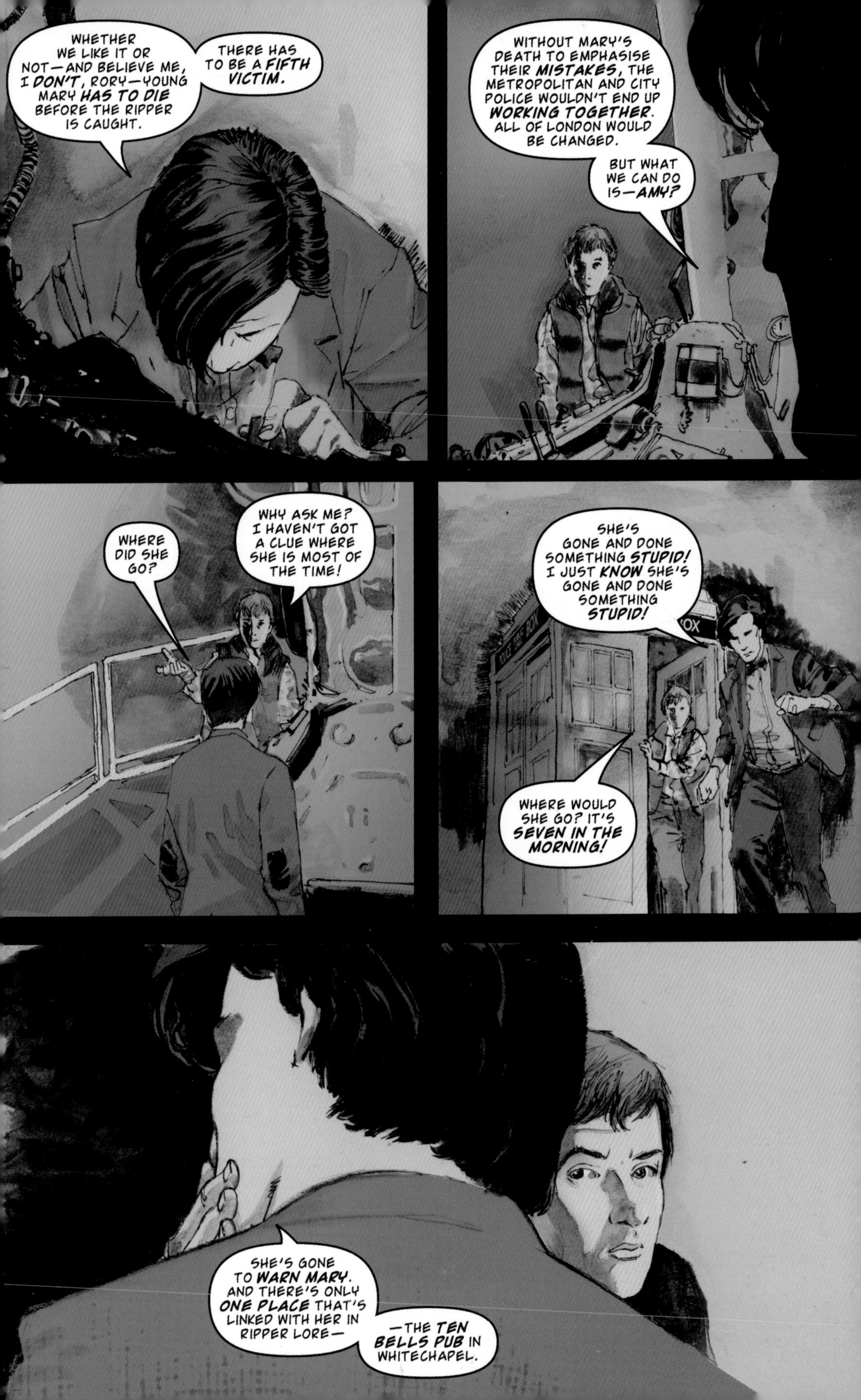
WHETHER WE LIKE IT OR NOT—AND BELIEVE ME, I DON'T, RORY—YOUNG MARY HAS TO DIE BEFORE THE RIPPER IS CAUGHT.
THERE HAS TO BE A FIFTH VICTIM.
WITHOUT MARY'S DEATH TO EMPHASISE THEIR MISTAKES, THE METROPOLITAN AND CITY POLICE WOULDN'T END UP WORKING TOGETHER. ALL OF LONDON WOULD BE CHANGED.
BUT WHAT WE CAN DO IS—AMY?
WHERE DID SHE GO?
WHY ASK ME? I HAVEN'T GOT A CLUE WHERE SHE IS MOST OF THE TIME!
SHE'S GONE AND DONE SOMETHING STUPID! I JUST KNOW SHE'S GONE AND DONE SOMETHING STUPID!
WHERE WOULD SHE GO? IT'S SEVEN IN THE MORNING!
SHE'S GONE TO WARN MARY. AND THERE'S ONLY ONE PLACE THAT'S LINKED WITH HER IN RIPPER LORE—
—THE TEN BELLS PUB IN WHITECHAPEL.

THEN WE'D BETTER **STOP** HER!

GOOD PLAN. YOU TRY THE **TEN BELLS**, I'LL TRY THE **POLICE STATION**, JUST IN CASE.

IF YOU FIND HER, **BRING HER BACK** HERE!

OW!

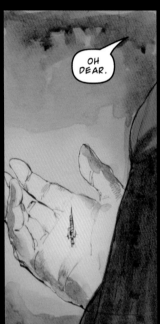

OH DEAR.

CLATTER

WHUR... WHAA...

THERE NOW, HUSH—YOU'RE FIGHTING THE **PARALYSIS**. LET IT TAKE YOU.

I'M ONLY HERE TO **TALK**.

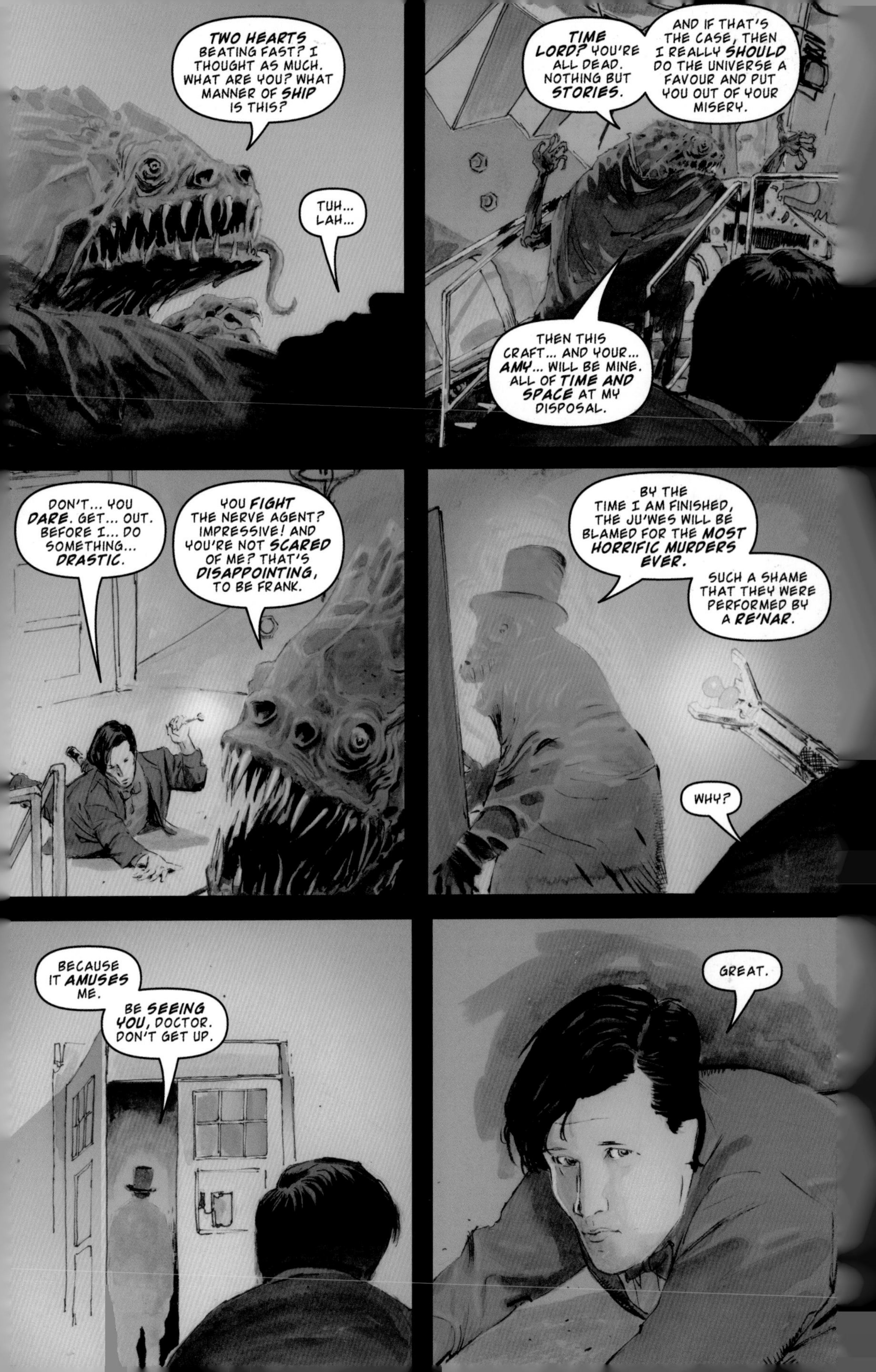
TWO HEARTS BEATING FAST? I THOUGHT AS MUCH. WHAT ARE YOU? WHAT MANNER OF SHIP IS THIS?
TUH... LAH...
TIME LORD? YOU'RE ALL DEAD. NOTHING BUT STORIES.
AND IF THAT'S THE CASE, THEN I REALLY SHOULD DO THE UNIVERSE A FAVOUR AND PUT YOU OUT OF YOUR MISERY.
THEN THIS CRAFT... AND YOUR... AMY... WILL BE MINE. ALL OF TIME AND SPACE AT MY DISPOSAL.
DON'T... YOU DARE. GET... OUT. BEFORE I... DO SOMETHING... DRASTIC.
YOU FIGHT THE NERVE AGENT? IMPRESSIVE! AND YOU'RE NOT SCARED OF ME? THAT'S DISAPPOINTING, TO BE FRANK.
BY THE TIME I AM FINISHED, THE JU'WES WILL BE BLAMED FOR THE MOST HORRIFIC MURDERS EVER.
SUCH A SHAME THAT THEY WERE PERFORMED BY A RE'NAR.
WHY?
BECAUSE IT AMUSES ME.
BE SEEING YOU, DOCTOR. DON'T GET UP.
GREAT.

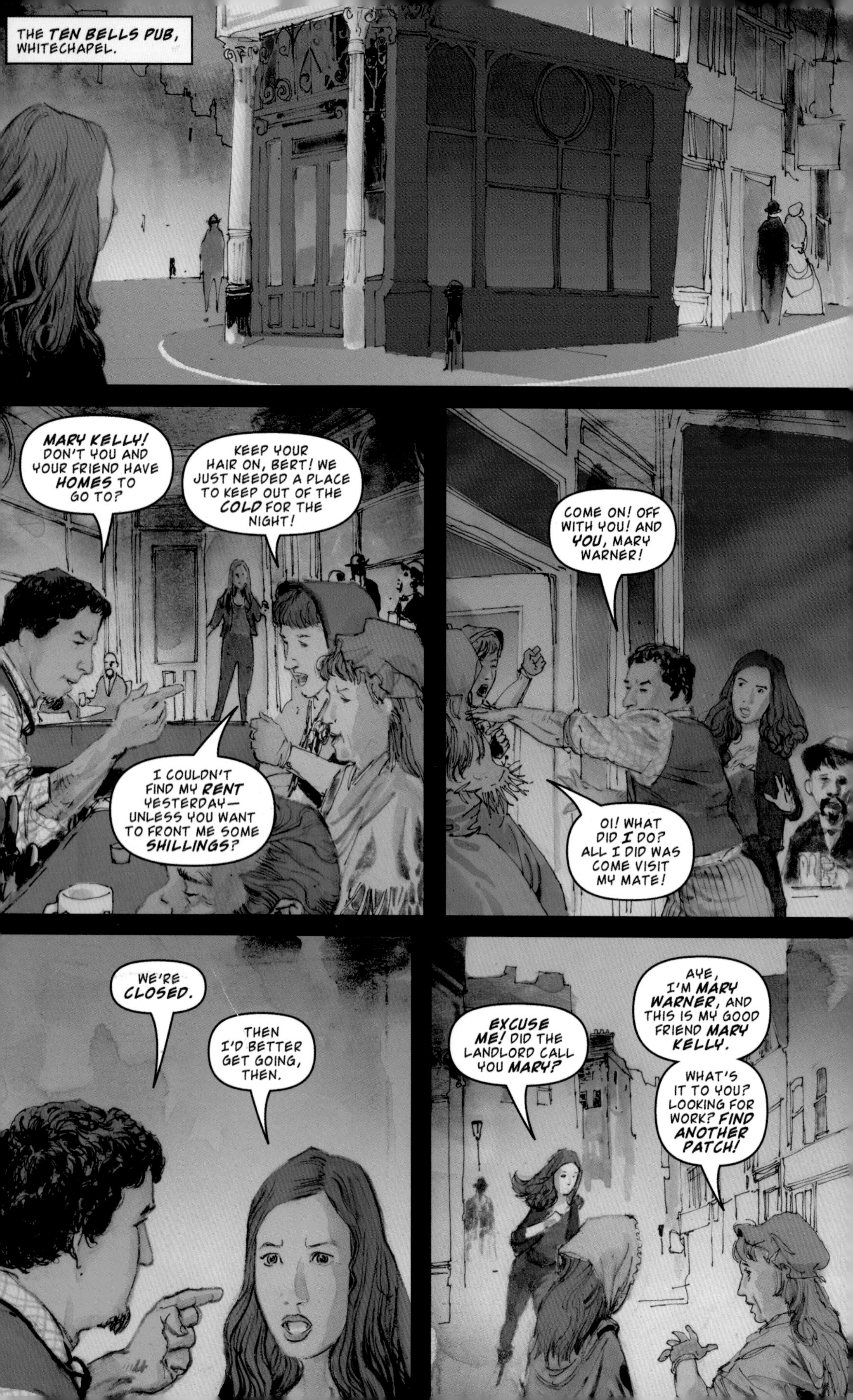

THE TEN BELLS PUB, WHITECHAPEL.
MARY KELLY! DON'T YOU AND YOUR FRIEND HAVE HOMES TO GO TO?
KEEP YOUR HAIR ON, BERT! WE JUST NEEDED A PLACE TO KEEP OUT OF THE COLD FOR THE NIGHT!
I COULDN'T FIND MY RENT YESTERDAY— UNLESS YOU WANT TO FRONT ME SOME SHILLINGS?
COME ON! OFF WITH YOU! AND YOU, MARY WARNER!
OI! WHAT DID I DO? ALL I DID WAS COME VISIT MY MATE!
WE'RE CLOSED.
THEN I'D BETTER GET GOING, THEN.
EXCUSE ME! DID THE LANDLORD CALL YOU MARY?
AYE, I'M MARY WARNER, AND THIS IS MY GOOD FRIEND MARY KELLY.
WHAT'S IT TO YOU? LOOKING FOR WORK? FIND ANOTHER PATCH!

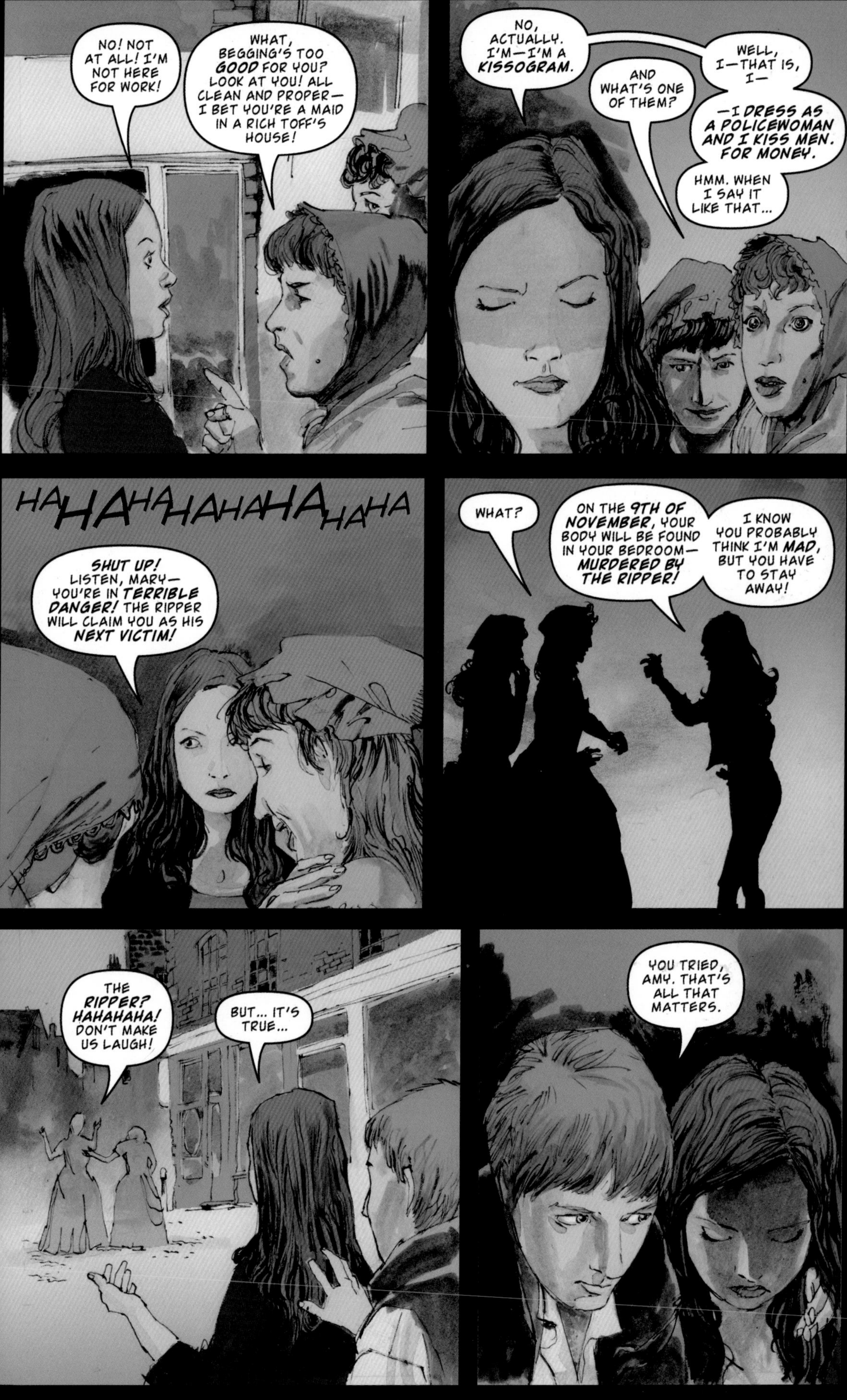
NO! NOT AT ALL! I'M NOT HERE FOR WORK!
WHAT, BEGGING'S TOO GOOD FOR YOU? LOOK AT YOU! ALL CLEAN AND PROPER— I BET YOU'RE A MAID IN A RICH TOFF'S HOUSE!
NO, ACTUALLY. I'M—I'M A KISSOGRAM.
AND WHAT'S ONE OF THEM?
WELL, I—THAT IS, I—
—I DRESS AS A POLICEWOMAN AND I KISS MEN. FOR MONEY.
HMM. WHEN I SAY IT LIKE THAT...
HAHAHAHAHAHAHAHAHA
SHUT UP! LISTEN, MARY— YOU'RE IN TERRIBLE DANGER! THE RIPPER WILL CLAIM YOU AS HIS NEXT VICTIM!
WHAT?
ON THE 9TH OF NOVEMBER, YOUR BODY WILL BE FOUND IN YOUR BEDROOM— MURDERED BY THE RIPPER!
I KNOW YOU PROBABLY THINK I'M MAD, BUT YOU HAVE TO STAY AWAY!
THE RIPPER? HAHAHAHA! DON'T MAKE US LAUGH!
BUT... IT'S TRUE...
YOU TRIED, AMY. THAT'S ALL THAT MATTERS.

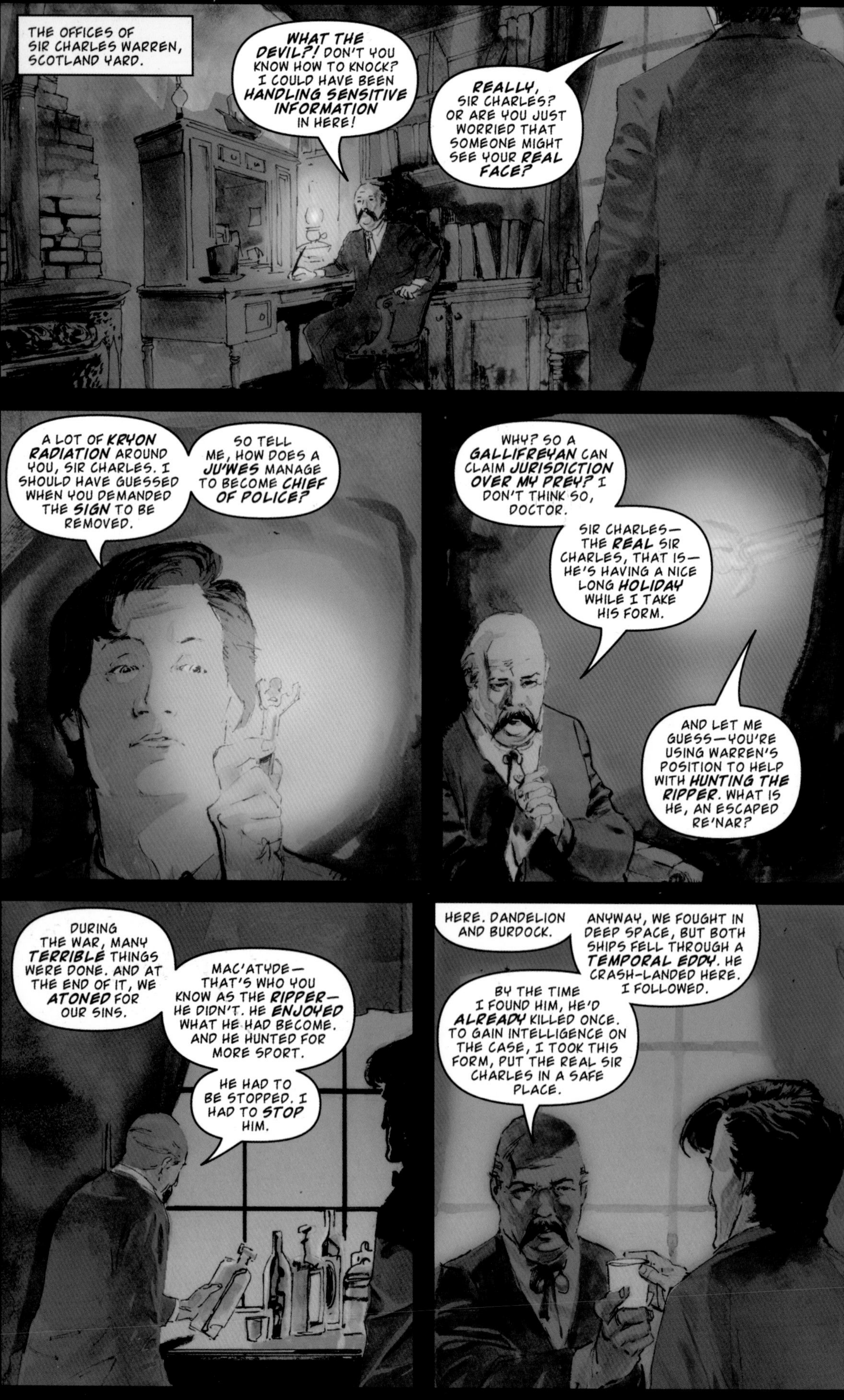
THE OFFICES OF SIR CHARLES WARREN, SCOTLAND YARD.
WHAT THE DEVIL?! DON'T YOU KNOW HOW TO KNOCK? I COULD HAVE BEEN HANDLING SENSITIVE INFORMATION IN HERE!
REALLY, SIR CHARLES? OR ARE YOU JUST WORRIED THAT SOMEONE MIGHT SEE YOUR REAL FACE?
A LOT OF KRYON RADIATION AROUND YOU, SIR CHARLES. I SHOULD HAVE GUESSED WHEN YOU DEMANDED THE SIGN TO BE REMOVED.
SO TELL ME, HOW DOES A JU'WES MANAGE TO BECOME CHIEF OF POLICE?
WHY? SO A GALLIFREYAN CAN CLAIM JURISDICTION OVER MY PREY? I DON'T THINK SO, DOCTOR.
SIR CHARLES— THE REAL SIR CHARLES, THAT IS— HE'S HAVING A NICE LONG HOLIDAY WHILE I TAKE HIS FORM.
AND LET ME GUESS—YOU'RE USING WARREN'S POSITION TO HELP WITH HUNTING THE RIPPER. WHAT IS HE, AN ESCAPED RE'NAR?
DURING THE WAR, MANY TERRIBLE THINGS WERE DONE. AND AT THE END OF IT, WE ATONED FOR OUR SINS.
MAC'ATYDE— THAT'S WHO YOU KNOW AS THE RIPPER— HE DIDN'T. HE ENJOYED WHAT HE HAD BECOME. AND HE HUNTED FOR MORE SPORT.
HE HAD TO BE STOPPED. I HAD TO STOP HIM.
HERE. DANDELION AND BURDOCK.
ANYWAY, WE FOUGHT IN DEEP SPACE, BUT BOTH SHIPS FELL THROUGH A TEMPORAL EDDY. HE CRASH-LANDED HERE. I FOLLOWED.
BY THE TIME I FOUND HIM, HE'D ALREADY KILLED ONCE. TO GAIN INTELLIGENCE ON THE CASE, I TOOK THIS FORM, PUT THE REAL SIR CHARLES IN A SAFE PLACE.

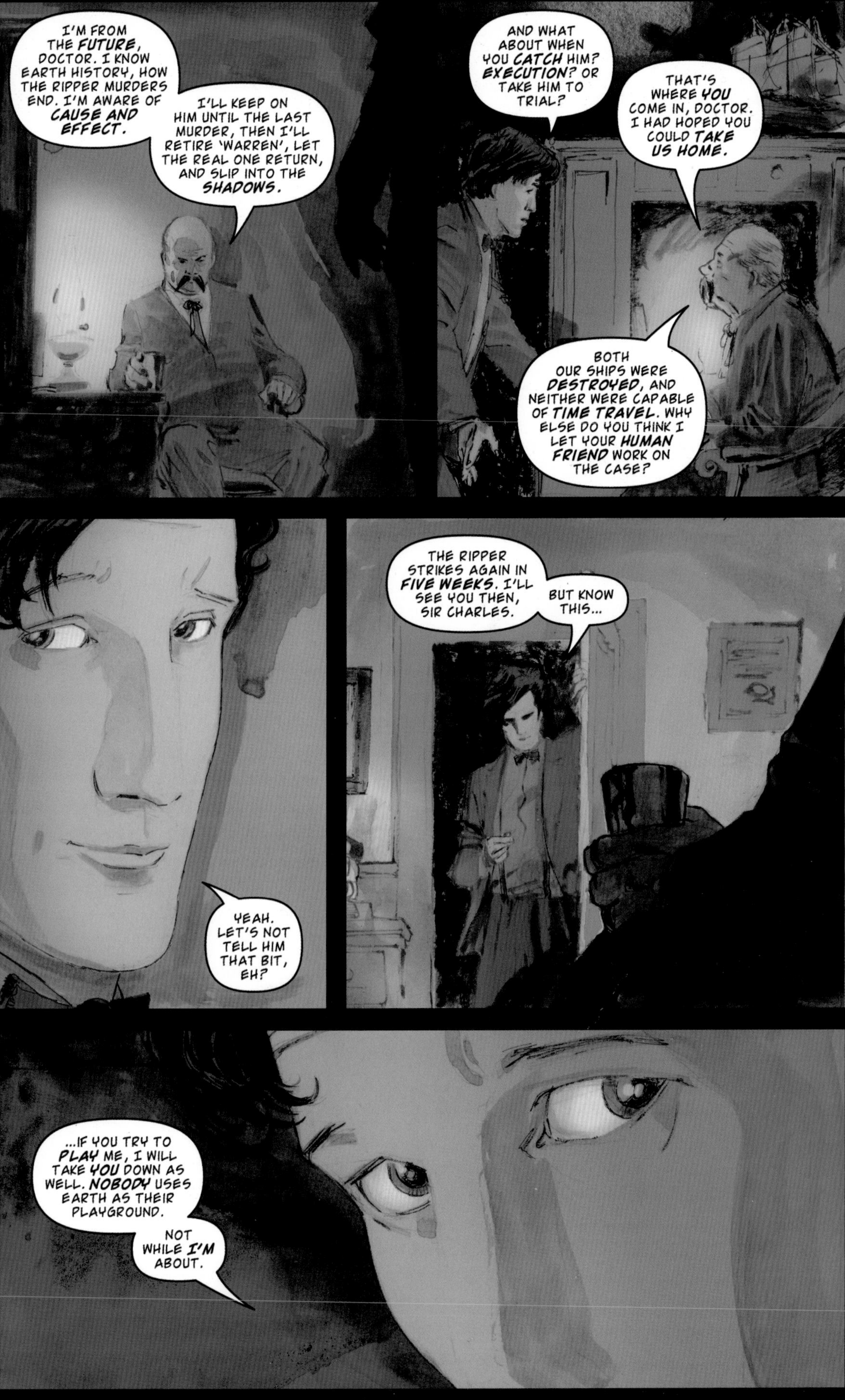
I'M FROM THE FUTURE, DOCTOR. I KNOW EARTH HISTORY, HOW THE RIPPER MURDERS END. I'M AWARE OF CAUSE AND EFFECT.
I'LL KEEP ON HIM UNTIL THE LAST MURDER, THEN I'LL RETIRE 'WARREN', LET THE REAL ONE RETURN, AND SLIP INTO THE SHADOWS.
AND WHAT ABOUT WHEN YOU CATCH HIM? EXECUTION? OR TAKE HIM TO TRIAL?
THAT'S WHERE YOU COME IN, DOCTOR. I HAD HOPED YOU COULD TAKE US HOME.
BOTH OUR SHIPS WERE DESTROYED, AND NEITHER WERE CAPABLE OF TIME TRAVEL. WHY ELSE DO YOU THINK I LET YOUR HUMAN FRIEND WORK ON THE CASE?
YEAH. LET'S NOT TELL HIM THAT BIT, EH?
THE RIPPER STRIKES AGAIN IN FIVE WEEKS. I'LL SEE YOU THEN, SIR CHARLES.
BUT KNOW THIS...
...IF YOU TRY TO PLAY ME, I WILL TAKE YOU DOWN AS WELL. NOBODY USES EARTH AS THEIR PLAYGROUND.
NOT WHILE I'M ABOUT.

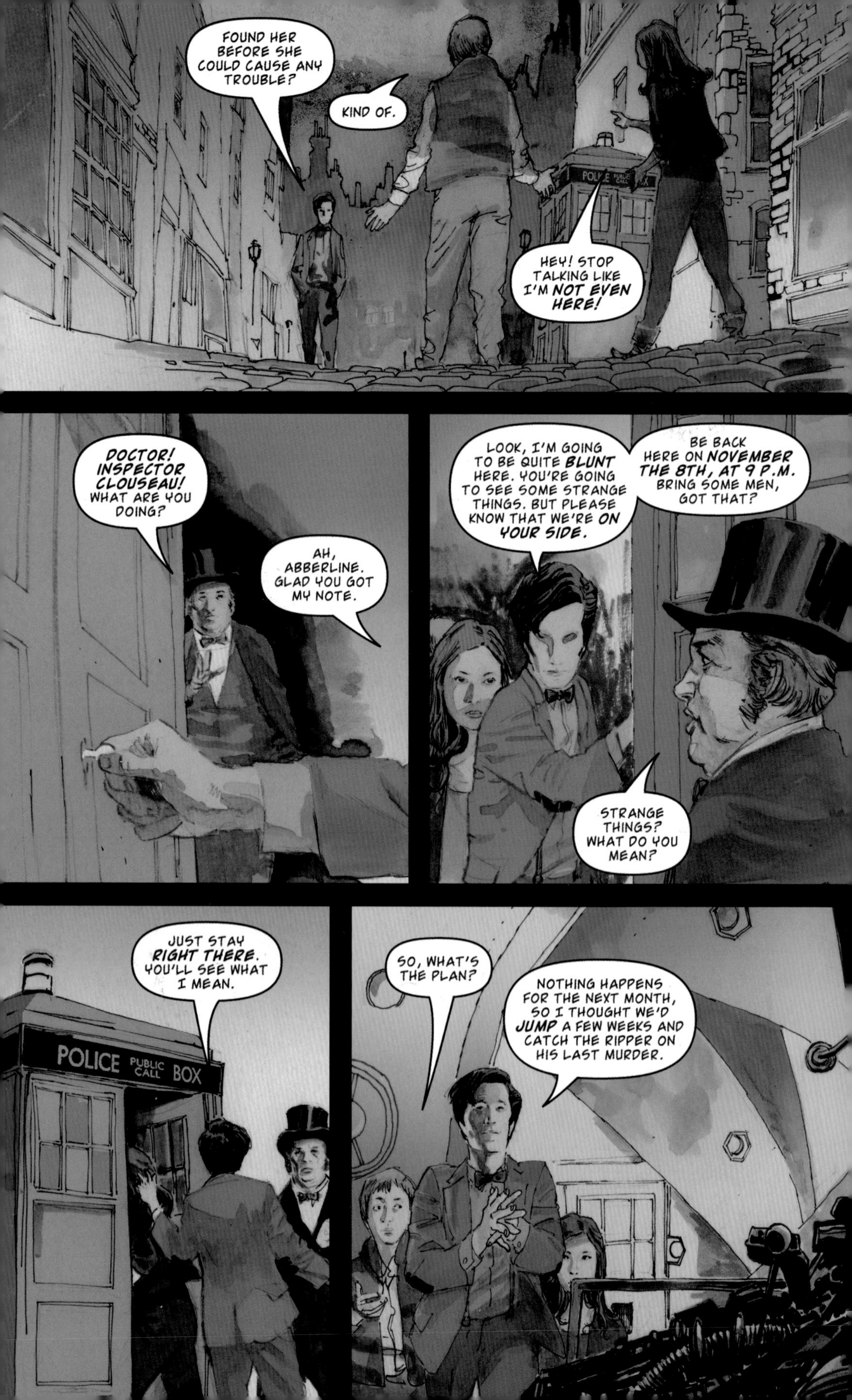
FOUND HER BEFORE SHE COULD CAUSE ANY TROUBLE?
KIND OF.
HEY! STOP TALKING LIKE I'M NOT EVEN HERE!
DOCTOR! INSPECTOR CLOUSEAU! WHAT ARE YOU DOING?
AH, ABBERLINE. GLAD YOU GOT MY NOTE.
LOOK, I'M GOING TO BE QUITE BLUNT HERE. YOU'RE GOING TO SEE SOME STRANGE THINGS. BUT PLEASE KNOW THAT WE'RE ON YOUR SIDE.
BE BACK HERE ON NOVEMBER THE 8TH, AT 9 P.M. BRING SOME MEN, GOT THAT?
STRANGE THINGS? WHAT DO YOU MEAN?
JUST STAY RIGHT THERE. YOU'LL SEE WHAT I MEAN.
POLICE PUBLIC CALL BOX
SO, WHAT'S THE PLAN?
NOTHING HAPPENS FOR THE NEXT MONTH, SO I THOUGHT WE'D JUMP A FEW WEEKS AND CATCH THE RIPPER ON HIS LAST MURDER.

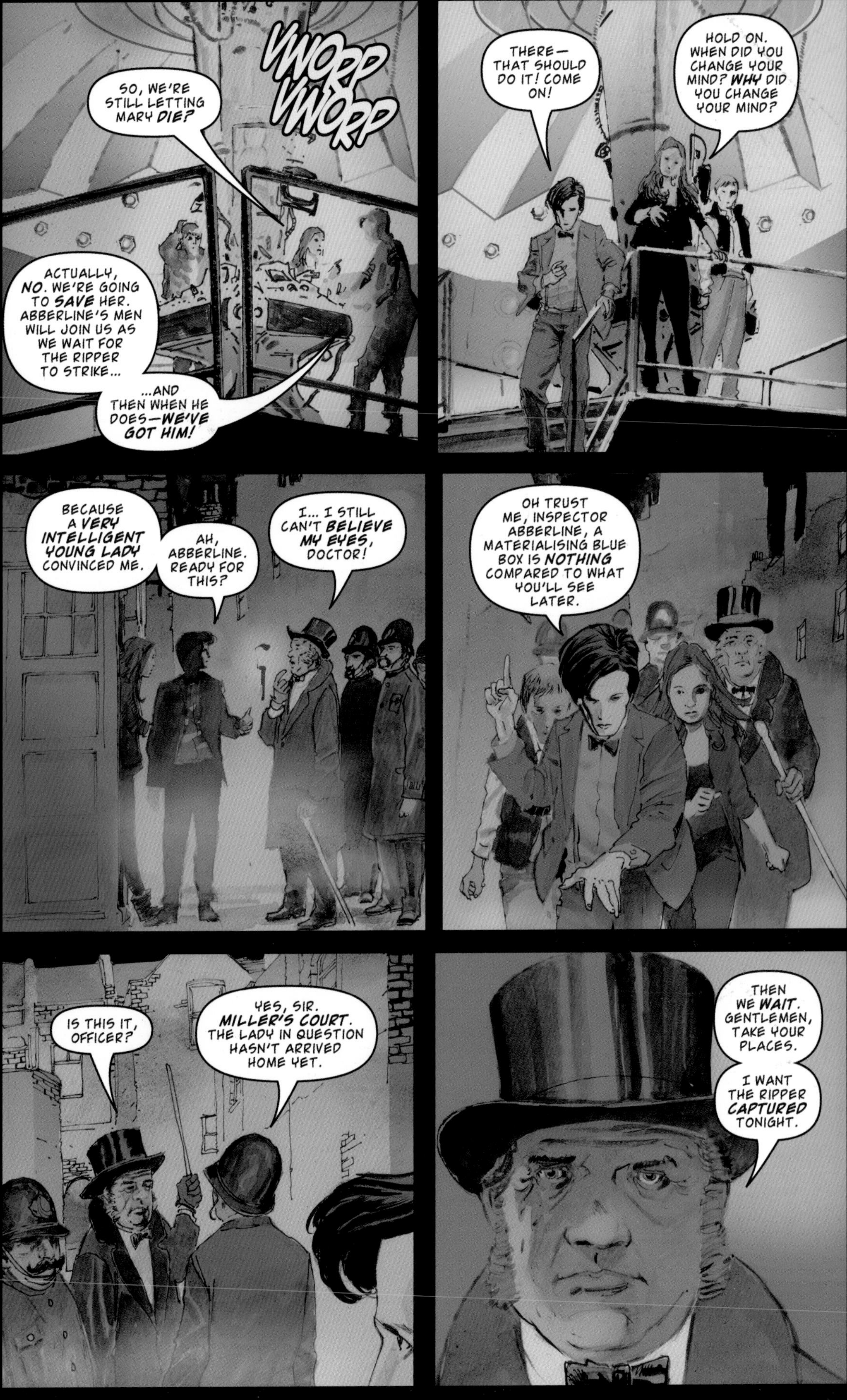
VWORP VWORP
SO, WE'RE STILL LETTING MARY DIE?
ACTUALLY, NO. WE'RE GOING TO SAVE HER. ABBERLINE'S MEN WILL JOIN US AS WE WAIT FOR THE RIPPER TO STRIKE...
...AND THEN WHEN HE DOES—WE'VE GOT HIM!
THERE—THAT SHOULD DO IT! COME ON!
HOLD ON. WHEN DID YOU CHANGE YOUR MIND? WHY DID YOU CHANGE YOUR MIND?
BECAUSE A VERY INTELLIGENT YOUNG LADY CONVINCED ME.
AH, ABBERLINE. READY FOR THIS?
I... I STILL CAN'T BELIEVE MY EYES, DOCTOR!
OH TRUST ME, INSPECTOR ABBERLINE, A MATERIALISING BLUE BOX IS NOTHING COMPARED TO WHAT YOU'LL SEE LATER.
IS THIS IT, OFFICER?
YES, SIR. MILLER'S COURT. THE LADY IN QUESTION HASN'T ARRIVED HOME YET.
THEN WE WAIT. GENTLEMEN, TAKE YOUR PLACES.
I WANT THE RIPPER CAPTURED TONIGHT.

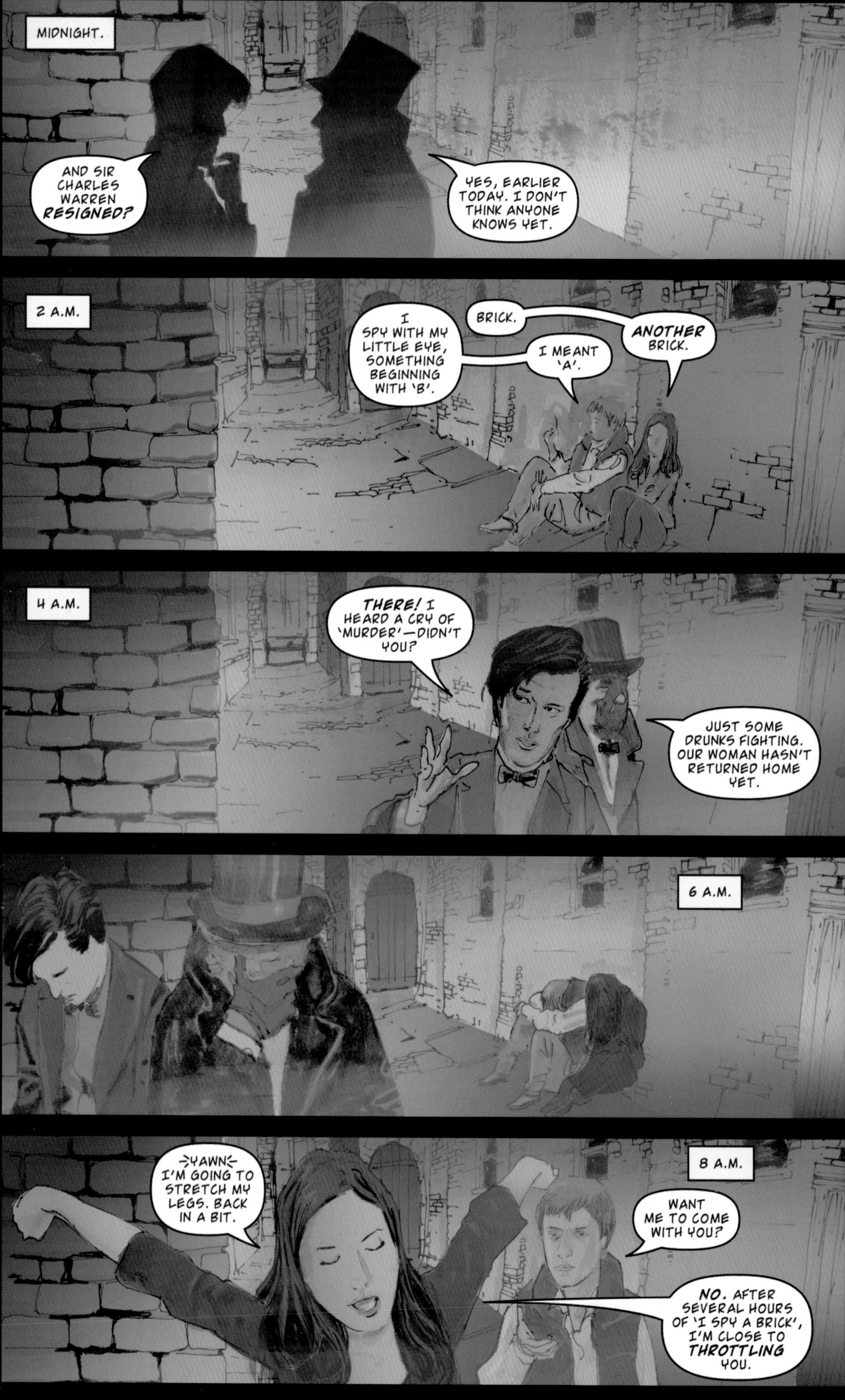
MIDNIGHT.
AND SIR CHARLES WARREN RESIGNED?
YES, EARLIER TODAY. I DON'T THINK ANYONE KNOWS YET.
2 A.M.
I SPY WITH MY LITTLE EYE, SOMETHING BEGINNING WITH 'B'.
BRICK.
I MEANT 'A'.
ANOTHER BRICK.
4 A.M.
THERE! I HEARD A CRY OF 'MURDER'—DIDN'T YOU?
JUST SOME DRUNKS FIGHTING. OUR WOMAN HASN'T RETURNED HOME YET.
6 A.M.
8 A.M.
>YAWN< I'M GOING TO STRETCH MY LEGS. BACK IN A BIT.
WANT ME TO COME WITH YOU?
NO. AFTER SEVERAL HOURS OF 'I SPY A BRICK', I'M CLOSE TO THROTTLING YOU.

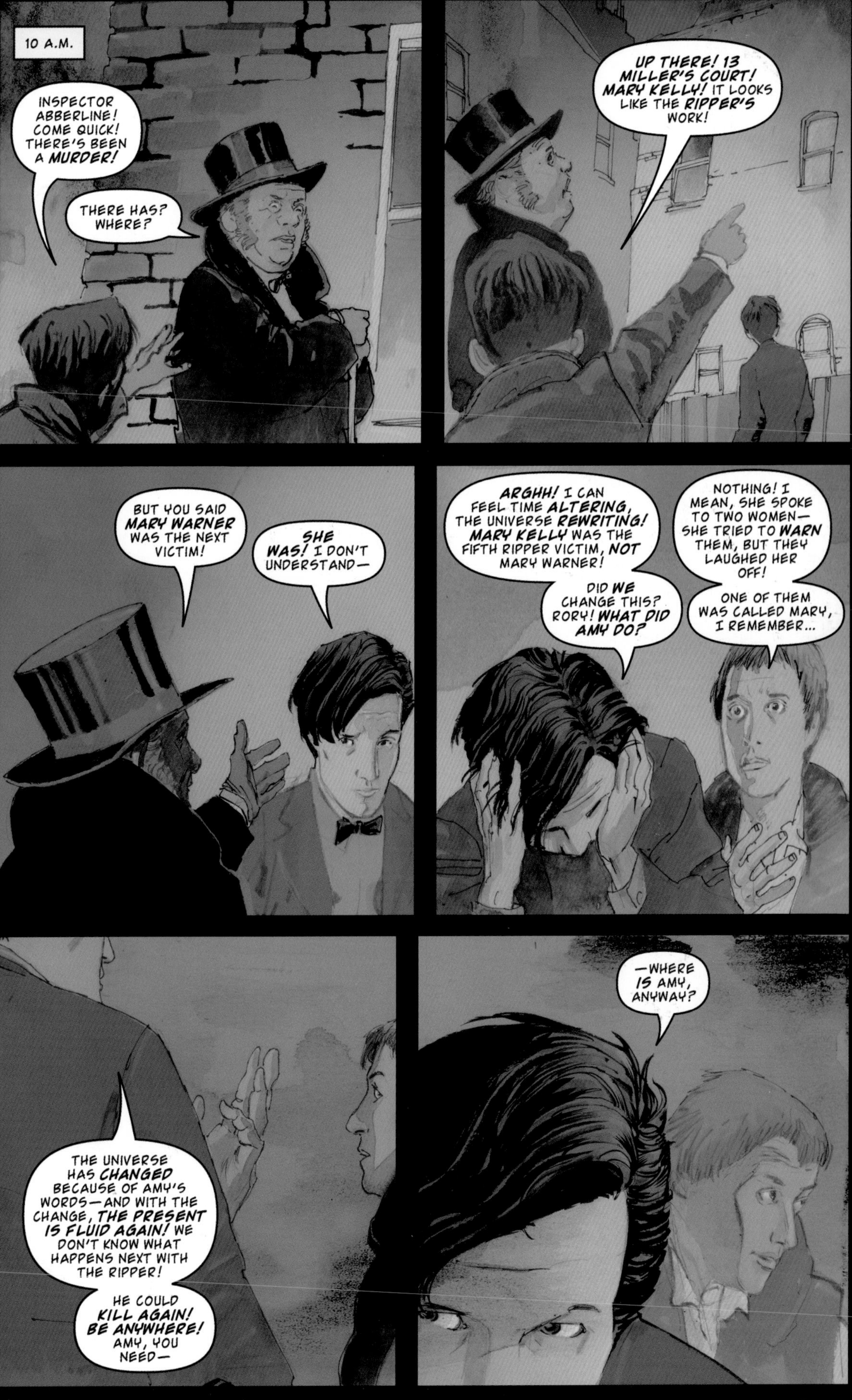
10 A.M.
INSPECTOR ABBERLINE! COME QUICK! THERE'S BEEN A MURDER!
THERE HAS? WHERE?
UP THERE! 13 MILLER'S COURT! MARY KELLY! IT LOOKS LIKE THE RIPPER'S WORK!
BUT YOU SAID MARY WARNER WAS THE NEXT VICTIM!
SHE WAS! I DON'T UNDERSTAND—
ARGHH! I CAN FEEL TIME ALTERING, THE UNIVERSE REWRITING! MARY KELLY WAS THE FIFTH RIPPER VICTIM, NOT MARY WARNER!
DID WE CHANGE THIS? RORY! WHAT DID AMY DO?
NOTHING! I MEAN, SHE SPOKE TO TWO WOMEN—SHE TRIED TO WARN THEM, BUT THEY LAUGHED HER OFF!
ONE OF THEM WAS CALLED MARY, I REMEMBER...
THE UNIVERSE HAS CHANGED BECAUSE OF AMY'S WORDS—AND WITH THE CHANGE, THE PRESENT IS FLUID AGAIN! WE DON'T KNOW WHAT HAPPENS NEXT WITH THE RIPPER!
HE COULD KILL AGAIN! BE ANYWHERE! AMY, YOU NEED—
—WHERE IS AMY, ANYWAY?

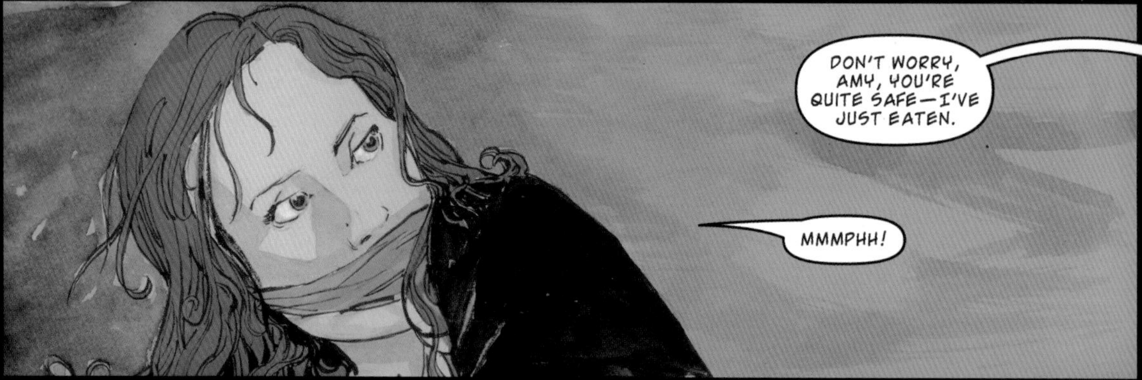
DON'T WORRY, AMY, YOU'RE QUITE SAFE—I'VE JUST EATEN.
MMMPHH!

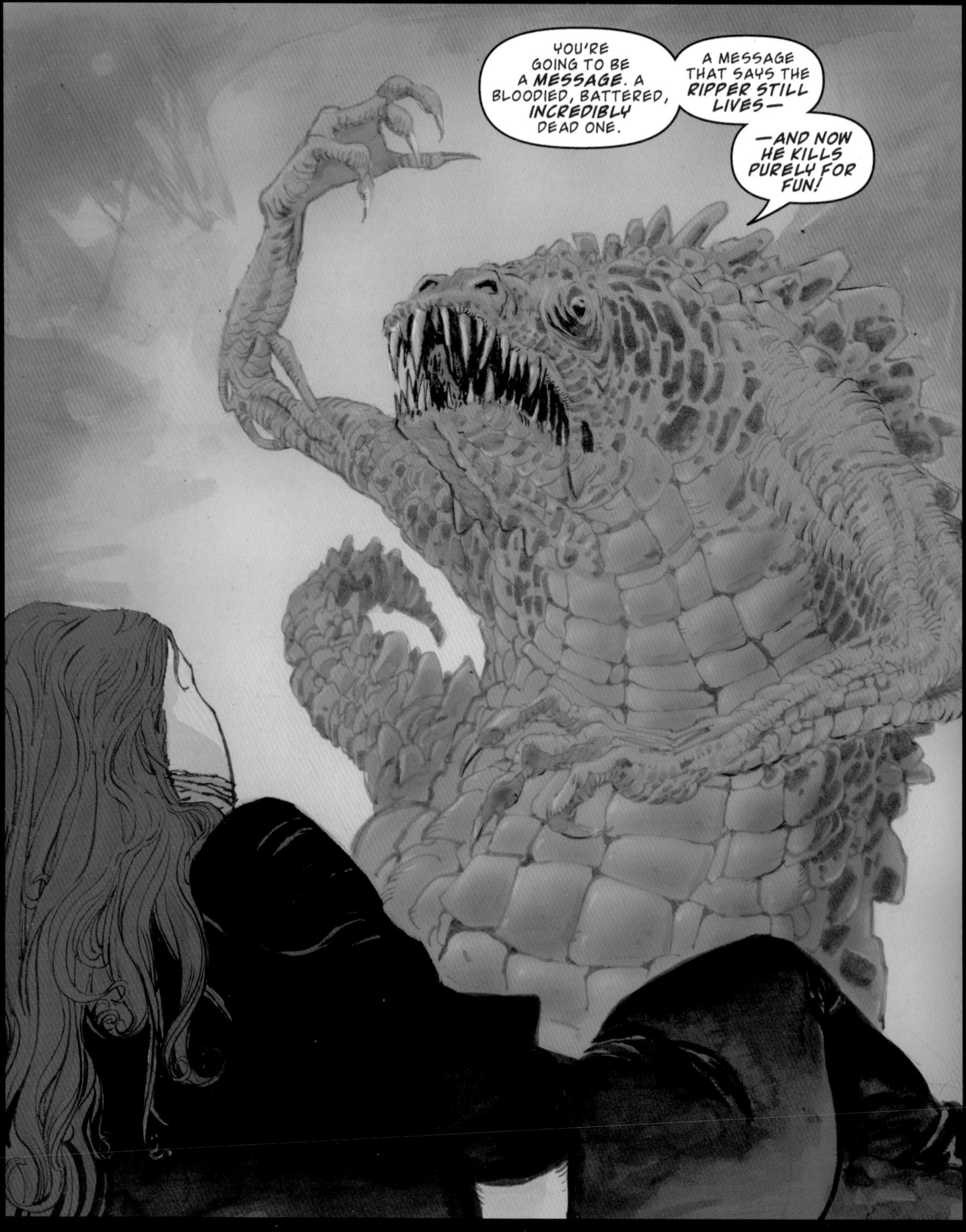
YOU'RE GOING TO BE A **MESSAGE**. A BLOODIED, BATTERED, **INCREDIBLY** DEAD ONE.
A MESSAGE THAT SAYS THE ***RIPPER STILL LIVES***—
—AND NOW HE KILLS PURELY FOR FUN!

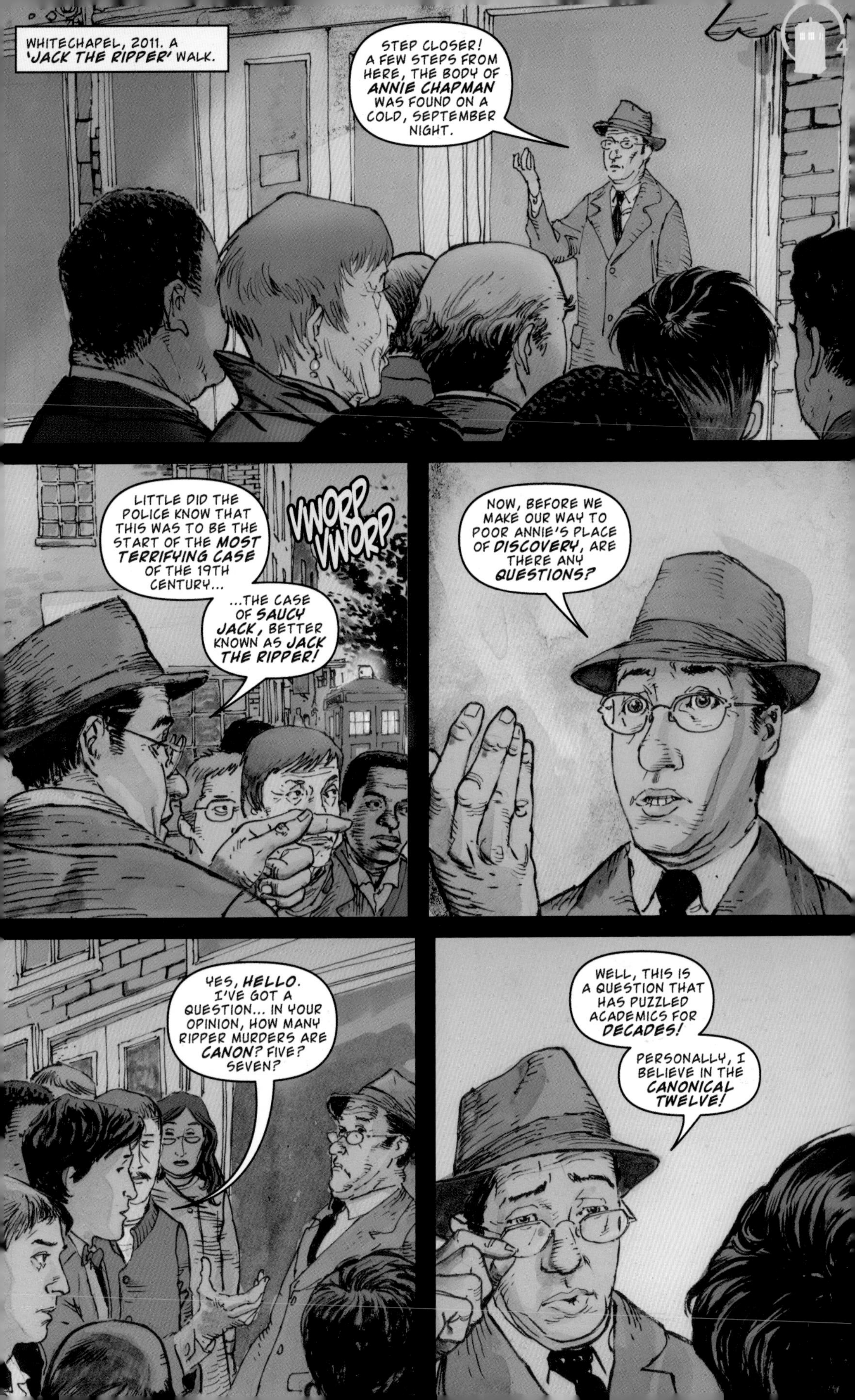
WHITECHAPEL, 2011. A 'JACK THE RIPPER' WALK.
STEP CLOSER! A FEW STEPS FROM HERE, THE BODY OF ANNIE CHAPMAN WAS FOUND ON A COLD, SEPTEMBER NIGHT.
LITTLE DID THE POLICE KNOW THAT THIS WAS TO BE THE START OF THE MOST TERRIFYING CASE OF THE 19TH CENTURY...
VWORP VWORP
...THE CASE OF SAUCY JACK, BETTER KNOWN AS JACK THE RIPPER!
NOW, BEFORE WE MAKE OUR WAY TO POOR ANNIE'S PLACE OF DISCOVERY, ARE THERE ANY QUESTIONS?
YES, HELLO. I'VE GOT A QUESTION... IN YOUR OPINION, HOW MANY RIPPER MURDERS ARE CANON? FIVE? SEVEN?
WELL, THIS IS A QUESTION THAT HAS PUZZLED ACADEMICS FOR DECADES!
PERSONALLY, I BELIEVE IN THE CANONICAL TWELVE!

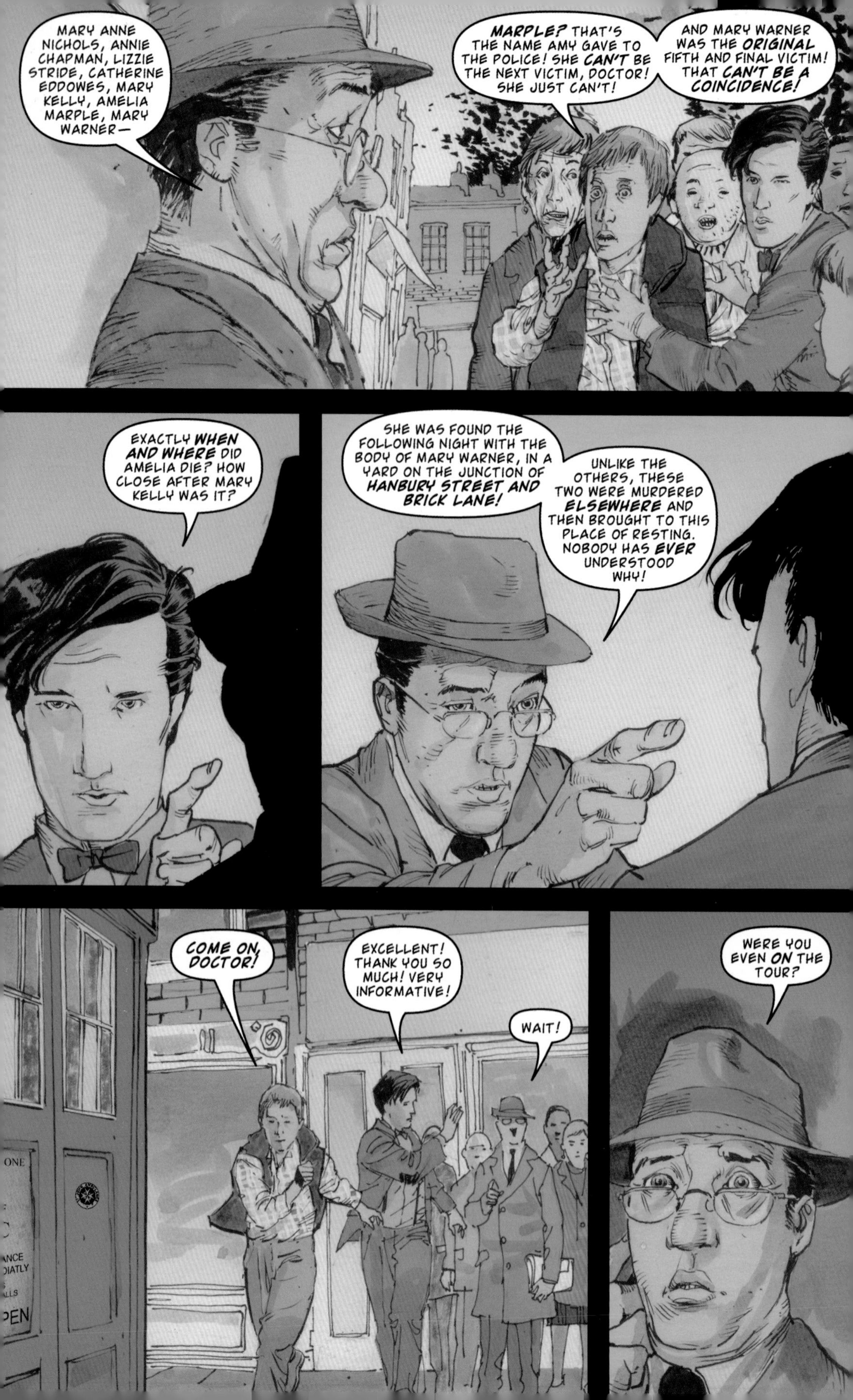

MARY ANNE NICHOLS, ANNIE CHAPMAN, LIZZIE STRIDE, CATHERINE EDDOWES, MARY KELLY, AMELIA MARPLE, MARY WARNER—
MARPLE? THAT'S THE NAME AMY GAVE TO THE POLICE! SHE CAN'T BE THE NEXT VICTIM, DOCTOR! SHE JUST CAN'T!
AND MARY WARNER WAS THE ORIGINAL FIFTH AND FINAL VICTIM! THAT CAN'T BE A COINCIDENCE!
EXACTLY WHEN AND WHERE DID AMELIA DIE? HOW CLOSE AFTER MARY KELLY WAS IT?
SHE WAS FOUND THE FOLLOWING NIGHT WITH THE BODY OF MARY WARNER, IN A YARD ON THE JUNCTION OF HANBURY STREET AND BRICK LANE!
UNLIKE THE OTHERS, THESE TWO WERE MURDERED ELSEWHERE AND THEN BROUGHT TO THIS PLACE OF RESTING. NOBODY HAS EVER UNDERSTOOD WHY!
COME ON, DOCTOR!
EXCELLENT! THANK YOU SO MUCH! VERY INFORMATIVE!
WAIT!
WERE YOU EVEN ON THE TOUR?

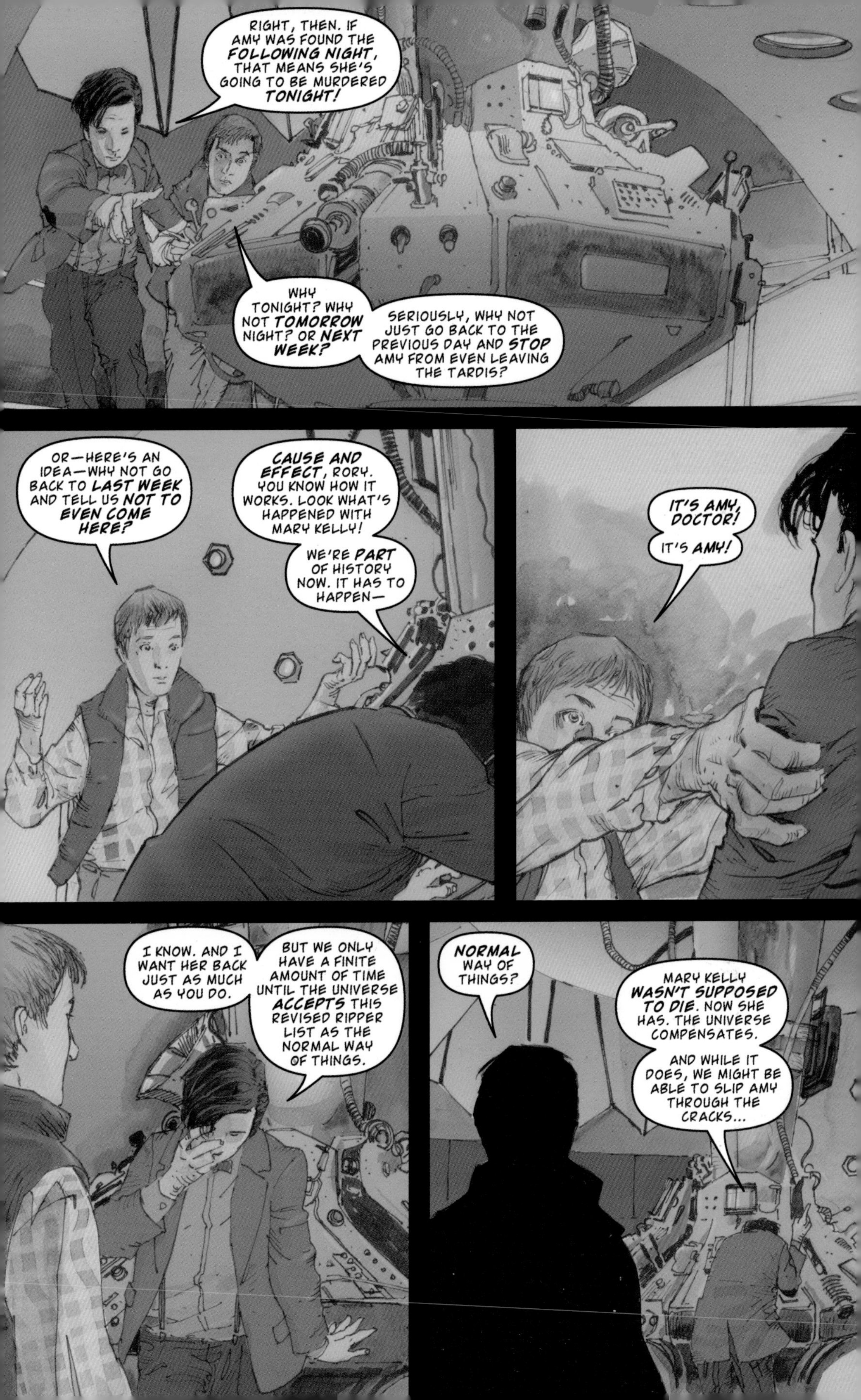
RIGHT, THEN. IF AMY WAS FOUND THE FOLLOWING NIGHT, THAT MEANS SHE'S GOING TO BE MURDERED TONIGHT!
WHY TONIGHT? WHY NOT TOMORROW NIGHT? OR NEXT WEEK?
SERIOUSLY, WHY NOT JUST GO BACK TO THE PREVIOUS DAY AND STOP AMY FROM EVEN LEAVING THE TARDIS?
OR—HERE'S AN IDEA—WHY NOT GO BACK TO LAST WEEK AND TELL US NOT TO EVEN COME HERE?
CAUSE AND EFFECT, RORY. YOU KNOW HOW IT WORKS. LOOK WHAT'S HAPPENED WITH MARY KELLY!
WE'RE PART OF HISTORY NOW. IT HAS TO HAPPEN—
IT'S AMY, DOCTOR!
IT'S AMY!
I KNOW. AND I WANT HER BACK JUST AS MUCH AS YOU DO.
BUT WE ONLY HAVE A FINITE AMOUNT OF TIME UNTIL THE UNIVERSE ACCEPTS THIS REVISED RIPPER LIST AS THE NORMAL WAY OF THINGS.
NORMAL WAY OF THINGS?
MARY KELLY WASN'T SUPPOSED TO DIE. NOW SHE HAS. THE UNIVERSE COMPENSATES.
AND WHILE IT DOES, WE MIGHT BE ABLE TO SLIP AMY THROUGH THE CRACKS...

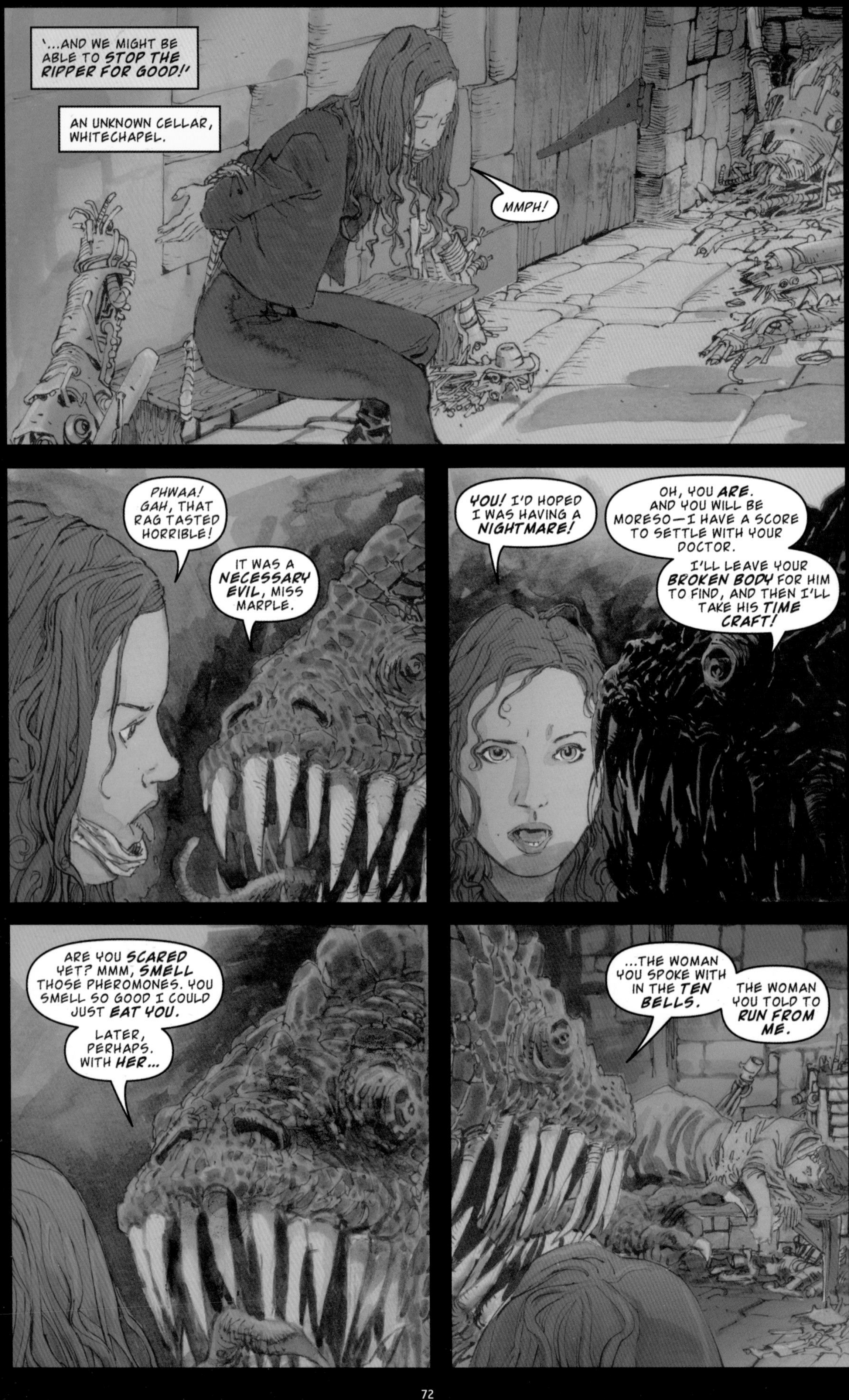
'...AND WE MIGHT BE ABLE TO STOP THE RIPPER FOR GOOD!'
AN UNKNOWN CELLAR, WHITECHAPEL.
MMPH!
PHWAA! GAH, THAT RAG TASTED HORRIBLE!
IT WAS A NECESSARY EVIL, MISS MARPLE.
YOU! I'D HOPED I WAS HAVING A NIGHTMARE!
OH, YOU ARE. AND YOU WILL BE MORESO—I HAVE A SCORE TO SETTLE WITH YOUR DOCTOR.
I'LL LEAVE YOUR BROKEN BODY FOR HIM TO FIND, AND THEN I'LL TAKE HIS TIME CRAFT!
ARE YOU SCARED YET? MMM, SMELL THOSE PHEROMONES. YOU SMELL SO GOOD I COULD JUST EAT YOU.
LATER, PERHAPS. WITH HER...
...THE WOMAN YOU SPOKE WITH IN THE TEN BELLS.
THE WOMAN YOU TOLD TO RUN FROM ME.

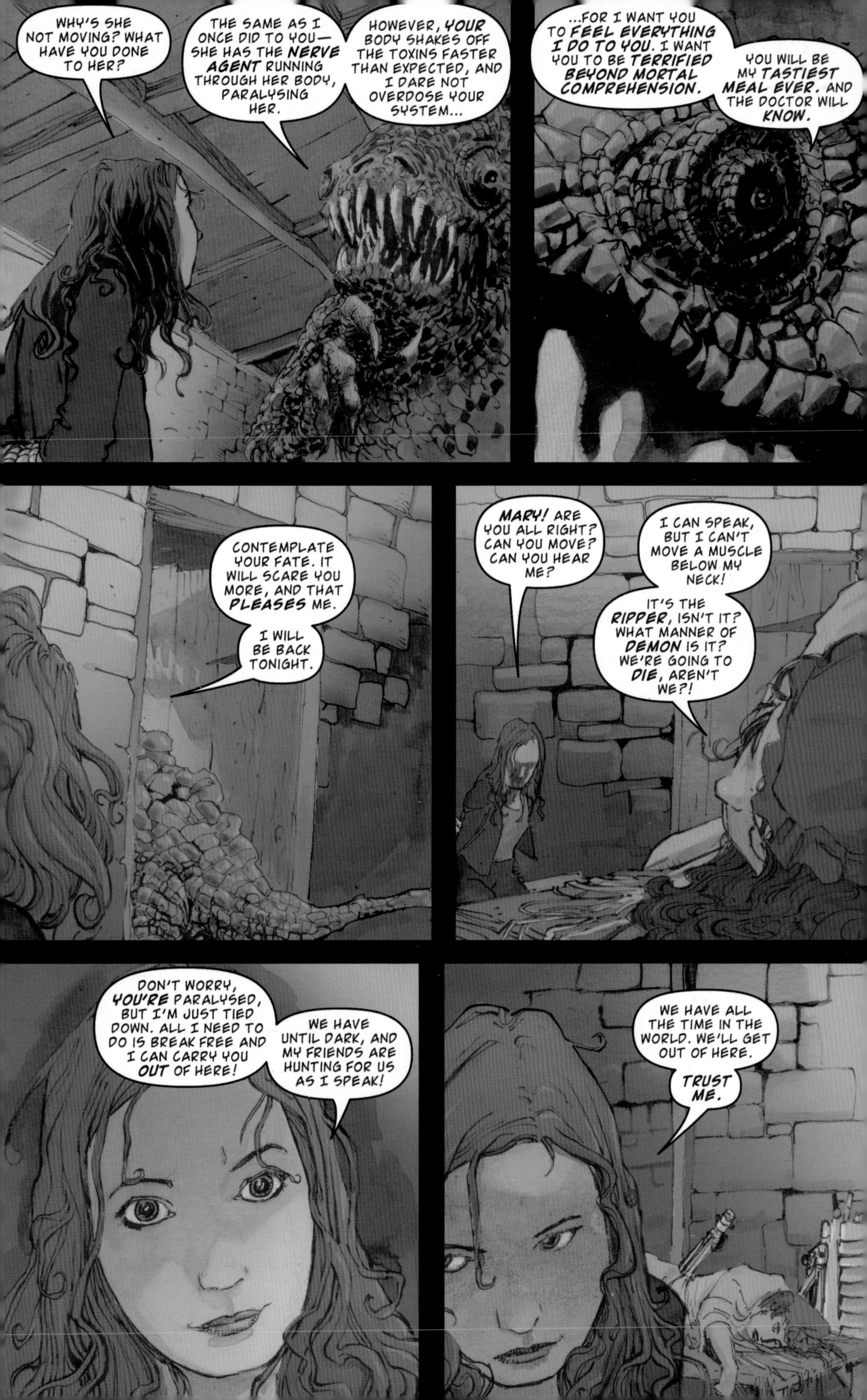
WHY'S SHE NOT MOVING? WHAT HAVE YOU DONE TO HER?
THE SAME AS I ONCE DID TO YOU—SHE HAS THE NERVE AGENT RUNNING THROUGH HER BODY, PARALYSING HER.
HOWEVER, YOUR BODY SHAKES OFF THE TOXINS FASTER THAN EXPECTED, AND I DARE NOT OVERDOSE YOUR SYSTEM...
...FOR I WANT YOU TO FEEL EVERYTHING I DO TO YOU. I WANT YOU TO BE TERRIFIED BEYOND MORTAL COMPREHENSION.
YOU WILL BE MY TASTIEST MEAL EVER. AND THE DOCTOR WILL KNOW.
CONTEMPLATE YOUR FATE. IT WILL SCARE YOU MORE, AND THAT PLEASES ME.
I WILL BE BACK TONIGHT.
MARY! ARE YOU ALL RIGHT? CAN YOU MOVE? CAN YOU HEAR ME?
I CAN SPEAK, BUT I CAN'T MOVE A MUSCLE BELOW MY NECK!
IT'S THE RIPPER, ISN'T IT? WHAT MANNER OF DEMON IS IT? WE'RE GOING TO DIE, AREN'T WE?!
DON'T WORRY, YOU'RE PARALYSED, BUT I'M JUST TIED DOWN. ALL I NEED TO DO IS BREAK FREE AND I CAN CARRY YOU OUT OF HERE!
WE HAVE UNTIL DARK, AND MY FRIENDS ARE HUNTING FOR US AS I SPEAK!
WE HAVE ALL THE TIME IN THE WORLD. WE'LL GET OUT OF HERE.
TRUST ME.

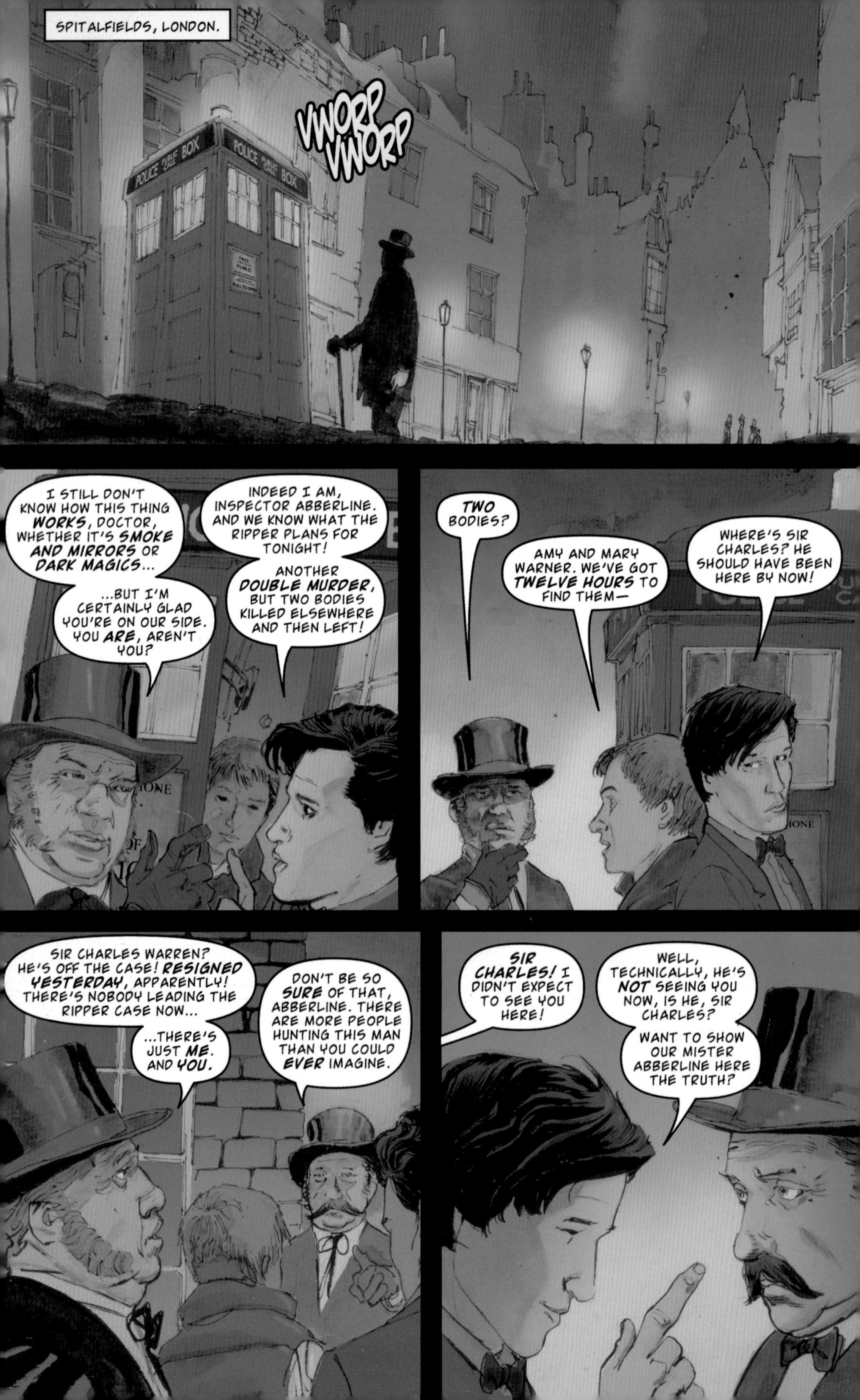
SPITALFIELDS, LONDON.
VWORP VWORP
POLICE PUBLIC CALL BOX
I STILL DON'T KNOW HOW THIS THING WORKS, DOCTOR, WHETHER IT'S SMOKE AND MIRRORS OR DARK MAGICS...
...BUT I'M CERTAINLY GLAD YOU'RE ON OUR SIDE. YOU ARE, AREN'T YOU?
INDEED I AM, INSPECTOR ABBERLINE. AND WE KNOW WHAT THE RIPPER PLANS FOR TONIGHT!
ANOTHER DOUBLE MURDER, BUT TWO BODIES KILLED ELSEWHERE AND THEN LEFT!
TWO BODIES?
AMY AND MARY WARNER. WE'VE GOT TWELVE HOURS TO FIND THEM—
WHERE'S SIR CHARLES? HE SHOULD HAVE BEEN HERE BY NOW!
SIR CHARLES WARREN? HE'S OFF THE CASE! RESIGNED YESTERDAY, APPARENTLY! THERE'S NOBODY LEADING THE RIPPER CASE NOW...
...THERE'S JUST ME. AND YOU.
DON'T BE SO SURE OF THAT, ABBERLINE. THERE ARE MORE PEOPLE HUNTING THIS MAN THAN YOU COULD EVER IMAGINE.
SIR CHARLES! I DIDN'T EXPECT TO SEE YOU HERE!
WELL, TECHNICALLY, HE'S NOT SEEING YOU NOW, IS HE, SIR CHARLES?
WANT TO SHOW OUR MISTER ABBERLINE HERE THE TRUTH?

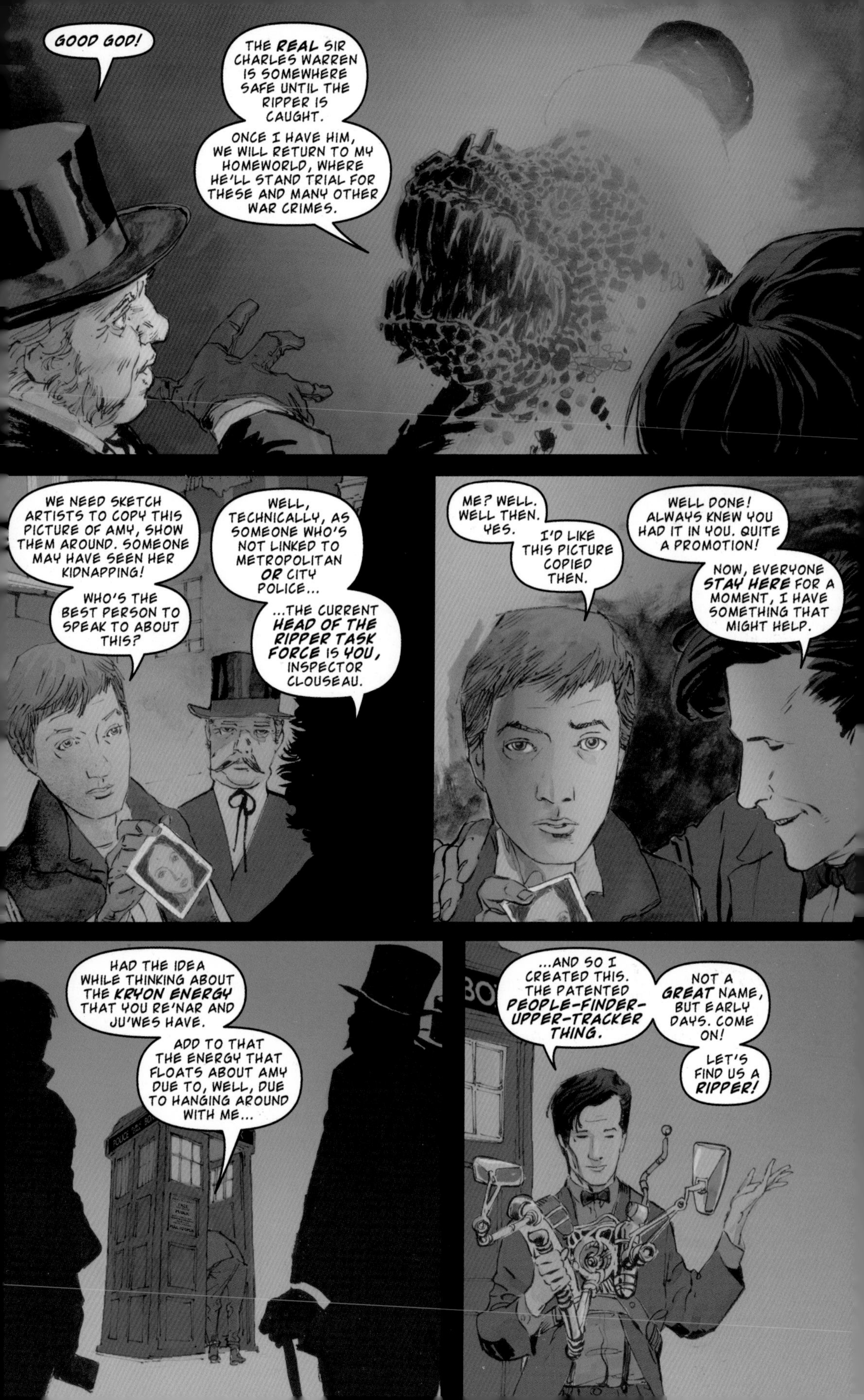
GOOD GOD!
THE REAL SIR CHARLES WARREN IS SOMEWHERE SAFE UNTIL THE RIPPER IS CAUGHT.
ONCE I HAVE HIM, WE WILL RETURN TO MY HOMEWORLD, WHERE HE'LL STAND TRIAL FOR THESE AND MANY OTHER WAR CRIMES.
WE NEED SKETCH ARTISTS TO COPY THIS PICTURE OF AMY, SHOW THEM AROUND. SOMEONE MAY HAVE SEEN HER KIDNAPPING!
WHO'S THE BEST PERSON TO SPEAK TO ABOUT THIS?
WELL, TECHNICALLY, AS SOMEONE WHO'S NOT LINKED TO METROPOLITAN OR CITY POLICE...
...THE CURRENT HEAD OF THE RIPPER TASK FORCE IS YOU, INSPECTOR CLOUSEAU.
ME? WELL. WELL THEN. YES.
I'D LIKE THIS PICTURE COPIED THEN.
WELL DONE! ALWAYS KNEW YOU HAD IT IN YOU. QUITE A PROMOTION!
NOW, EVERYONE STAY HERE FOR A MOMENT, I HAVE SOMETHING THAT MIGHT HELP.
HAD THE IDEA WHILE THINKING ABOUT THE KRYON ENERGY THAT YOU RE'NAR AND JU'WES HAVE.
ADD TO THAT THE ENERGY THAT FLOATS ABOUT AMY DUE TO, WELL, DUE TO HANGING AROUND WITH ME...
...AND SO I CREATED THIS. THE PATENTED PEOPLE-FINDER-UPPER-TRACKER THING.
NOT A GREAT NAME, BUT EARLY DAYS. COME ON!
LET'S FIND US A RIPPER!

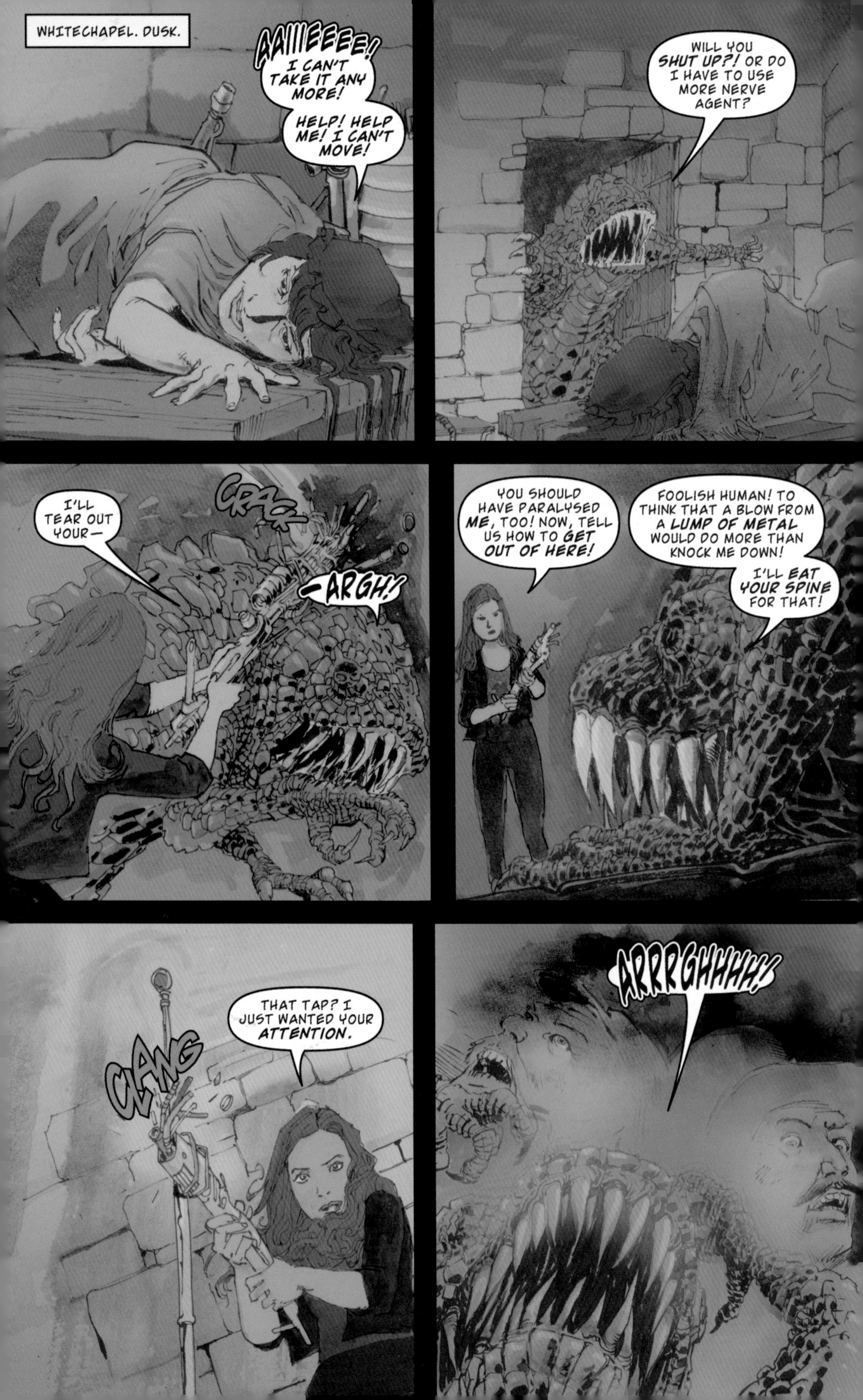
WHITECHAPEL. DUSK.
AAIIIEEEEE! I CAN'T TAKE IT ANY MORE!
HELP! HELP ME! I CAN'T MOVE!
WILL YOU SHUT UP?! OR DO I HAVE TO USE MORE NERVE AGENT?
I'LL TEAR OUT YOUR—
CRACK
—ARGH!
YOU SHOULD HAVE PARALYSED ME, TOO! NOW, TELL US HOW TO GET OUT OF HERE!
FOOLISH HUMAN! TO THINK THAT A BLOW FROM A LUMP OF METAL WOULD DO MORE THAN KNOCK ME DOWN!
I'LL EAT YOUR SPINE FOR THAT!
CLANG
THAT TAP? I JUST WANTED YOUR ATTENTION.
ARRRGHHHH!

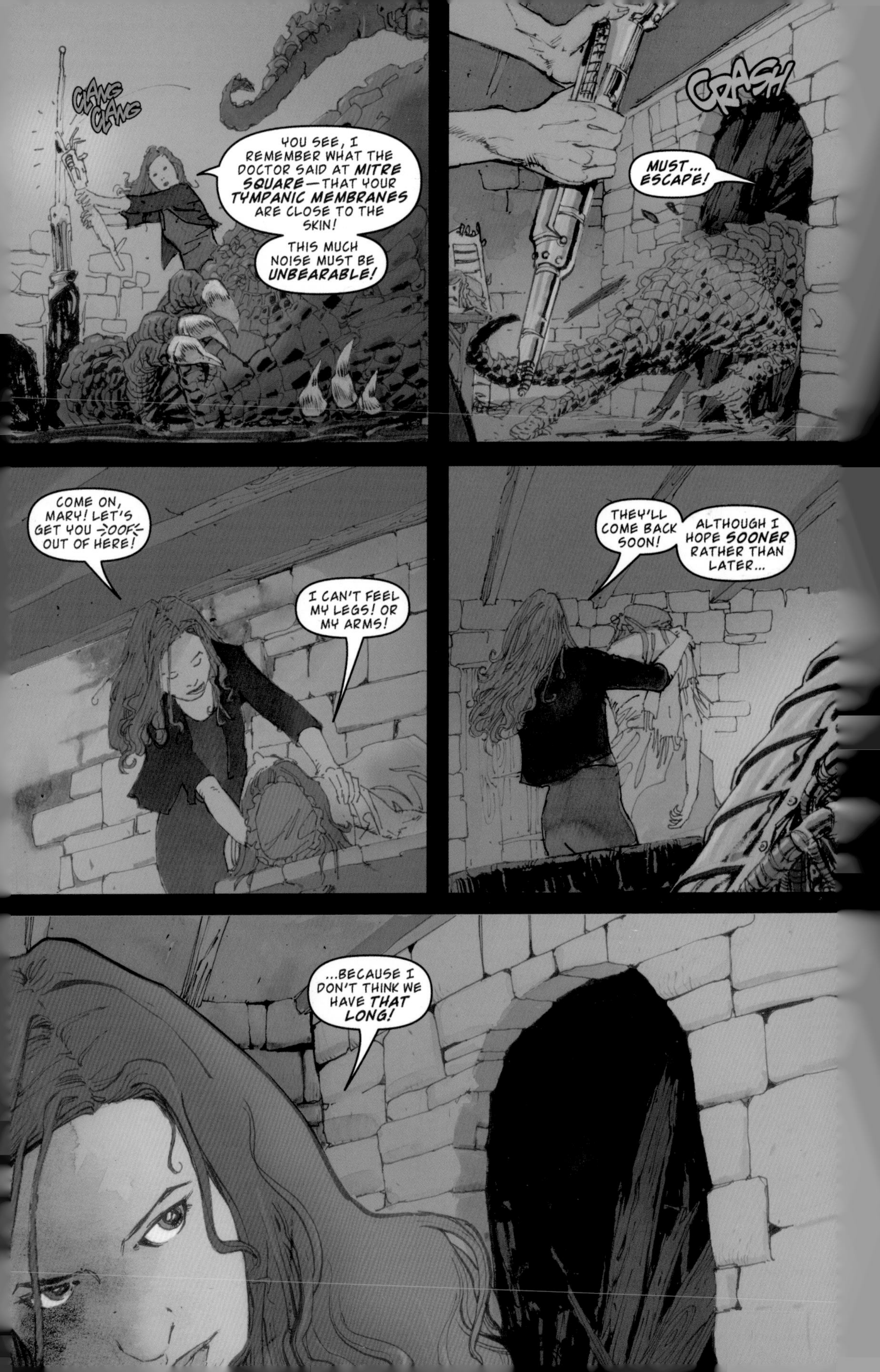
CLANG CLANG
YOU SEE, I REMEMBER WHAT THE DOCTOR SAID AT MITRE SQUARE—THAT YOUR TYMPANIC MEMBRANES ARE CLOSE TO THE SKIN!
THIS MUCH NOISE MUST BE UNBEARABLE!
CRASH
MUST... ESCAPE!
COME ON, MARY! LET'S GET YOU -OOF- OUT OF HERE!
I CAN'T FEEL MY LEGS! OR MY ARMS!
THEY'LL COME BACK SOON!
ALTHOUGH I HOPE SOONER RATHER THAN LATER...
...BECAUSE I DON'T THINK WE HAVE THAT LONG!

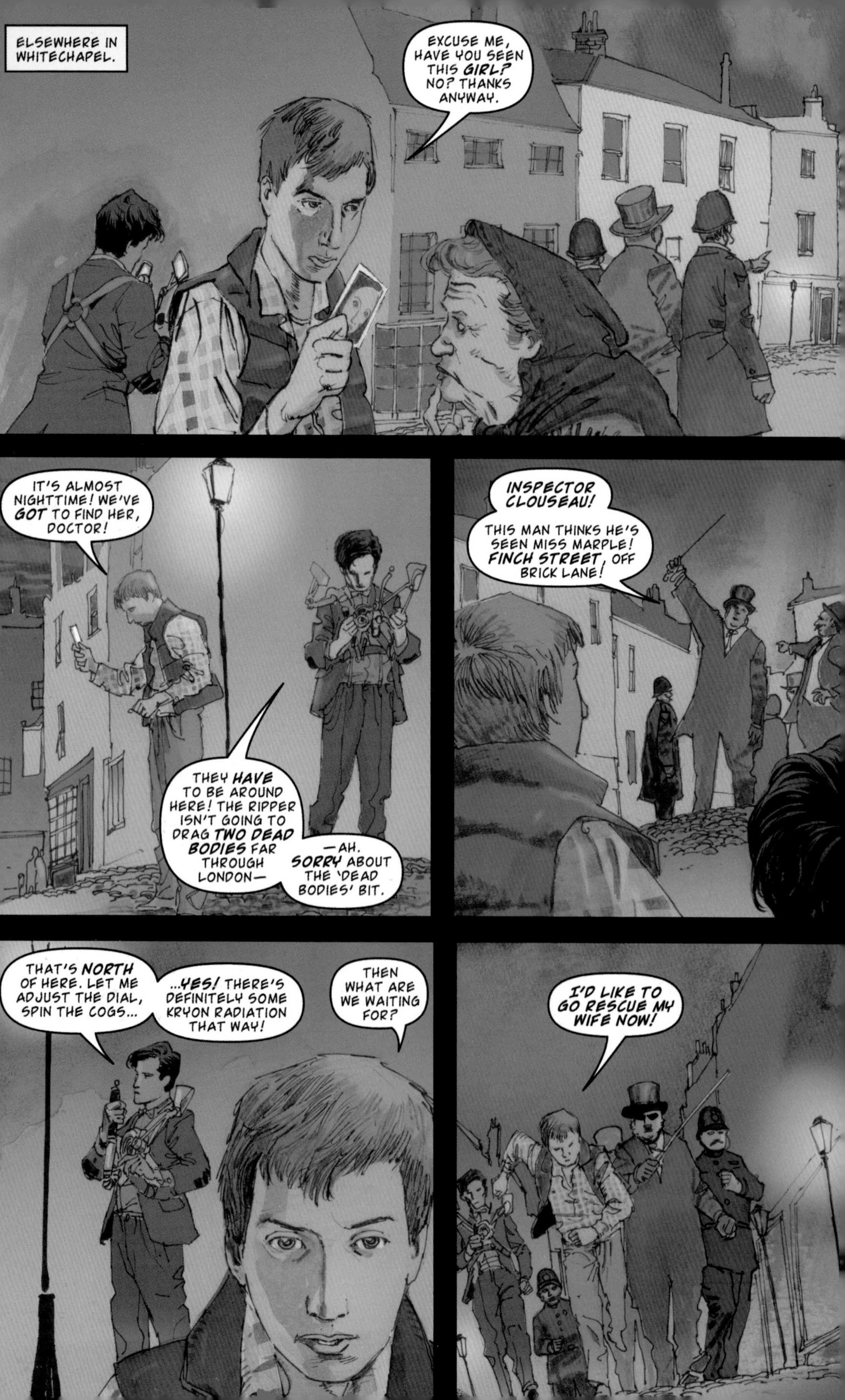

ELSEWHERE IN WHITECHAPEL.
EXCUSE ME, HAVE YOU SEEN THIS GIRL? NO? THANKS ANYWAY.
IT'S ALMOST NIGHTTIME! WE'VE GOT TO FIND HER, DOCTOR!
THEY HAVE TO BE AROUND HERE! THE RIPPER ISN'T GOING TO DRAG TWO DEAD BODIES FAR THROUGH LONDON—
—AH. SORRY ABOUT THE 'DEAD BODIES' BIT.
INSPECTOR CLOUSEAU!
THIS MAN THINKS HE'S SEEN MISS MARPLE! FINCH STREET, OFF BRICK LANE!
THAT'S NORTH OF HERE. LET ME ADJUST THE DIAL, SPIN THE COGS...
...YES! THERE'S DEFINITELY SOME KRYON RADIATION THAT WAY!
THEN WHAT ARE WE WAITING FOR?
I'D LIKE TO GO RESCUE MY WIFE NOW!

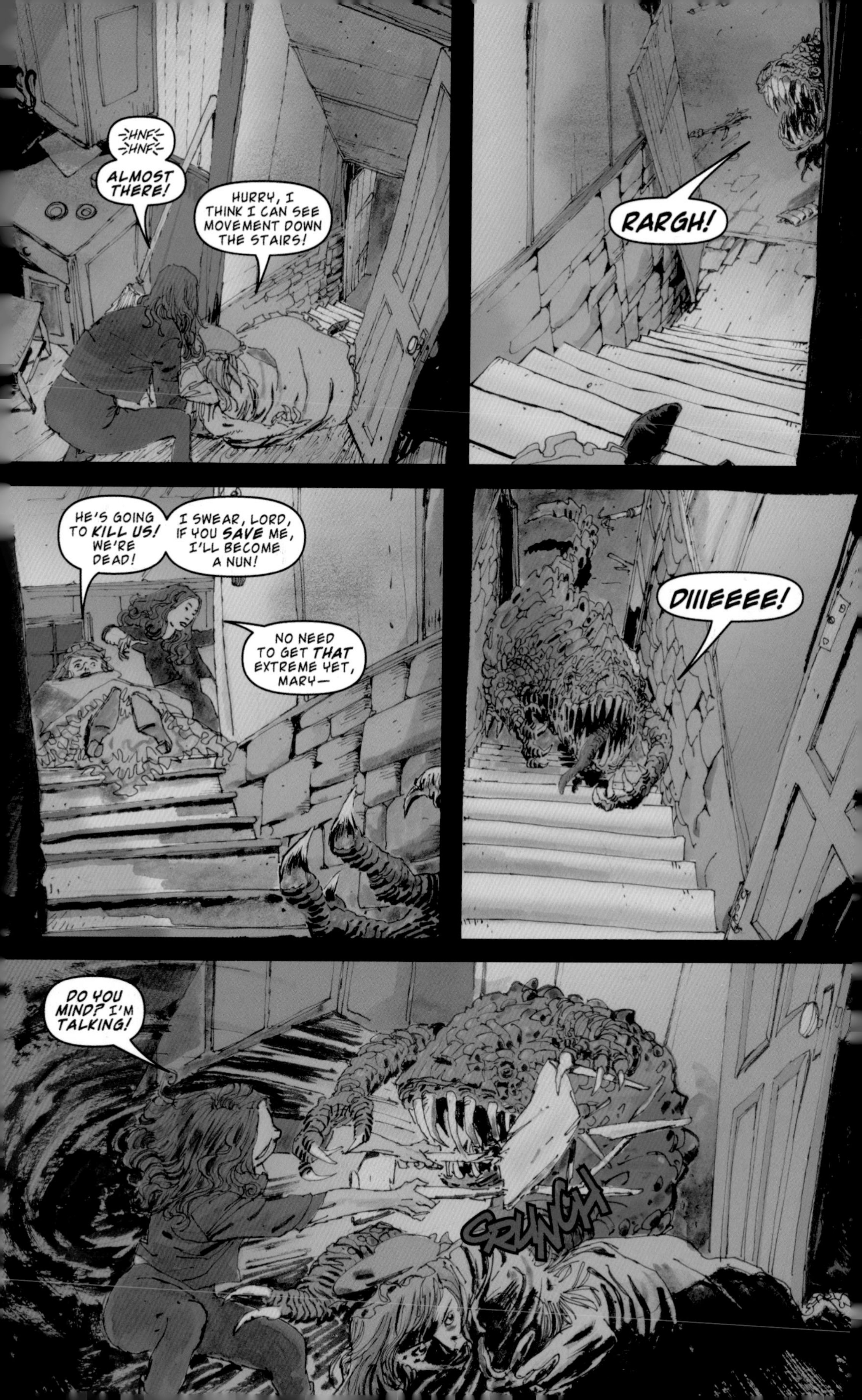

HNF HNF
ALMOST THERE!
HURRY, I THINK I CAN SEE MOVEMENT DOWN THE STAIRS!
RARGH!
HE'S GOING TO KILL US! WE'RE DEAD!
I SWEAR, LORD, IF YOU SAVE ME, I'LL BECOME A NUN!
NO NEED TO GET THAT EXTREME YET, MARY—
DIIIEEEE!
DO YOU MIND? I'M TALKING!
CRUNCH

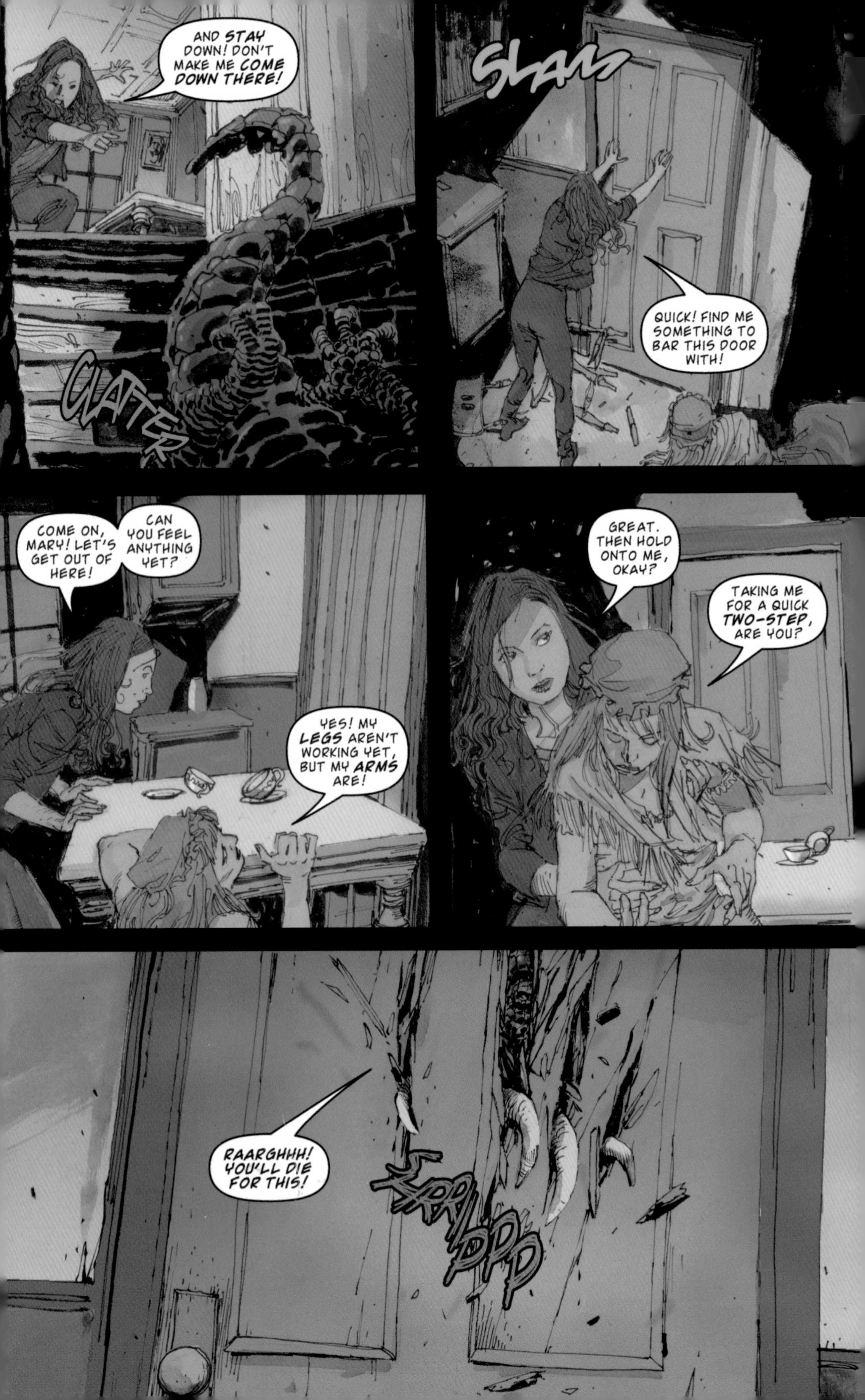

AND STAY DOWN! DON'T MAKE ME COME DOWN THERE!
CLATTER
SLAM
QUICK! FIND ME SOMETHING TO BAR THIS DOOR WITH!
COME ON, MARY! LET'S GET OUT OF HERE!
CAN YOU FEEL ANYTHING YET?
YES! MY LEGS AREN'T WORKING YET, BUT MY ARMS ARE!
GREAT. THEN HOLD ONTO ME, OKAY?
TAKING ME FOR A QUICK TWO-STEP, ARE YOU?
RAARGHHH! YOU'LL DIE FOR THIS!
SKRRRIPPP

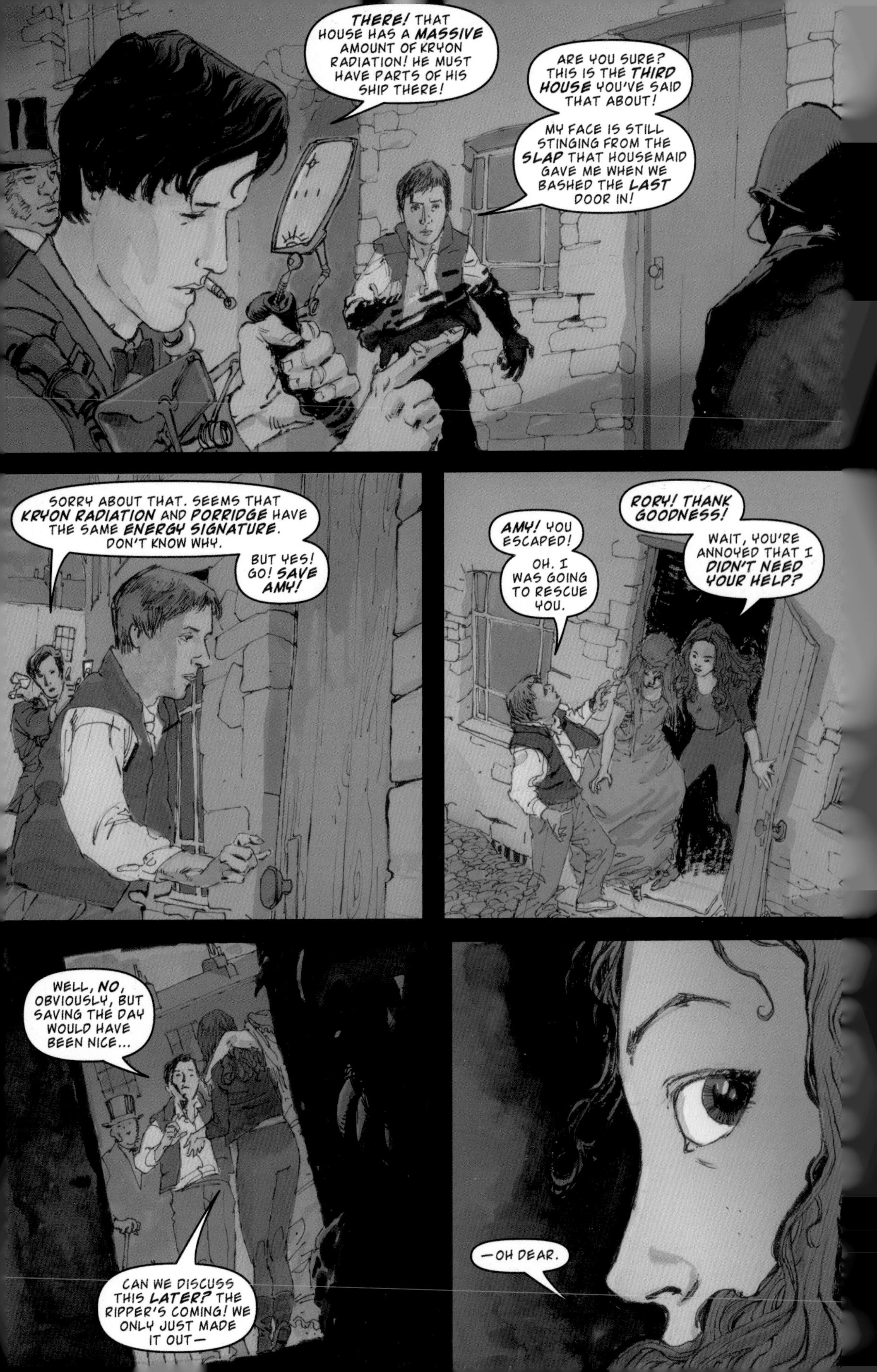
THERE! THAT HOUSE HAS A MASSIVE AMOUNT OF KRYON RADIATION! HE MUST HAVE PARTS OF HIS SHIP THERE!
ARE YOU SURE? THIS IS THE THIRD HOUSE YOU'VE SAID THAT ABOUT!
MY FACE IS STILL STINGING FROM THE SLAP THAT HOUSEMAID GAVE ME WHEN WE BASHED THE LAST DOOR IN!
SORRY ABOUT THAT. SEEMS THAT KRYON RADIATION AND PORRIDGE HAVE THE SAME ENERGY SIGNATURE. DON'T KNOW WHY.
BUT YES! GO! SAVE AMY!
AMY! YOU ESCAPED!
OH. I WAS GOING TO RESCUE YOU.
RORY! THANK GOODNESS!
WAIT, YOU'RE ANNOYED THAT I DIDN'T NEED YOUR HELP?
WELL, NO, OBVIOUSLY, BUT SAVING THE DAY WOULD HAVE BEEN NICE...
CAN WE DISCUSS THIS LATER? THE RIPPER'S COMING! WE ONLY JUST MADE IT OUT—
—OH DEAR.

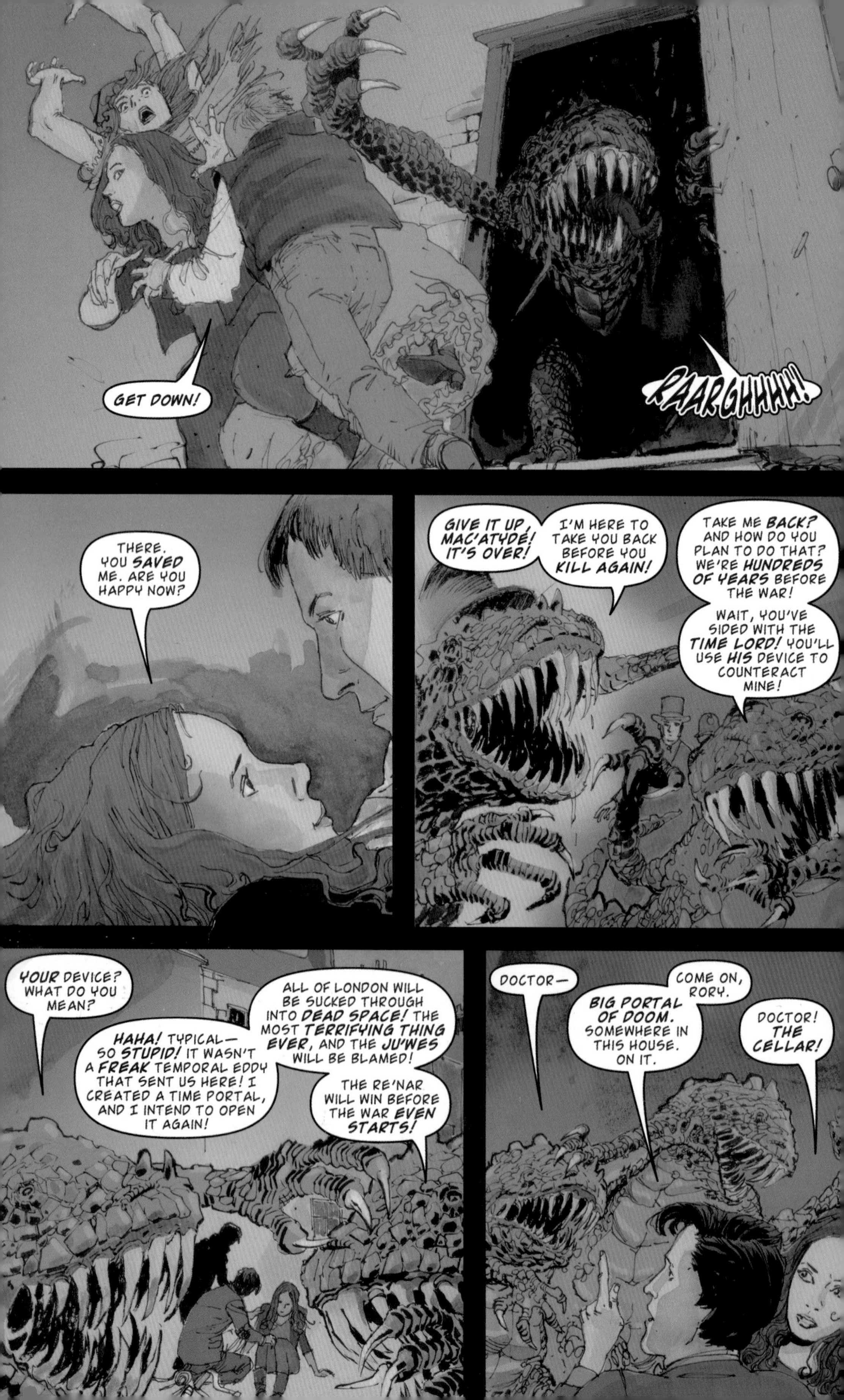
GET DOWN!
RAARGHHHH!
THERE. YOU SAVED ME. ARE YOU HAPPY NOW?
GIVE IT UP, MAC'ATYDÉ! IT'S OVER!
I'M HERE TO TAKE YOU BACK BEFORE YOU KILL AGAIN!
TAKE ME BACK? AND HOW DO YOU PLAN TO DO THAT? WE'RE HUNDREDS OF YEARS BEFORE THE WAR!
WAIT, YOU'VE SIDED WITH THE TIME LORD! YOU'LL USE HIS DEVICE TO COUNTERACT MINE!
YOUR DEVICE? WHAT DO YOU MEAN?
HAHA! TYPICAL— SO STUPID! IT WASN'T A FREAK TEMPORAL EDDY THAT SENT US HERE! I CREATED A TIME PORTAL, AND I INTEND TO OPEN IT AGAIN!
ALL OF LONDON WILL BE SUCKED THROUGH INTO DEAD SPACE! THE MOST TERRIFYING THING EVER, AND THE JU'WES WILL BE BLAMED!
THE RE'NAR WILL WIN BEFORE THE WAR EVEN STARTS!
DOCTOR—
COME ON, RORY.
BIG PORTAL OF DOOM. SOMEWHERE IN THIS HOUSE. ON IT.
DOCTOR! THE CELLAR!

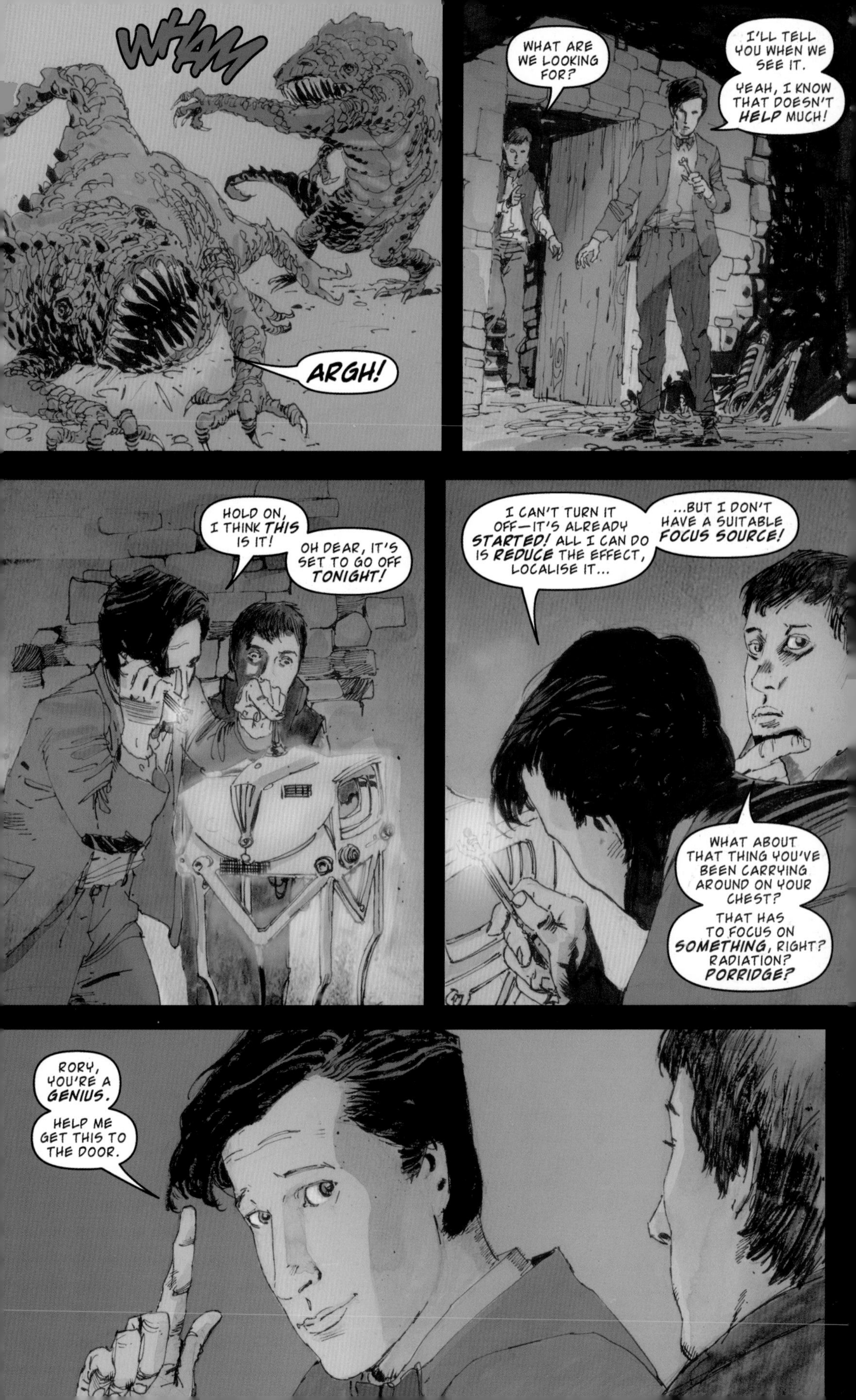
WHAM
ARGH!
WHAT ARE WE LOOKING FOR?
I'LL TELL YOU WHEN WE SEE IT.
YEAH, I KNOW THAT DOESN'T HELP MUCH!
HOLD ON, I THINK THIS IS IT!
OH DEAR, IT'S SET TO GO OFF TONIGHT!
I CAN'T TURN IT OFF—IT'S ALREADY STARTED! ALL I CAN DO IS REDUCE THE EFFECT, LOCALISE IT...
...BUT I DON'T HAVE A SUITABLE FOCUS SOURCE!
WHAT ABOUT THAT THING YOU'VE BEEN CARRYING AROUND ON YOUR CHEST?
THAT HAS TO FOCUS ON SOMETHING, RIGHT? RADIATION? PORRIDGE?
RORY, YOU'RE A GENIUS.
HELP ME GET THIS TO THE DOOR.

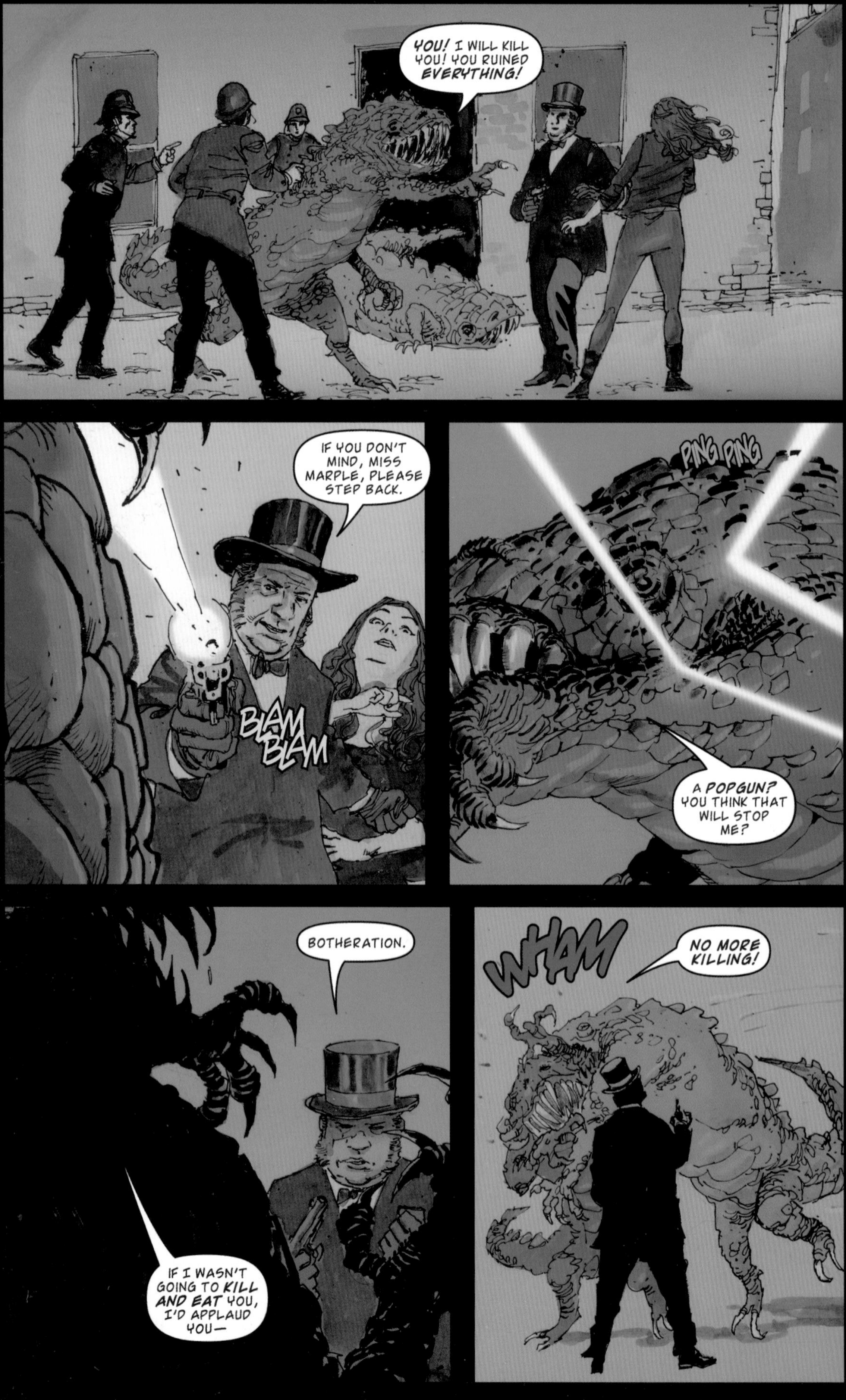
YOU! I WILL KILL YOU! YOU RUINED EVERYTHING!
IF YOU DON'T MIND, MISS MARPLE, PLEASE STEP BACK.
BLAM BLAM
PING PING
A POPGUN? YOU THINK THAT WILL STOP ME?
BOTHERATION.
IF I WASN'T GOING TO KILL AND EAT YOU, I'D APPLAUD YOU—
WHAM
NO MORE KILLING!

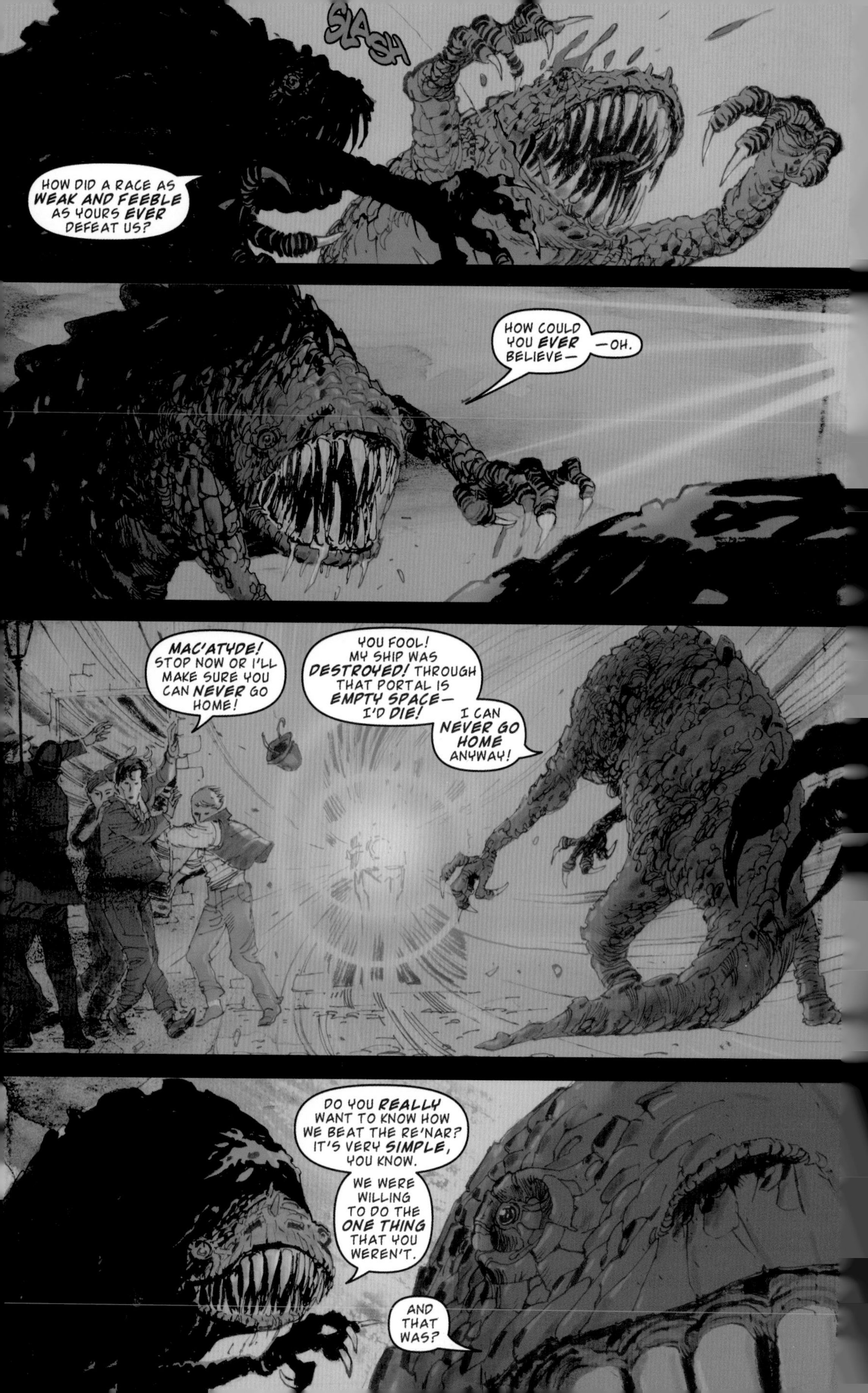
SLASH
HOW DID A RACE AS WEAK AND FEEBLE AS YOURS EVER DEFEAT US?
HOW COULD YOU EVER BELIEVE—
—OH.
MAC'ATYDE! STOP NOW OR I'LL MAKE SURE YOU CAN NEVER GO HOME!
YOU FOOL! MY SHIP WAS DESTROYED! THROUGH THAT PORTAL IS EMPTY SPACE— I'D DIE!
I CAN NEVER GO HOME ANYWAY!
DO YOU REALLY WANT TO KNOW HOW WE BEAT THE RE'NAR? IT'S VERY SIMPLE, YOU KNOW.
WE WERE WILLING TO DO THE ONE THING THAT YOU WEREN'T.
AND THAT WAS?

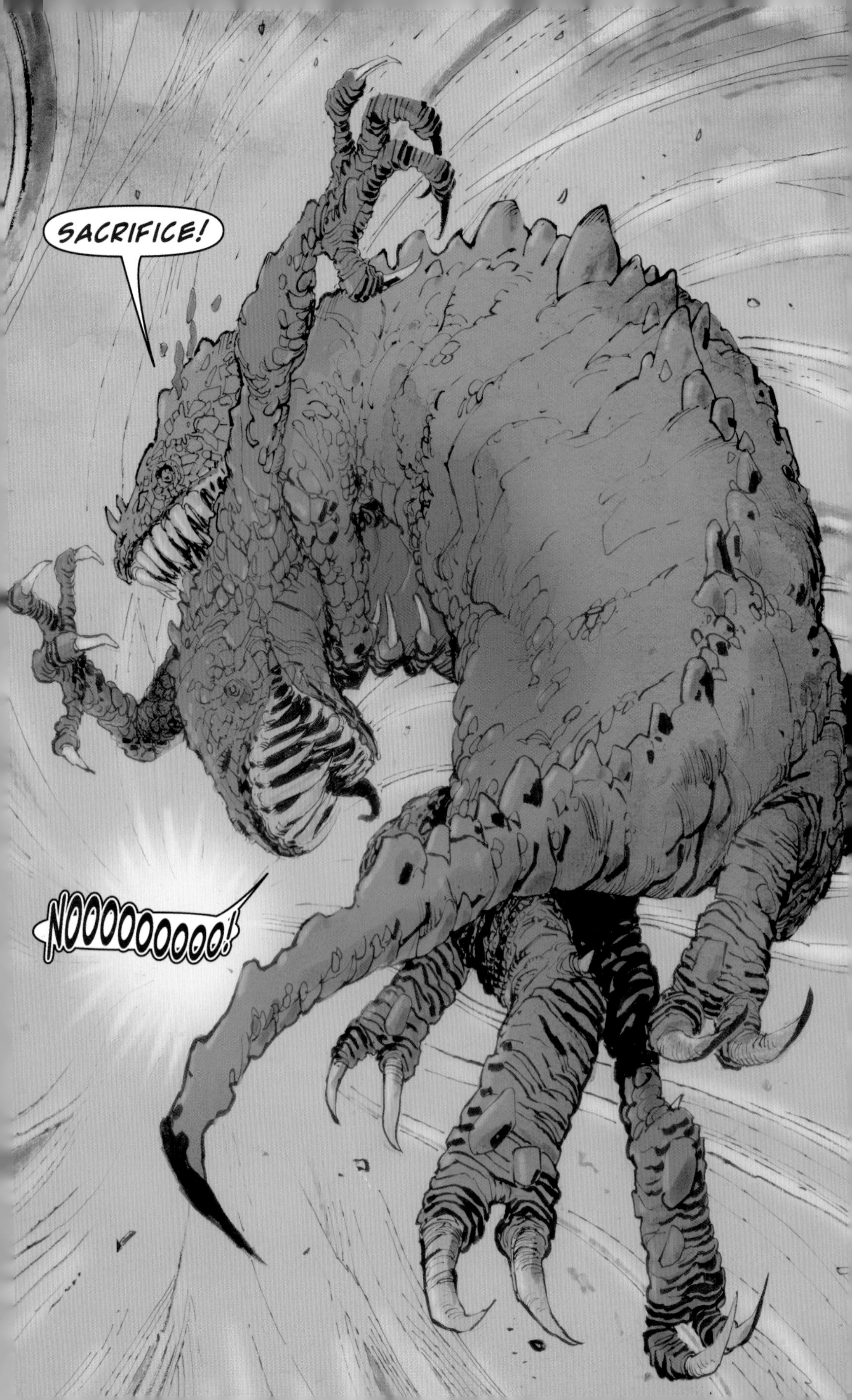
SACRIFICE!
NOOOOOOOOO!

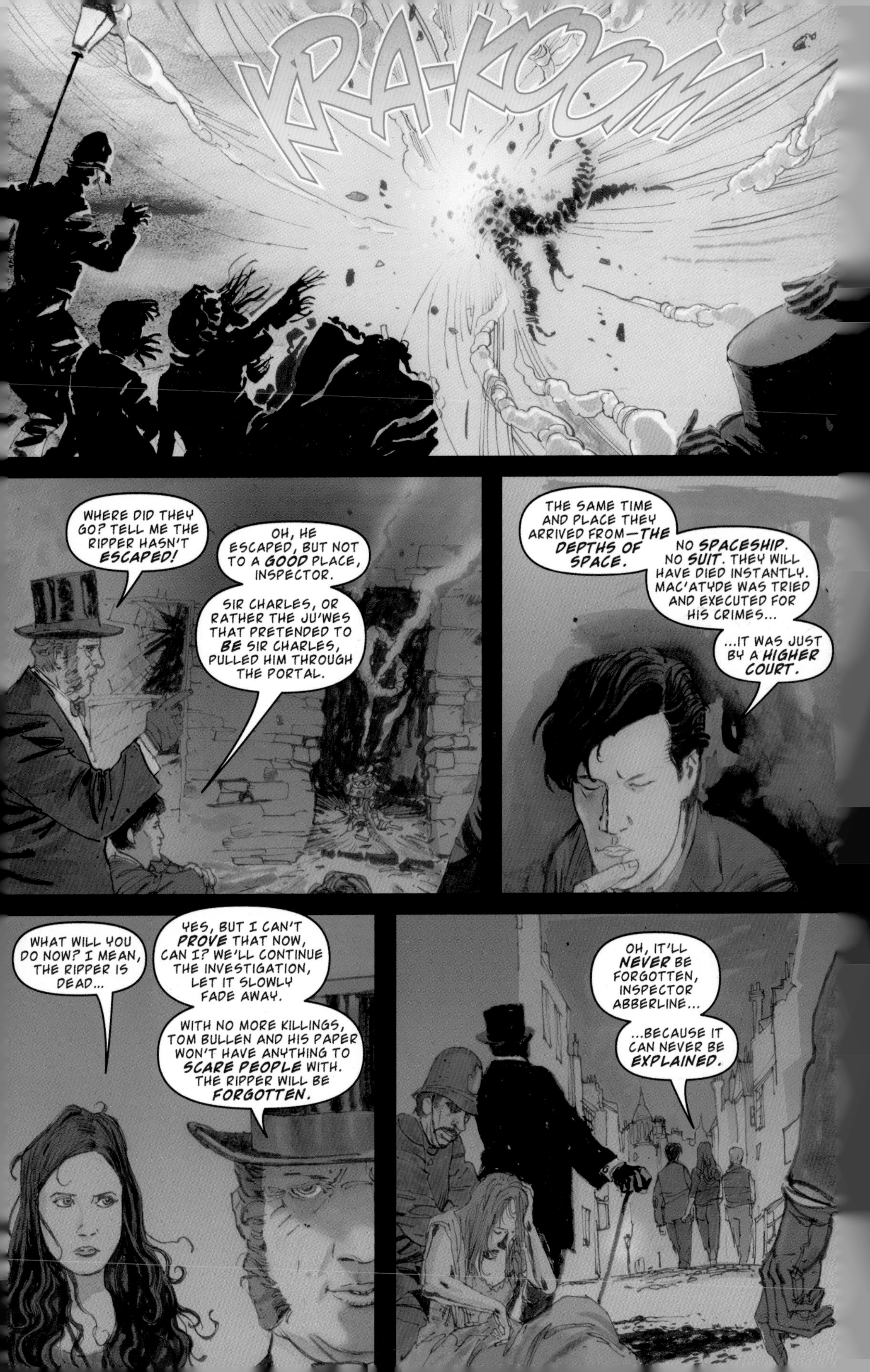
KRA-KOOM
WHERE DID THEY GO? TELL ME THE RIPPER HASN'T ESCAPED!
OH, HE ESCAPED, BUT NOT TO A GOOD PLACE, INSPECTOR.
SIR CHARLES, OR RATHER THE JU'WES THAT PRETENDED TO BE SIR CHARLES, PULLED HIM THROUGH THE PORTAL.
THE SAME TIME AND PLACE THEY ARRIVED FROM—THE DEPTHS OF SPACE.
NO SPACESHIP. NO SUIT. THEY WILL HAVE DIED INSTANTLY. MAC'ATYDE WAS TRIED AND EXECUTED FOR HIS CRIMES...
...IT WAS JUST BY A HIGHER COURT.
WHAT WILL YOU DO NOW? I MEAN, THE RIPPER IS DEAD...
YES, BUT I CAN'T PROVE THAT NOW, CAN I? WE'LL CONTINUE THE INVESTIGATION, LET IT SLOWLY FADE AWAY.
WITH NO MORE KILLINGS, TOM BULLEN AND HIS PAPER WON'T HAVE ANYTHING TO SCARE PEOPLE WITH. THE RIPPER WILL BE FORGOTTEN.
OH, IT'LL NEVER BE FORGOTTEN, INSPECTOR ABBERLINE...
...BECAUSE IT CAN NEVER BE EXPLAINED.

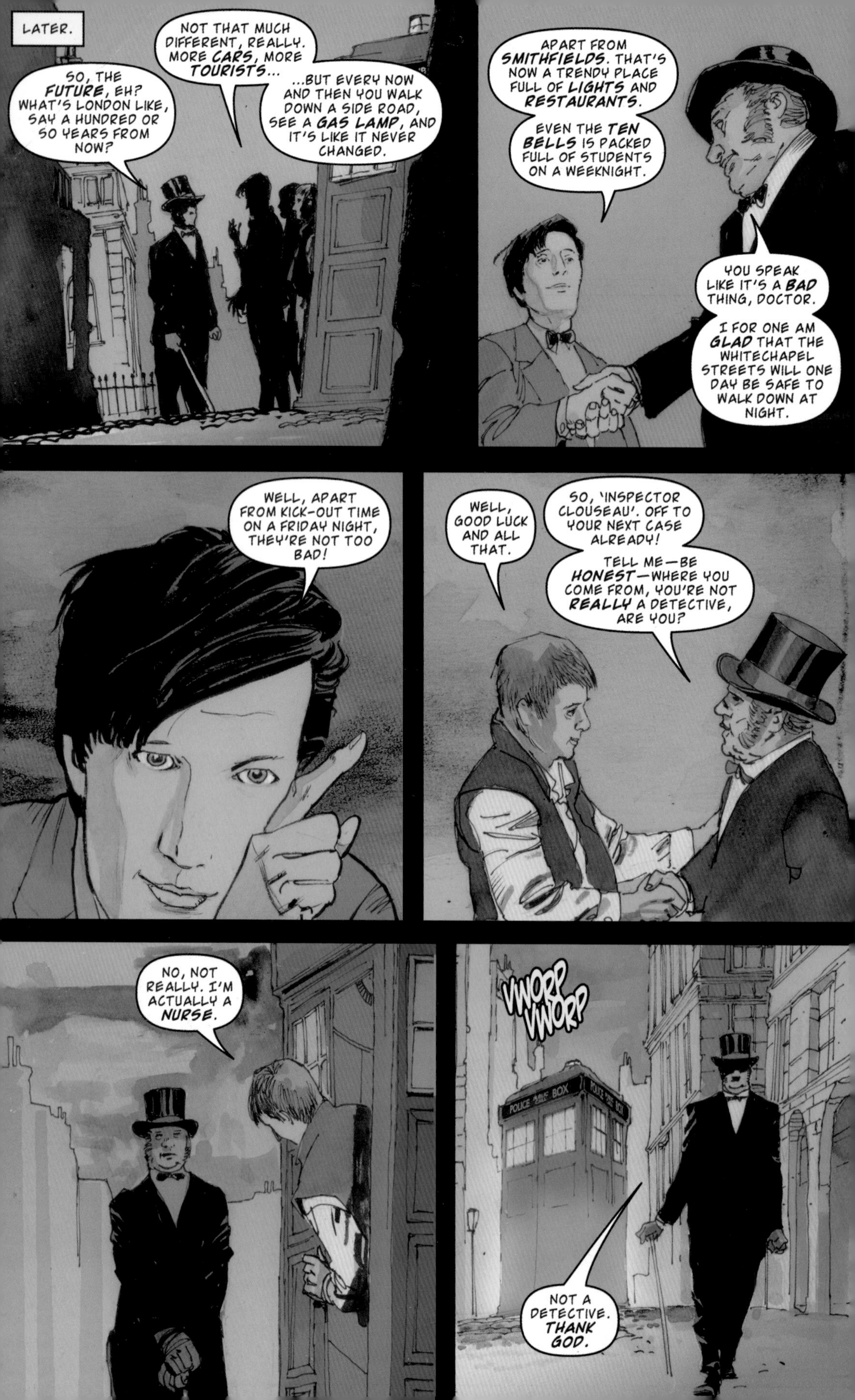
LATER.
SO, THE FUTURE, EH? WHAT'S LONDON LIKE, SAY A HUNDRED OR SO YEARS FROM NOW?
NOT THAT MUCH DIFFERENT, REALLY. MORE CARS, MORE TOURISTS...
...BUT EVERY NOW AND THEN YOU WALK DOWN A SIDE ROAD, SEE A GAS LAMP, AND IT'S LIKE IT NEVER CHANGED.
APART FROM SMITHFIELDS. THAT'S NOW A TRENDY PLACE FULL OF LIGHTS AND RESTAURANTS.
EVEN THE TEN BELLS IS PACKED FULL OF STUDENTS ON A WEEKNIGHT.
YOU SPEAK LIKE IT'S A BAD THING, DOCTOR.
I FOR ONE AM GLAD THAT THE WHITECHAPEL STREETS WILL ONE DAY BE SAFE TO WALK DOWN AT NIGHT.
WELL, APART FROM KICK-OUT TIME ON A FRIDAY NIGHT, THEY'RE NOT TOO BAD!
WELL, GOOD LUCK AND ALL THAT.
SO, 'INSPECTOR CLOUSEAU'. OFF TO YOUR NEXT CASE ALREADY!
TELL ME—BE HONEST—WHERE YOU COME FROM, YOU'RE NOT REALLY A DETECTIVE, ARE YOU?
NO, NOT REALLY. I'M ACTUALLY A NURSE.
VWORP VWORP
POLICE PUBLIC CALL BOX
NOT A DETECTIVE. THANK GOD.

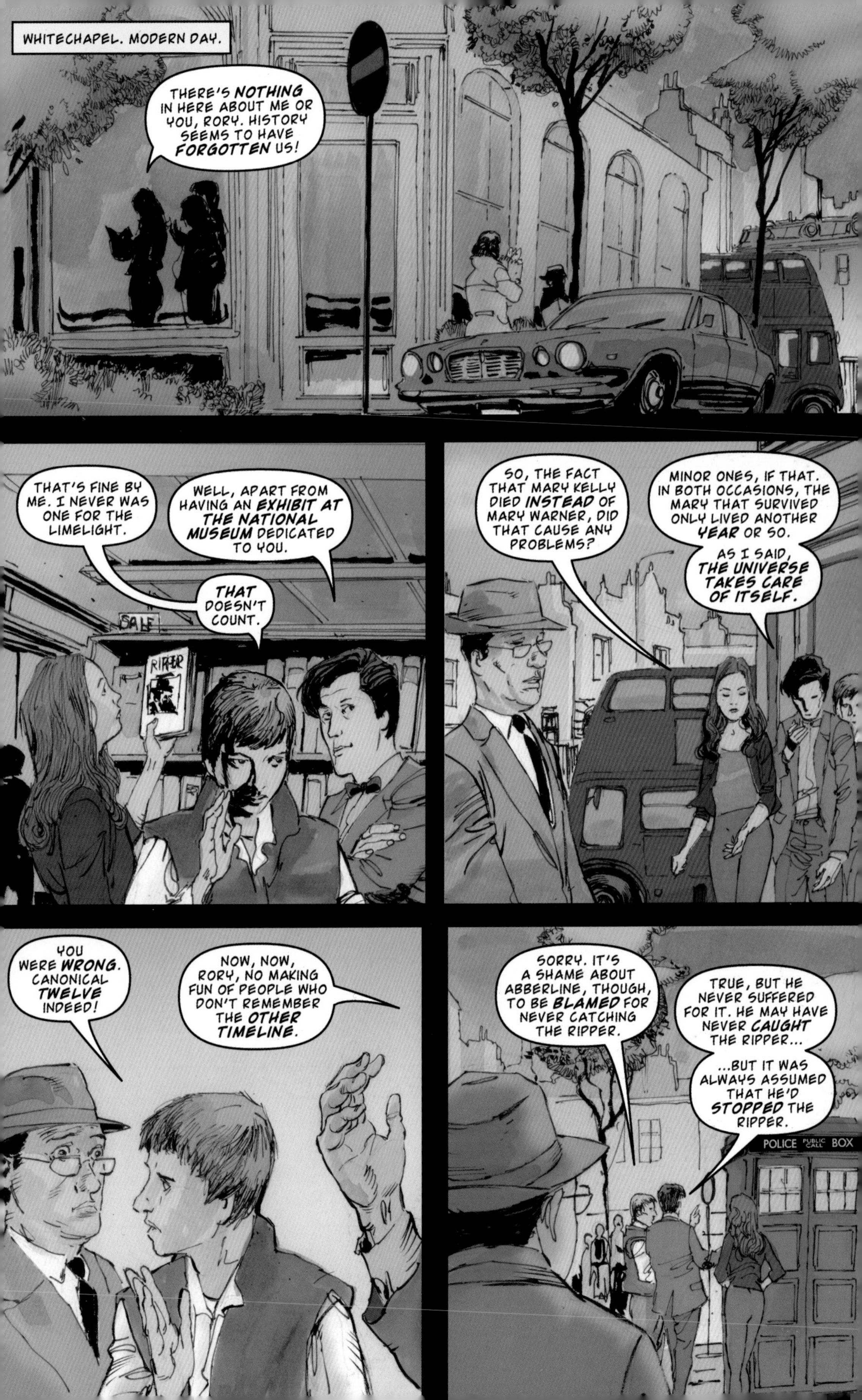
WHITECHAPEL. MODERN DAY.
THERE'S NOTHING IN HERE ABOUT ME OR YOU, RORY. HISTORY SEEMS TO HAVE FORGOTTEN US!
THAT'S FINE BY ME. I NEVER WAS ONE FOR THE LIMELIGHT.
WELL, APART FROM HAVING AN EXHIBIT AT THE NATIONAL MUSEUM DEDICATED TO YOU.
THAT DOESN'T COUNT.
SALE
RIPPER
SO, THE FACT THAT MARY KELLY DIED INSTEAD OF MARY WARNER, DID THAT CAUSE ANY PROBLEMS?
MINOR ONES, IF THAT. IN BOTH OCCASIONS, THE MARY THAT SURVIVED ONLY LIVED ANOTHER YEAR OR SO.
AS I SAID, THE UNIVERSE TAKES CARE OF ITSELF.
YOU WERE WRONG. CANONICAL TWELVE INDEED!
NOW, NOW, RORY, NO MAKING FUN OF PEOPLE WHO DON'T REMEMBER THE OTHER TIMELINE.
SORRY. IT'S A SHAME ABOUT ABBERLINE, THOUGH, TO BE BLAMED FOR NEVER CATCHING THE RIPPER.
TRUE, BUT HE NEVER SUFFERED FOR IT. HE MAY HAVE NEVER CAUGHT THE RIPPER...
...BUT IT WAS ALWAYS ASSUMED THAT HE'D STOPPED THE RIPPER.
POLICE PUBLIC CALL BOX

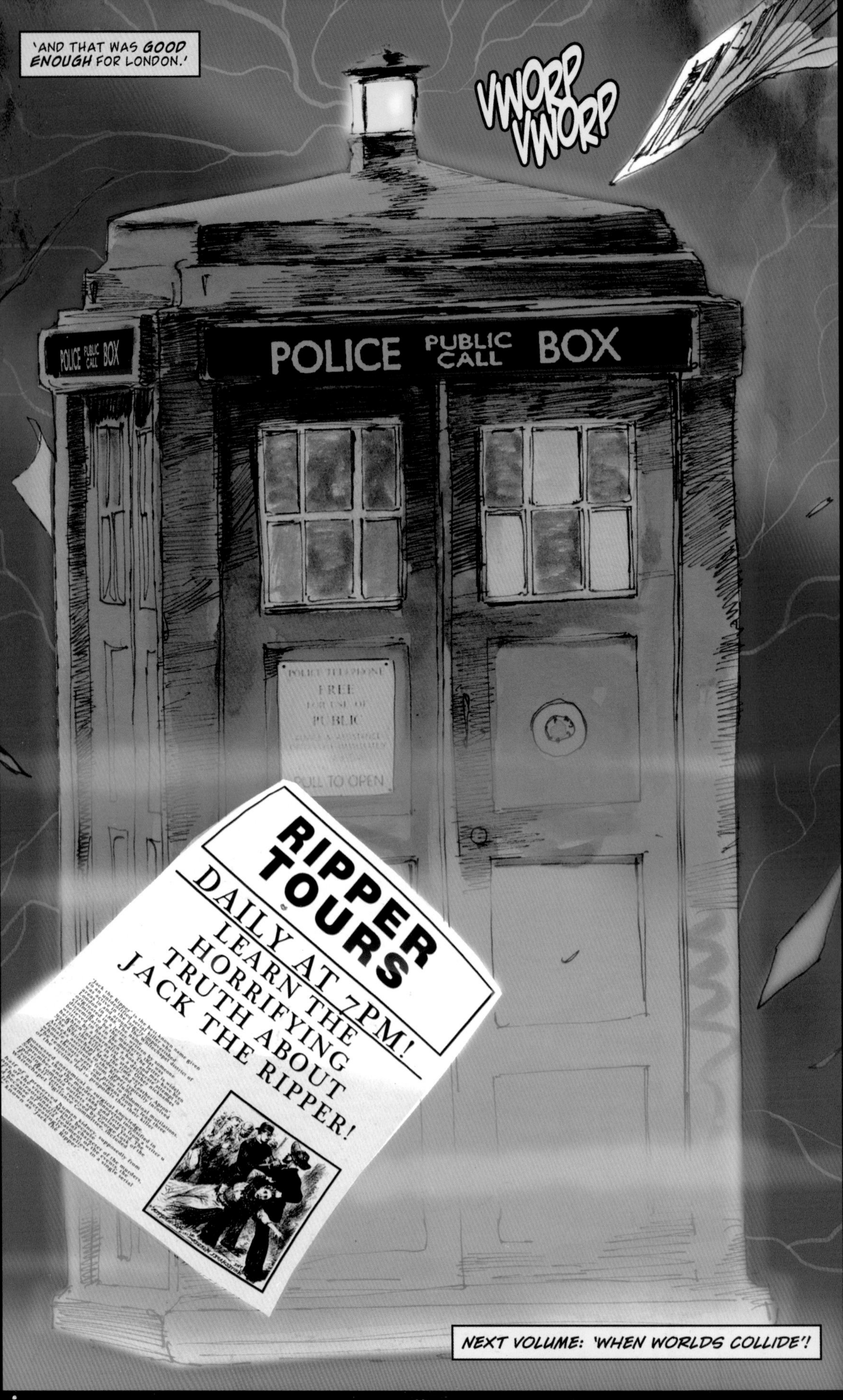
'AND THAT WAS GOOD ENOUGH FOR LONDON.'
VWORP VWORP
POLICE PUBLIC CALL BOX
POLICE PUBLIC CALL BOX
POLICE TELEPHONE
FREE
FOR USE OF
PUBLIC
PULL TO OPEN
RIPPER TOURS
DAILY AT 7PM!
LEARN THE HORRIFYING TRUTH ABOUT JACK THE RIPPER!
NEXT VOLUME: 'WHEN WORLDS COLLIDE'!

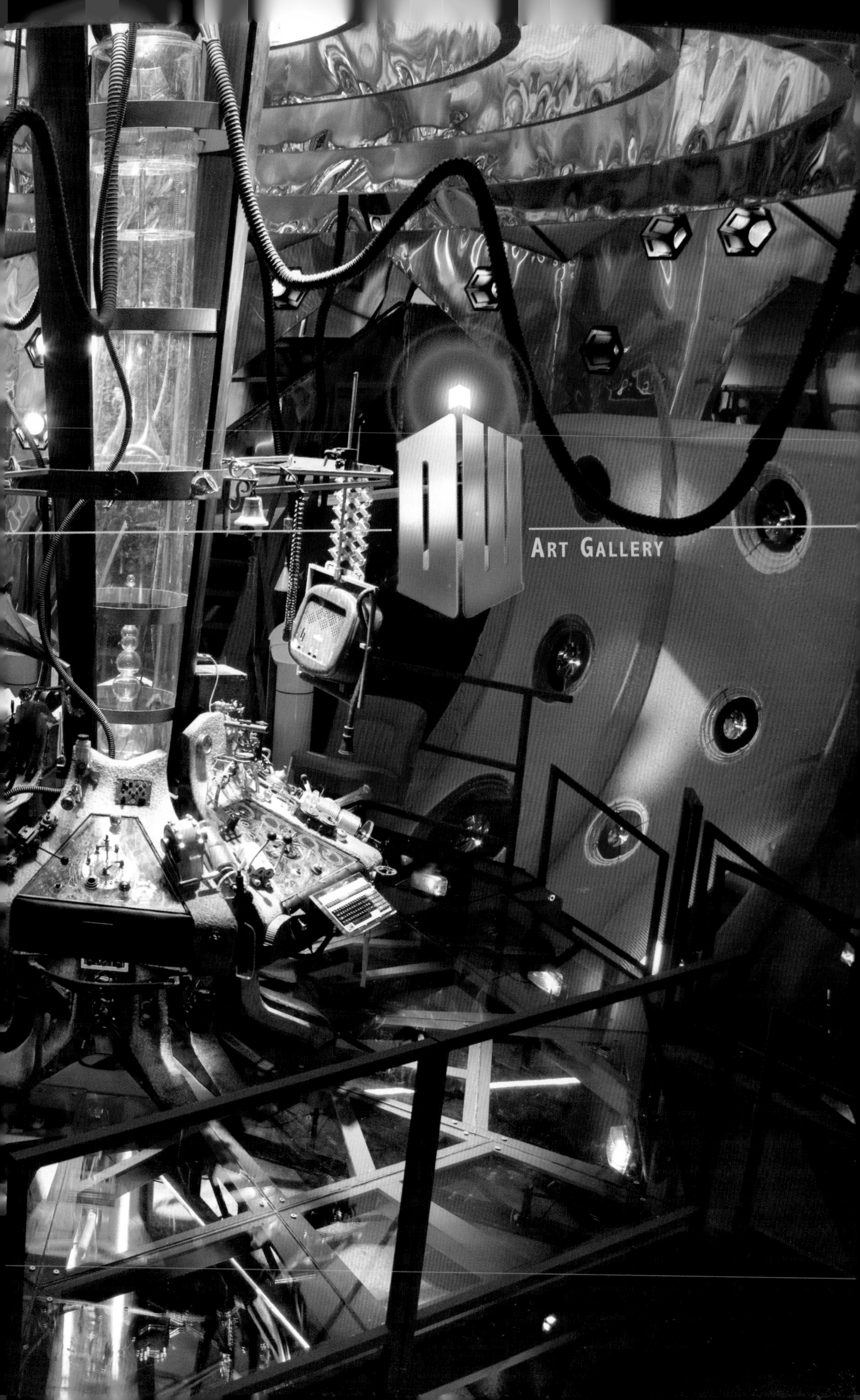

Art Gallery

ART BY TOMMY LEE EDWARDS

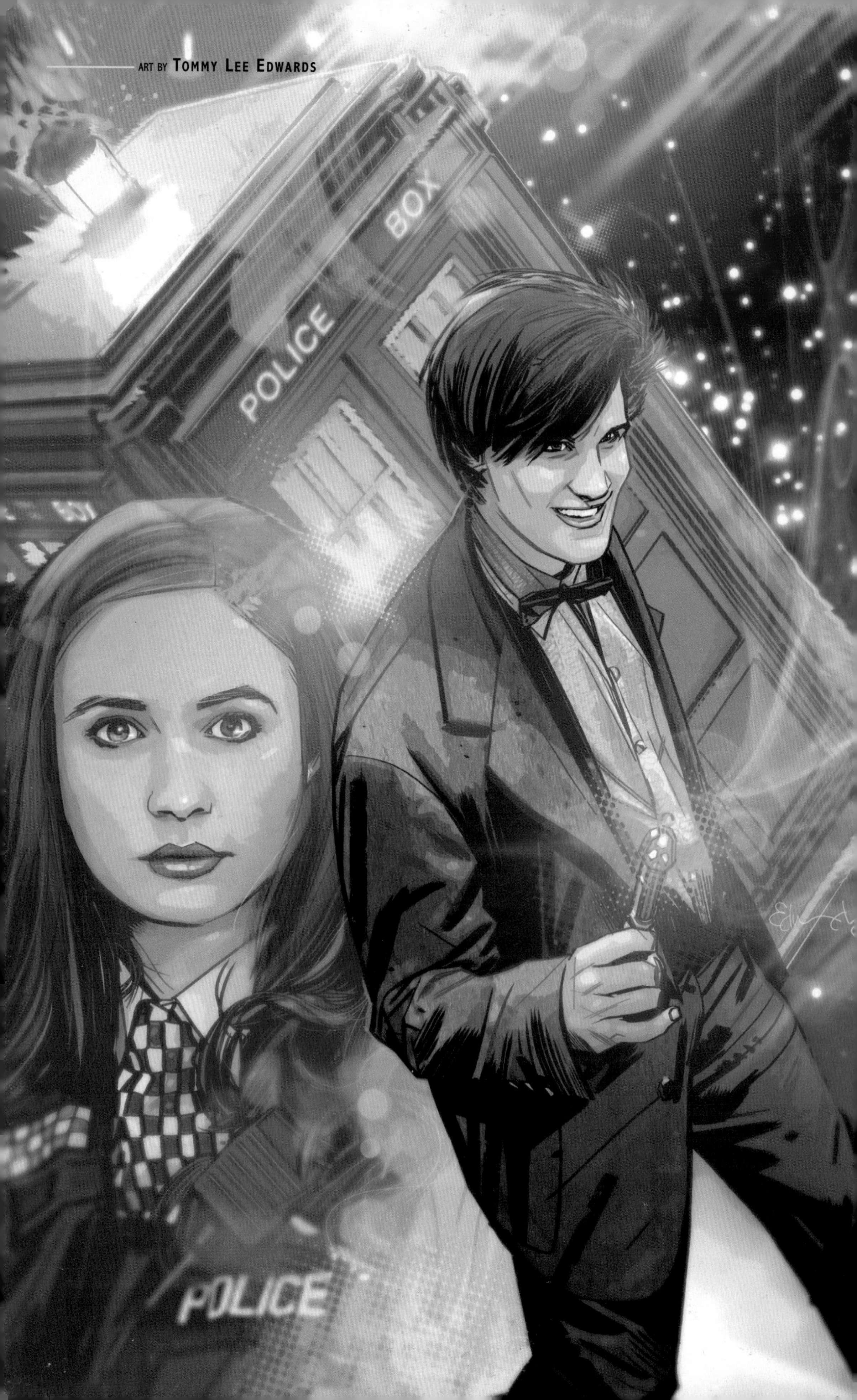
POLICE BOX
POLICE

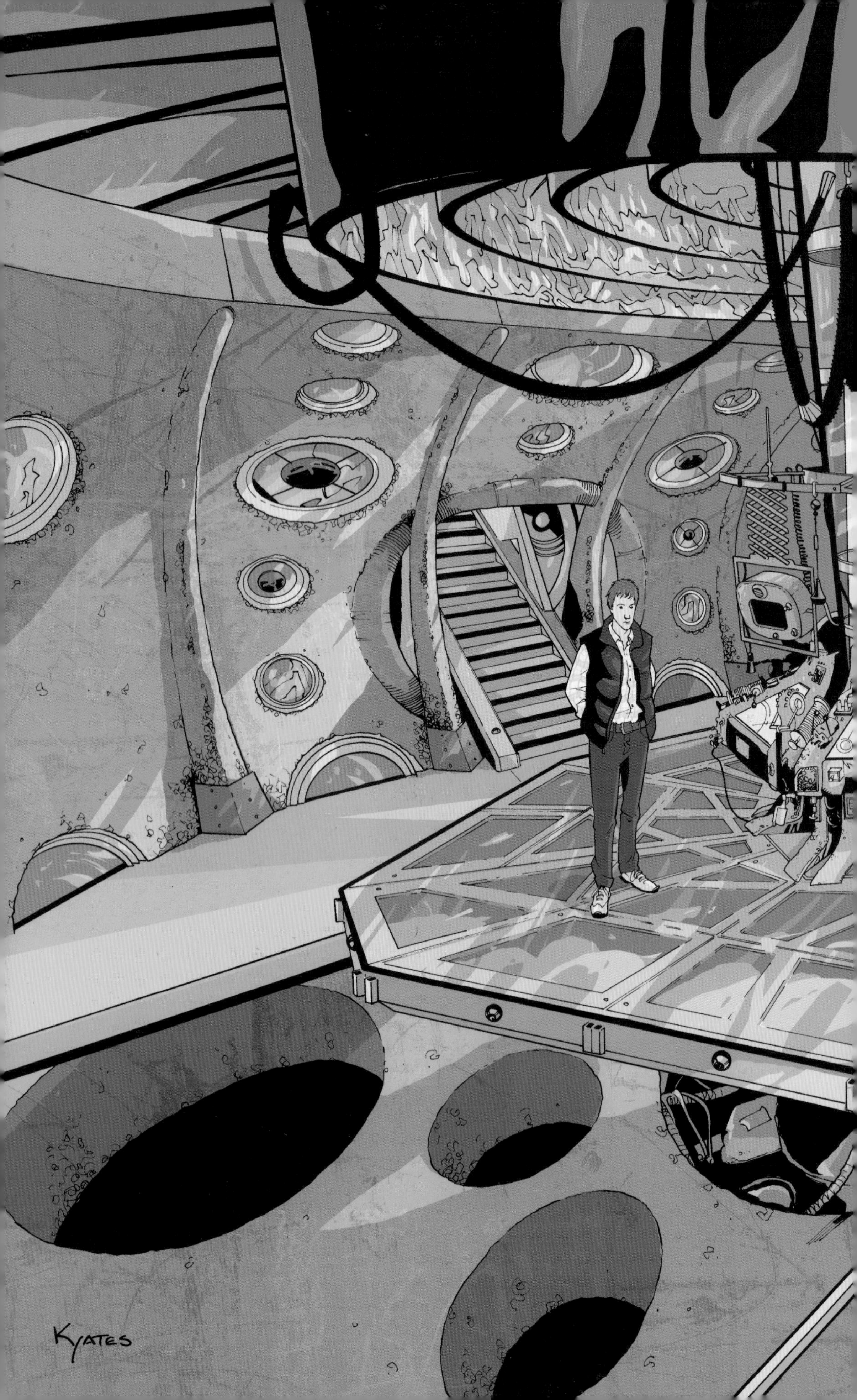
KYATES

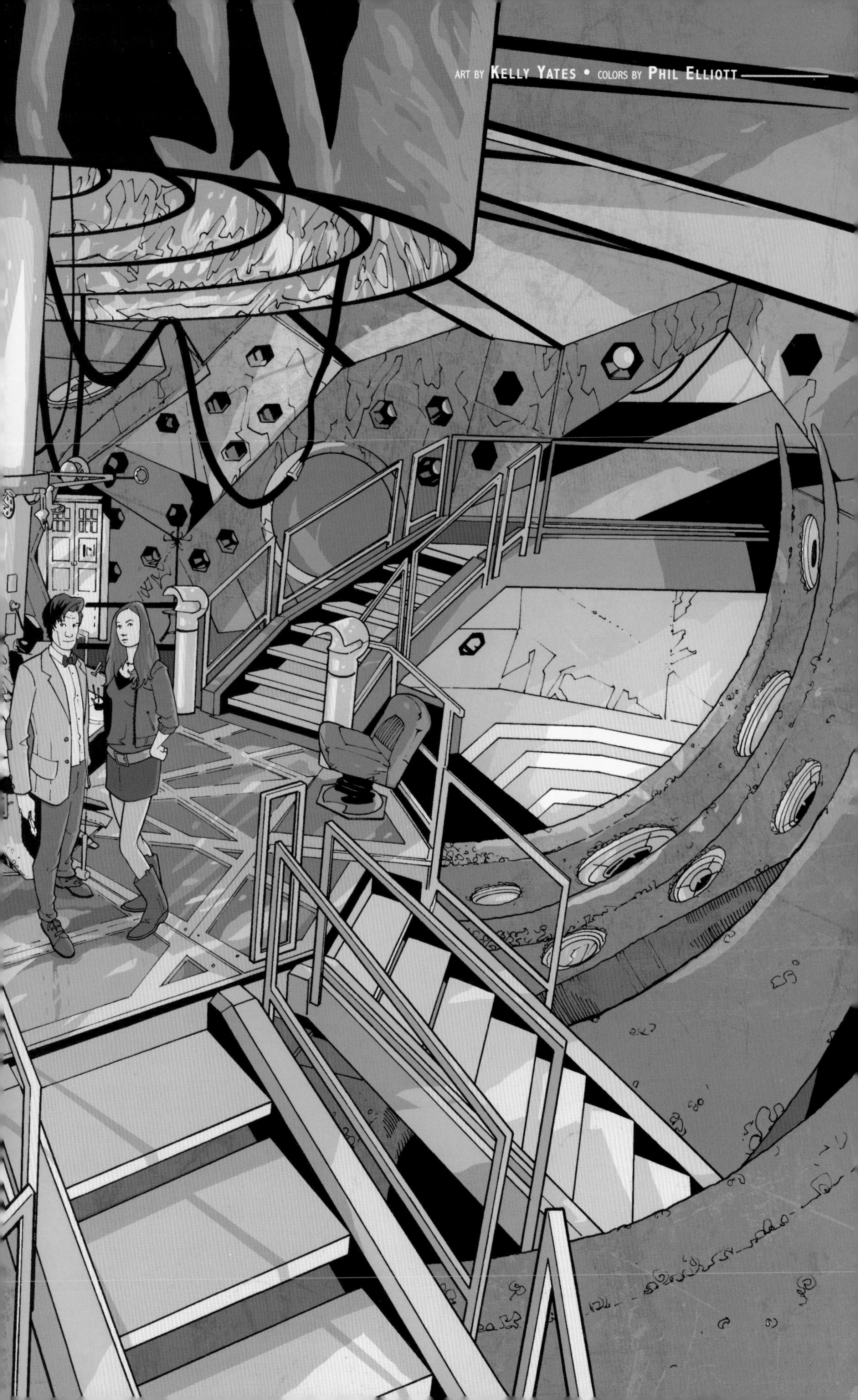
ART BY KELLY YATES • COLORS BY PHIL ELLIOTT

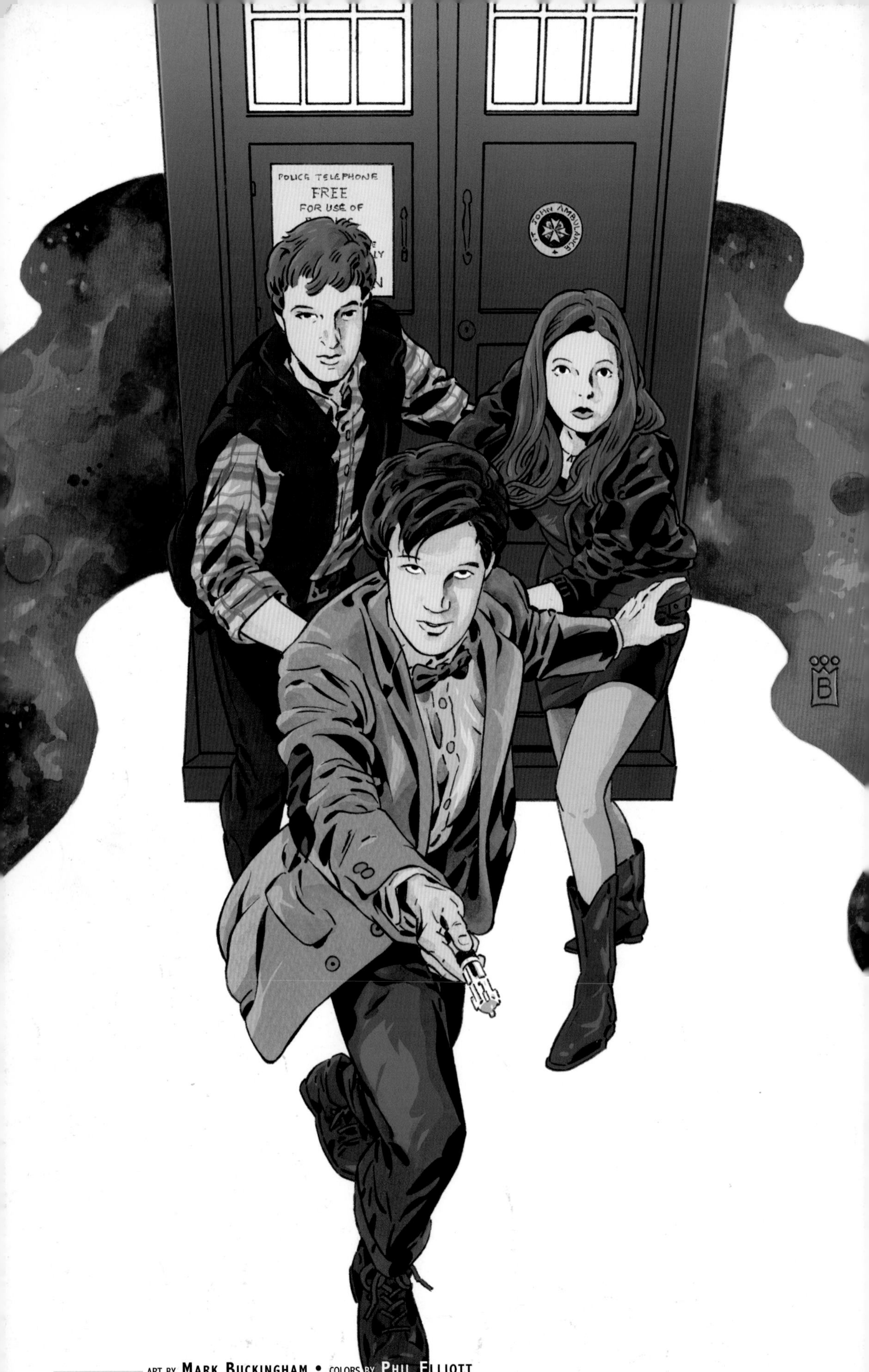
POLICE TELEPHONE
FREE
FOR USE OF

ART BY **MARK BUCKINGHAM** • COLORS BY **PHIL ELLIOTT**

ART BY TOMMY LEE EDWARDS

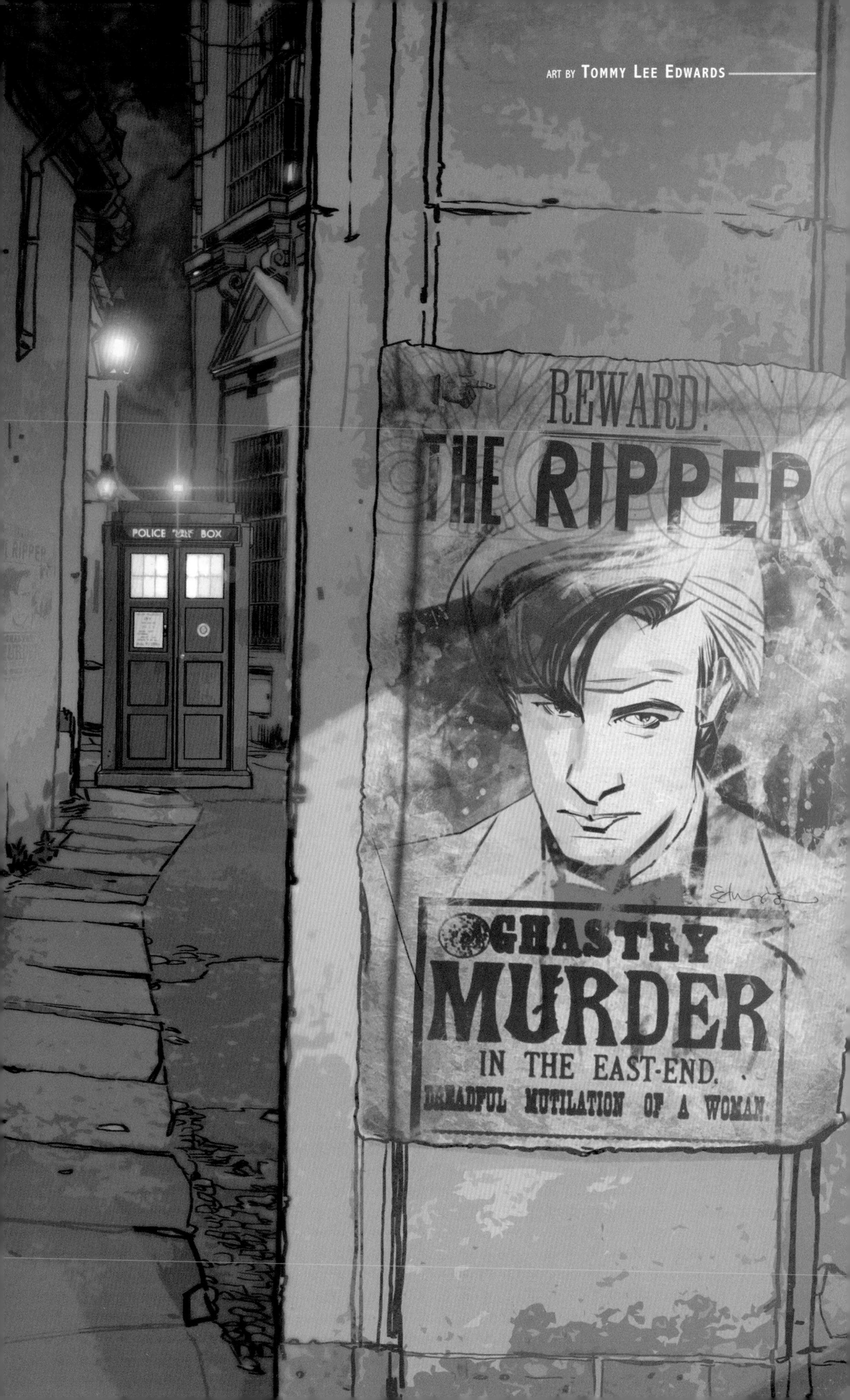

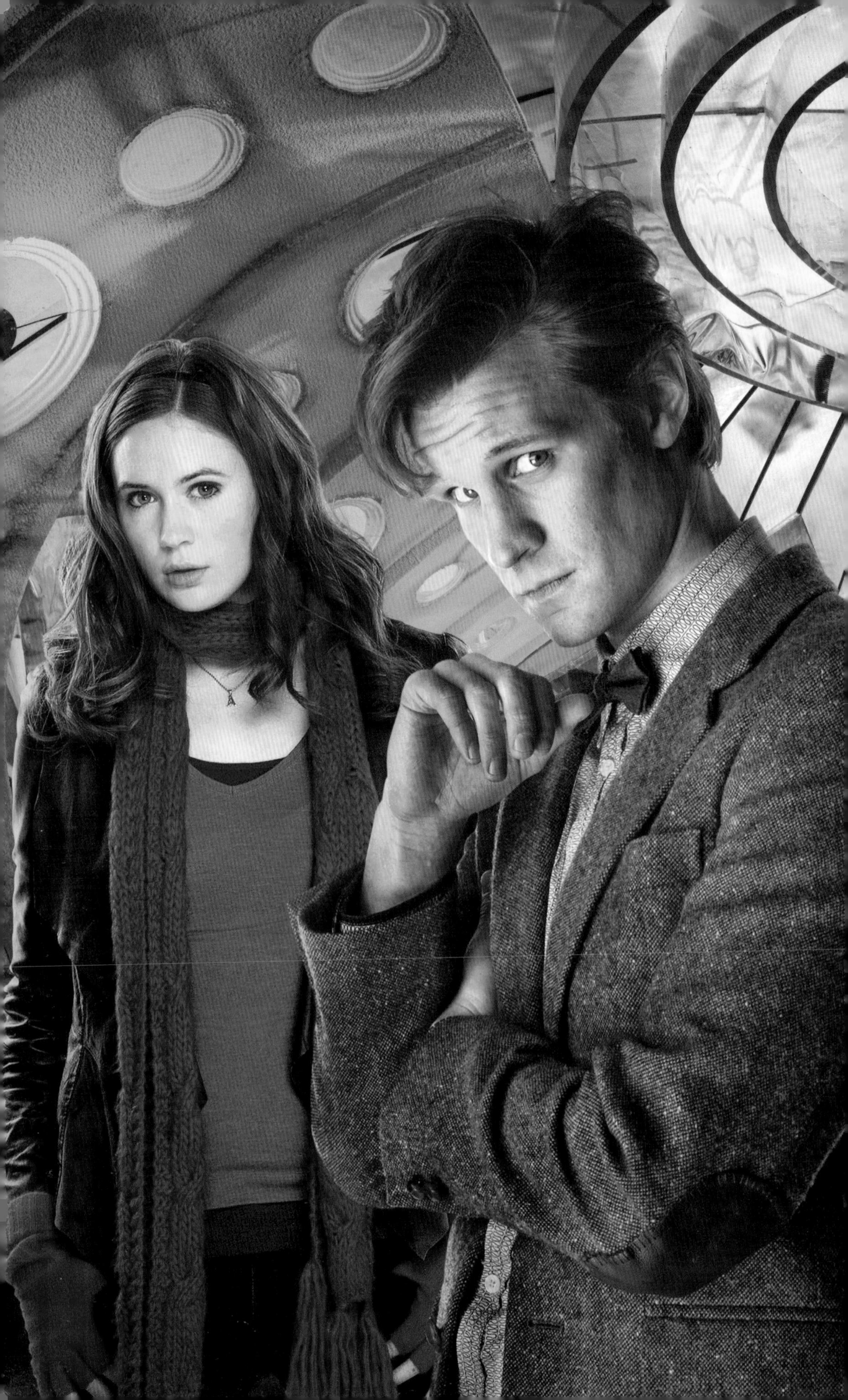

ART BY BEN TEMPLESMITH

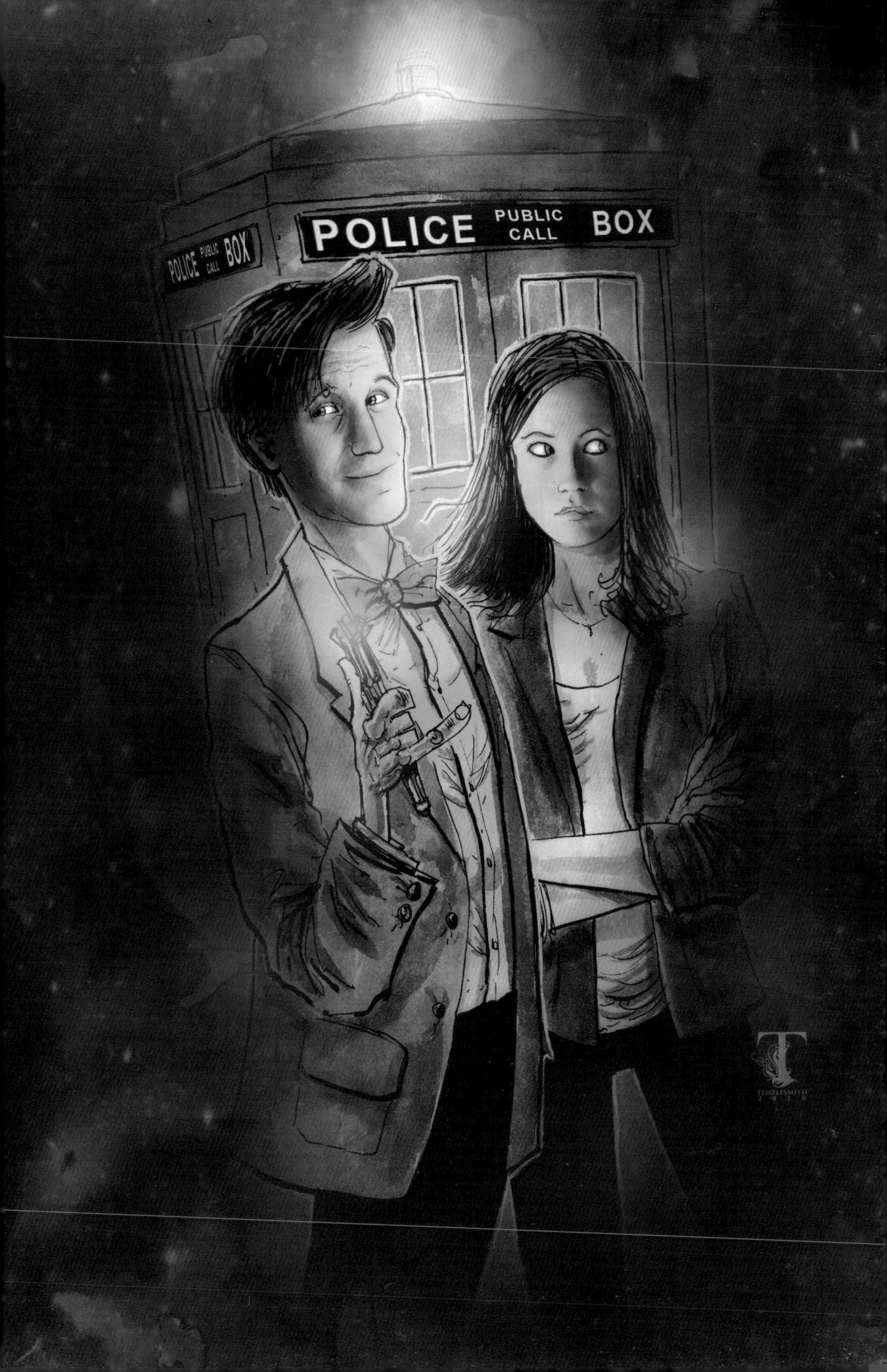
POLICE PUBLIC CALL BOX
POLICE PUBLIC CALL BOX
TEMPLESMITH

ART BY TOMMY LEE EDWARDS

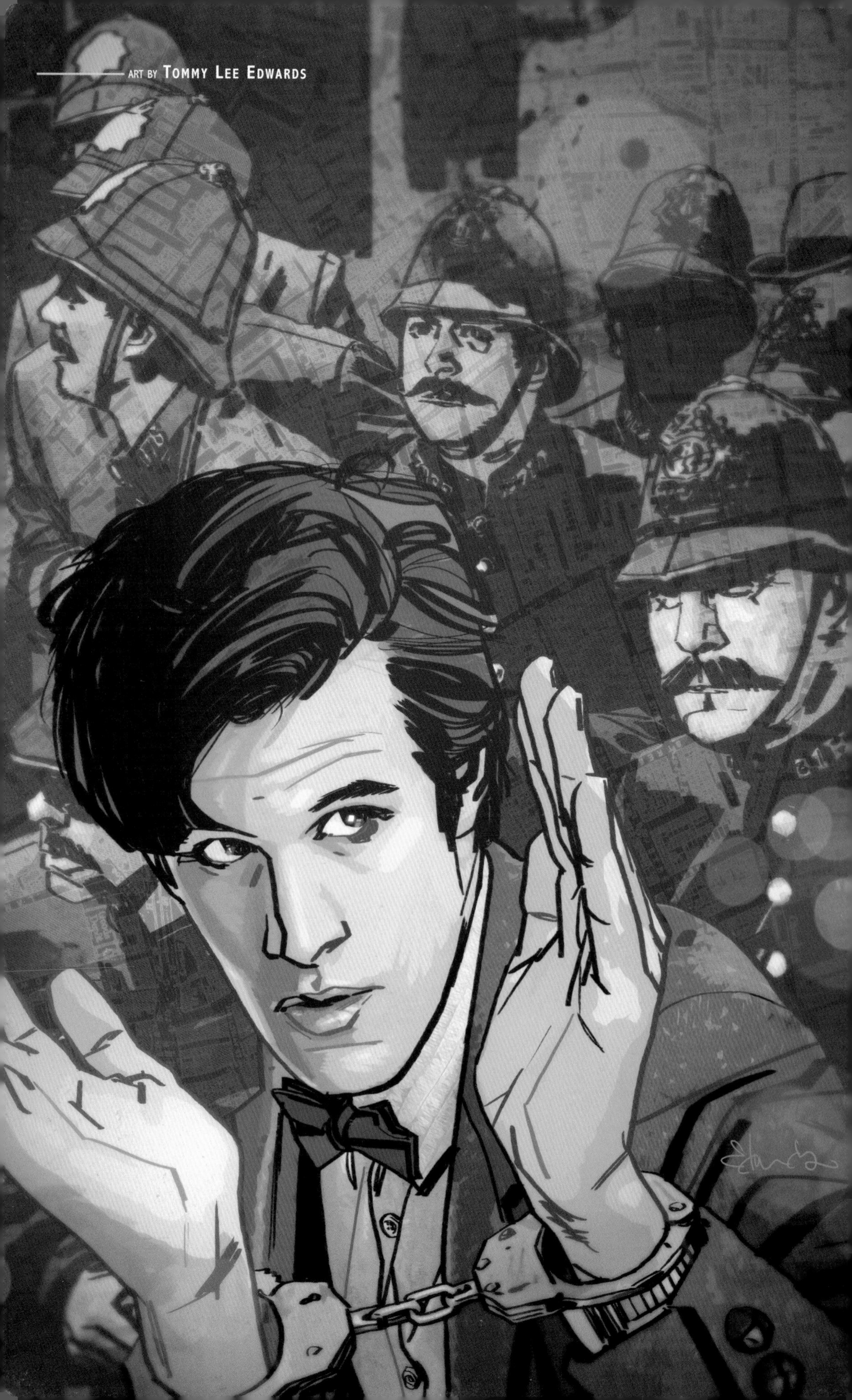

ART BY CHRIS SAMNEE • COLORS BY PHIL ELLIOTT

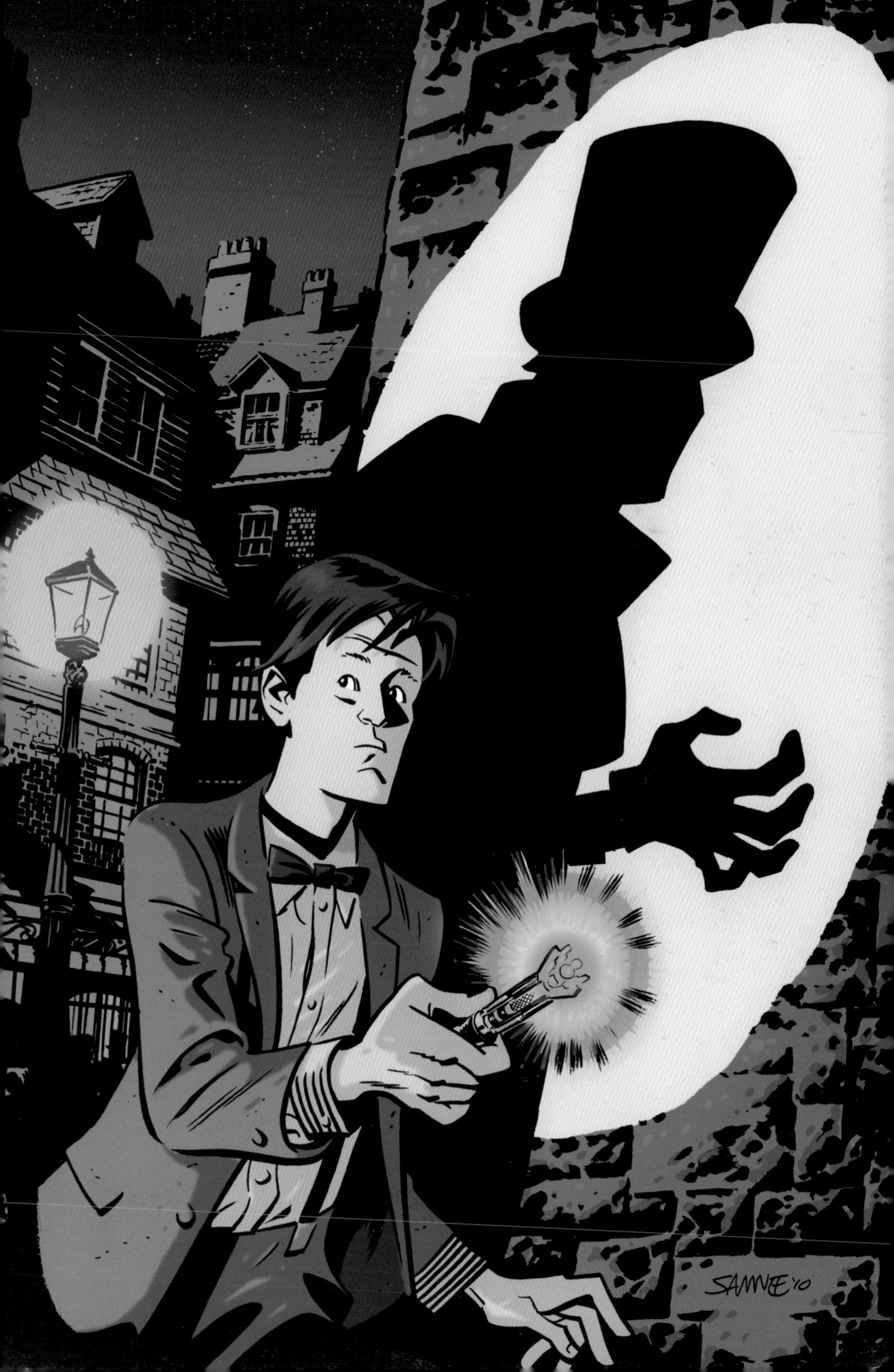
SAMNEE '10

ART BY TOMMY LEE EDWARDS

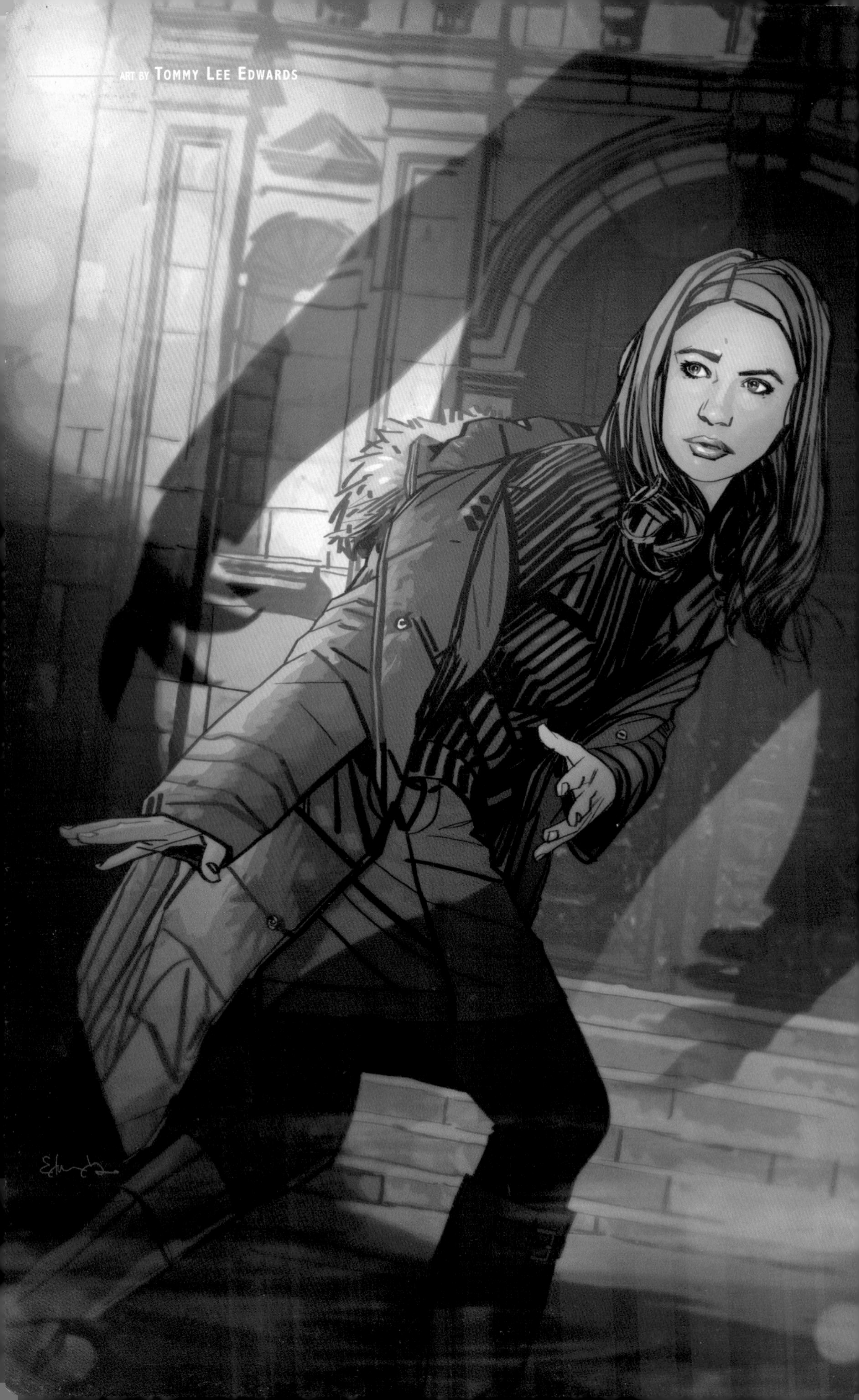

ART BY MATTHEW DOW SMITH • COLORS BY CHARLIE KIRCHOFF

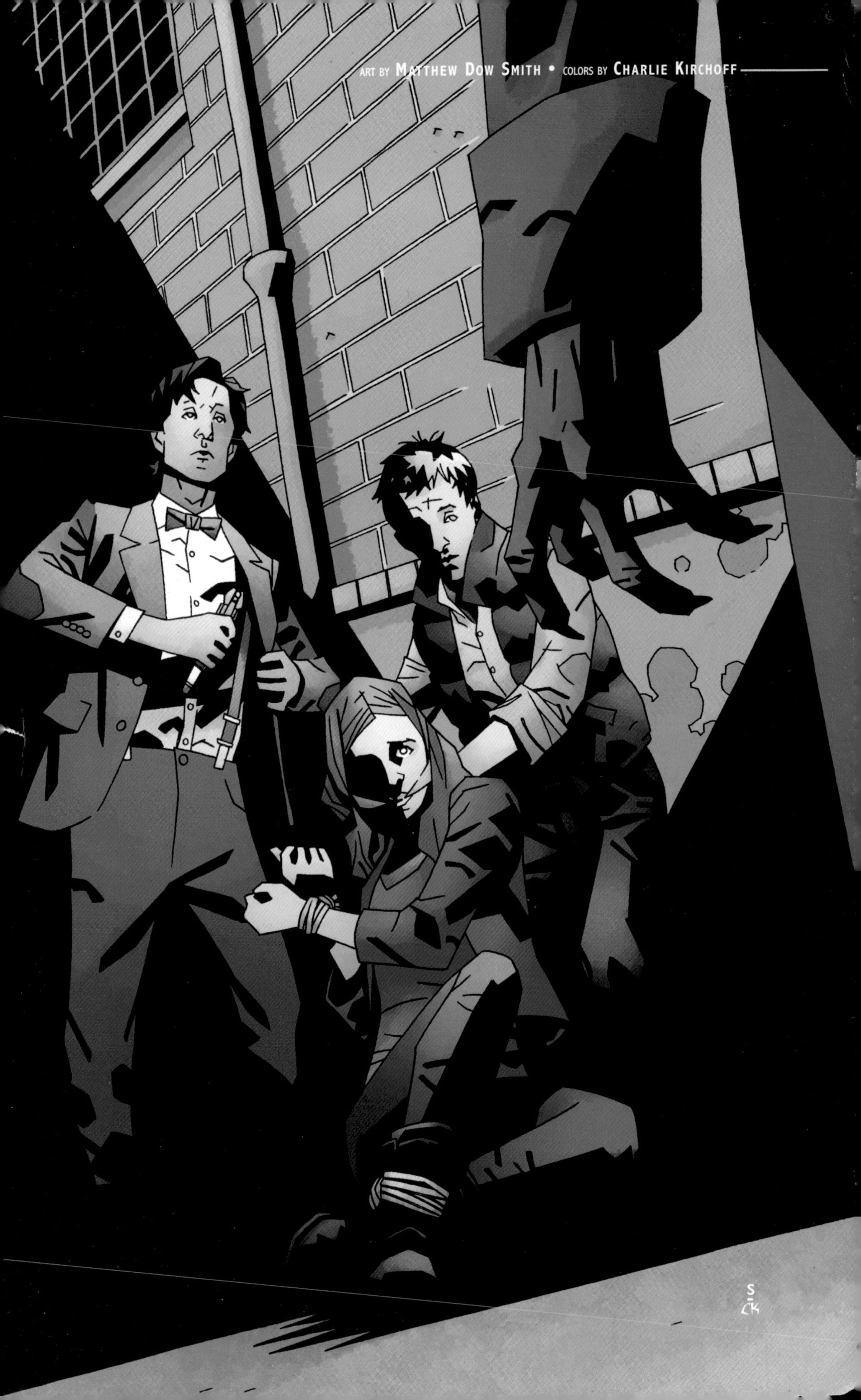

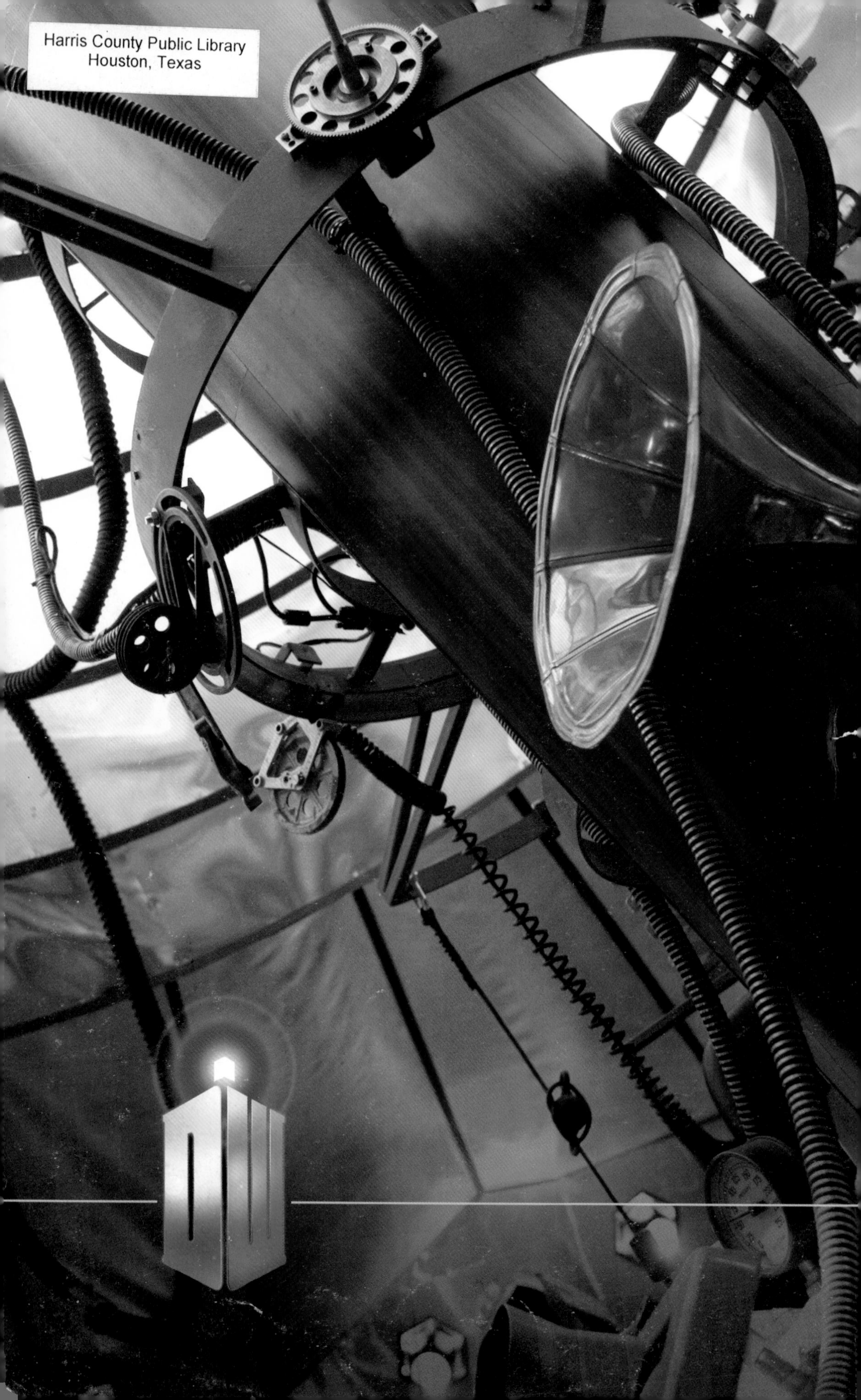